Quivering Daughters

"This important book breaks new ground by exposing the previously unknown world of the Christian fundamentalist Quiverfull movement. As the oldest of eleven children, this author knows first-hand the emotional and spiritual effects of life in a patriarchal family. Hillary's poetic words give voice to those quivering daughters who have grown up believing they have no voice. She offers hope and encouragement from a healthy Christian perspective by weaving her personal experiences as a quivering daughter into an inspirational book that illumines a path of healing and recovery for other daughters of patriarchy."

Wendy J. Duncan, M.A., L.B.S.W.
Author, *I Can't Hear God Anymore: Life in a Dallas Cult*
www.dallascult.com

"To women who have been hurt by the far-reaching consequences of Quiverfull teachings, Quivering Daughters offers compassion and encouragement on the journey back to God's grace. For the rest of us, Quiverfull daughter Hillary McFarland gives a biblical, non-judgmental view of a movement that is sometimes as harmful as it is sincere. I strongly recommend this book."

Meg Moseley
Author, *debut novel from WaterBrook Press, May 2011*
www.megmoseley.wordpress.com

"I was both convicted in my own heart and grieved as I read the stories of my sisters in Christ who are suffering for the sake of a manmade paradigm. Exposing a growing movement that is leaving many once-hopeful homeschooling families broken and wounded and parents needlessly estranged from their precious daughters and grandchildren, Hillary points the way to God's mercy and grace for those of us who have tasted the bitter fruits of patriocentricity. A must read for all homeschooling moms."

Karen Campbell, mom of six homeschooled children & ten homeschooling grandchildren. Host of the "thatmom" podcasts for homeschooling moms.
www.thatmom.com

Quivering Daughters

Hope and Healing
for the Daughters of Patriarchy

Hillary McFarland

Edited by Megan Lindsay

dlp

Darklight Press

Dallas, Texas

Cover design Abigail Paul, A Source of Joy Graphic Design
www.graphics.asourceofjoy.org
Special thanks to Brooke, who beautifully portrays the little girl; and her parents, for allowing me to photograph her.

Text and photography copyright © 2010 Hillary McFarland

Published by Darklight Press
PO BOX 796511, Dallas, TX 75379.

ISBN 978-0-9844686-0-7
Printed in the United States of America

Note: The views expressed by the author in this book are not necessarily those of its contributors. The information presented in this book is not a substitute for professional counsel. If you are suicidal, depressed, in physical or psychological danger, please seek professional help or call 911.

This book is dedicated

With love

To all of my sisters

In blood and in spirit.

"*Mercy is shown.*"

Hosea 2

Contents

Foreword

If you're reading this book, you probably already suspect something is wrong. Perhaps, for you, just holding this book in your hands is an incredible act of courage—or, as many parents might say, an act of rebellion. I'm here to tell you that I've sat where you sit today, with trembling fingers and a racing heart. I was terrified but I was also desperate to know the truth. And it's never rebellious to search for the truth. Here's what I can tell you for sure: be not afraid, sweet one. You are not alone.

The stories you read here will break your heart. But you'll find yourself weeping not only because what happens is tragic but because perhaps these stories also happened to you. Again, be not afraid. You are not alone.

Sometimes before we can build a new life and a new story for ourselves, we have to deconstruct our past. Hillary McFarland does this with such tenderness and with much grace. But like me, Hillary discovered that searching for the truth is not an act of rebellion—it is an act of courageous love.

The truth is, perhaps what you have suffered at the hands of Christians has distorted the true, loving nature of our Heavenly Father. If you're like me, your perception of God is that He's wrathful and eternally disappointed with you. By writing this book, Hillary offers hope to those of us whose abusive past (and yes, sweet one, it is abusive) hinders us from accepting the love of our gracious Abba. This book just might transform your understanding of God's true, loving nature.

This is why reading this book is not rebellion. In fact, it is an act of courageous love. Go ahead. Open this book. And remember: be not afraid. You are not alone.

Most of all: the truth will set you free.

—**Elizabeth Esther Henderson,** wife, mother, and author
www.elizabethesther.com

i

Christian Families on the Edge
Authoritarianism and Isolationism

Rachel D. Ramer

In response to antifamily trends in recent decades, there has been a resurgence within Christianity to restore family integrity and values. Christians may agree on the importance of these issues, but there are very different views of the role of family within Christianity and culture. Some Christian groups, who see culture as adversarial to Christianity, believe the role of family is to protect its members from culture. Family certainly is to be a place of security; however, the principles of authority and isolation these groups often recommend are problematic and result in the family becoming a legalistic subculture even within Christianity. These groups often promote principles of parental authority based on shame. Their application of ancient biblical examples to contemporary family situations is also questionable. Authoritarianism and isolationism provide a false sense of security from moral and spiritual evils, and merely result in a subculture that fails to interact with and transform culture in a redeeming way.

In an age of deteriorating families, deadbeat dads, and disregard for traditional family boundaries and values, Christians have responded by "focusing on the family." Many aberrant groups and cults, on the other hand, compel followers to forsake family, interrupting this natural and significant expression of God's protection and love. Yet some groups encourage forsaking nearly everything *but* family. In light of our "secularized" times, can the value of family be overrated?

Some Christians see family as the focal point of Christianity, relying on the teachings of leaders such as R. J. Rushdoony. Considered the father of Christian Reconstructionism, Rushdoony has stated, "All the basic governmental powers in society, save one, the death penalty, have been given [by God] to the family, not to the state nor to the church…A mark of anti-Christianity is the move to strip the family of these powers."[1] In agreement with this idea, voices such as *Patriarch* magazine promote "home education, home business, home church, home birth, family ministry, family health, family worship…courtship and betrothal, family-based welfare."[2] This view of the family may also include rejection of organized sports, church youth and singles' groups, along with neighborhood playmates.

Proponents portray this view as "balanced"[3] and acknowledge that the home is under the authority of the church. In this paradigm, however, the church is a "home church" made up of like-minded *families* who isolate themselves from non-family-focused activities and from other Christians who do not share their particular view of family life and child-rearing values.

From within this structure, church leaders who let their wives work outside the home, use credit, limit family size, send their children to public schools, and so on, are viewed in a negative light. Concerning such leaders, *Patriarch* asks, "Can I remain under the authority of someone who so denies the Bible by his life? Can my family continue to maintain fellowship in a church whose leaders so disregard the clear teachings of God's Word?"[4] *Patriarch* further suggests that youth groups and Sunday school programs demonstrate a "failure of the church to teach the principles of parental responsibility for child training and to reinforce it in the church's programs," and that the use of these programs in a church "may well be a reason to leave."[5]

Isolationist Jonathan Lindvall of *Bold Christian Living* tried to answer his critics by affirming: "Yes, I am sheltering my children! I am convinced this is what God calls me to do."[6] Most Christians would probably agree that children need a certain amount of sheltering. The *concept* of sheltering is not the issue, however; the *extent* of sheltering is the defining concern. Sheltering is a legitimate concept, but isolationists' rationale for sheltering often does not convey the extent of or limitations to the practice.

DISTURBING CHARACTERISTICS

Good can be found within this parenting movement, and proponents do express concern for protecting children from harmful leadership and disciplinary tactics. The principles and techniques advocated throughout much of their material, however, convey mixed messages and therefore should be evaluated. Not everyone on the authoritarian / isolationist side of the debate agrees fully on the issues addressed in this article, but there are, nevertheless, some disturbing characteristics of this movement.

Authority or Authoritarianism?

Excessive authority is of primary importance when evaluating harmful characteristics within child training / education materials. Many authoritarians mimic Bill Gothard's "chain of authority" or "chain of command" teachings.[7] While parents are to be in charge of children, demanding unquestioning obedience from children goes beyond what God instructed. In their article "Training Roseanna's Flesh," Michael and Debi Pearl, for example, argue that training a child properly is not a matter of focusing on any particular training issue itself, rather, "IT IS A MATTER OF ESTABLISHING AN UNDERSTANDING OF WHO IS IN CONTROL" (capitalization in original).[8] They continue, "You must look for opportunities to demonstrate that you have the last word, that your authority is to be obeyed without question....If, during the course of a day, no contest arises naturally, you should arrange one. Seek opportunity to thwart the child's will, to cause him to submit to your command."[9]

Kelly Crespin of the Eclectic Homeschool Association gave the Pearls' book, *To Train Up a Child*, a less-than-glowing review: "They compare the training of a child to the training of a dog or mouse. I feel that many children who receive this type of 'training' grow up to fear their parents, or any adult figure."[10]

Author Reb Bradley, however, echoes the Pearls: "Keep your objective in mind—subjection of their will...Teach your children to obey without being told 'why.'"[11] Authors William and Colleen Dedrick also concur: "When your child disregards or disobeys your command, he breaks fellowship with you and offends you as his God-ordained authority."[12] Concerning permissiveness, lack of restraint, and neglect, the Dedricks state, "Every minute you spend with your child there is a battle in one or more of these areas."[13]

Authoritarianism goes beyond healthy, positive discipline and demands absolute submission. From a biblical viewpoint, human authority is to be respected; yet, when the religious rulers were wrong, Peter and John disobeyed them (Acts 4:15–21). The Jewish midwives in Egypt also disobeyed authority for ethical reasons (Exod. 1:15–21). Parents who equate their authority with godlike sovereignty create confusion for a child. At some level, parents must become, for the child, models of humility instead of models of sovereignty. Parental overidentification with God's authority confuses the child who eventually witnesses the parents' imperfect/sinful humanity. This absolutizing of authority fails to recognize nuances and variables in human communication and situations and ignores possible emotional control issues and sinfulness within parents.

Some parenting books teach a calm, non-angry approach to asserting authority, while characterizing abuse as out-of-control reactions on the part of parents.[14] Out-of-control anger is obviously a negative manipulation, but manipulation can happen without anger, and often does. A calm approach to subjugating a child's will and leading him or her to equate the parent's will with godliness on all issues is simply a more insidious form of abuse.

Some authoritarians redefine child abuse as a lack of authority: "Real child abuse is allowing a child to be overtaken by the destructive forces of sin and rebellion."[15] Not so! Real child abuse is the misuse or overuse of authority. This overuse of authority can also occur with older children, for example, when parents make decisions for them in areas such as vocation, as well as some cases of courtship/betrothal. Jonathan Lindvall's Web site has an account of how one father micromanaged the relationship between his daughter and future son-in-law. He manipulated the couple emotionally into giving up their interest in each other, in order to test them, when he fully intended for them to marry.[16] This deception in the name of authority carries harmful moral implications, since ends do not justify means in this case any more than in a case of physical abuse.

In his book, *Imperative People: Those Who Must Be in Control*, Christian psychotherapist Les Carter points out the result of excessive control: "Listen for the words *should, supposed to, got to, have to, ought to, must, can't*....Technically speaking, nothing is wrong in stating what *should* be done. After all, in a world that shuns absolutes, it's refreshing to feel like you *do* stand for something." He adds, however, that "you are in essence stating, 'I'll accept you only after you meet my conditions.' And since each of us responds negatively to this kind of emotional blackmail, we become angry and tense" (emphases in original).[17] Children who emerge from such an environment may carry with them a distorted concept of God as an emotional blackmailer interested only in behavior. Parents who assert excessive control are prone to exasperate their children (Eph. 6:4), as the children's wills are consistently suppressed and their desires thwarted.

In contrast to the concept of establishing unquestioning obedience, Christian counselor Jeff Van Vonderen states:

Though most Christian parents have been trained to balk at this concept, it is our job to help [children] develop a strong *no*. They are going to need a strong no when they are fourteen years old and someone wants to be sexually intimate with them, or shoves a bottle of alcohol in their hand. Our job is to recognize opportunities for them to exercise their *no*—not to strip them of their will in the name of maintaining authority as a parent...In that light, actively look for opportunities to give them practice saying no, those times when a *no* would be an appropriate answer.[18]

Won't sheltering prevent 14-year-olds from being in situations where they need to say *no*? Not entirely. Children will also need to say *no* to the errant religions and philosophies presented from "authorities" they will encounter later in life. The ability to say *no* comes not simply from learning correct behavior and doctrine but from living in a healthy emotional environment. Moral behavior and correct doctrine are often sacrificed because of emotional neediness.

Arguing for strong parental authority, author J. Richard Fugate states, "It should be no surprise that leaderless children respond to cults, such as the Moonies and the Jones groups...These counterculture groups all have one thing in common—they **demand** followership. They each provide strong leadership, teach and enforce rules, and set a purpose for the life of the follower. Dare we as parents offer less?" (Emphasis in original).[19] Susceptibility to cults, however, can result not only from children being "leaderless" but also from being *overled*. Jesus contrasted authoritarianism with humble leadership: "You know that the rulers of the Gentiles lord it over them, and their high officials exercise authority over them. Not so with you. Instead, whoever wants to become great among you must be your servant" (Matt. 20:25–26 NIV). Humble leadership that is open to questioning and focused on relationship will provide emotional protection from cults; demanding leadership will not.

Head over Heart

Authoritarians tend to view all "heart issues" as sins, such as greed, rebellion, and lust. Blanket statements such as, "The loving parent will address the heart of the child through requiring confession"[20] center on Scriptures such as, "The heart is deceitful above all things, and desperately wicked" (Jer. 17:9 KJV). The sin aspect of the heart is not the only aspect to which the Bible refers, however. Consider the use of the term "heart" in "did not our heart burn within us?" (Luke 24:32 KJV) and "let not your heart be troubled" (John 14:1 KJV). Authoritarians mistakenly believe that emotional issues are being adequately dealt with by addressing all heart issues as sin issues. Tedd Tripp, author of *Shepherding a Child's Heart*, argues that addressing the heart's sin issues should also include concern for the emotional health of the child. He suggests approaching a child's heart issues by asking, "Help me understand what you are feeling."[21]

VanVonderen explains that in shame-based families, emotions and feelings are minimized: "Talking about feelings or needs leaves you feeling ashamed for being so 'selfish'...The measuring stick becomes: how things look; what people think; religious behavior....Children must learn to act like miniature adults in order to avoid shame...fault and blame are the order of the day."[22] The Pearls, for example, warn against expressing feelings, seeing them as selfishness: "For your children's own good, teach them to maintain control of their emotions. If you do not want to produce a sissy who uses adversity as a chance to get attention, then don't program them that way."[23]

VanVonderen notes that families who devalue emotions are "strong on 'head skills'" and "weak on 'heart skills.'"[24] He is suggesting the need for balance; he is not criticizing thinking skills. The perception that feelings need to be conquered, denied, and shamed creates the kind of environment that one former Jehovah's Witness likened to the dissonance he felt within the Watchtower structure. The head knows all the "right" answers, as defined by the system, but the repressed, controlled emotions leave a person susceptible to harm and error.[25]

Emotions, while not always accurate, *can* serve as an alarm, alerting one to distorted "truths." Rick Seelhoff, a former Children of God member, describes his release from the guilt he had experienced as a result of seeing nearly all feelings as sinful responses of the heart: "I had to come to the place where I regarded my feelings as friends rather than foes, that they weren't moral acts which I was judged for, but gifts of God given to help test reality."[26]

For many authoritarians, devaluing emotions also impacts the courtship/betrothal issue. John W. Thompson, for example, states, "Emotional romance, God says, is to be reserved for the betrothal stage of a relationship after a binding commitment to marry has been made, preventing the broken heart syndrome."[27] This approach, however, contributes to suppressed emotions, and, while it may prevent broken hearts before marriage, it does nothing to prevent broken hearts *after* marriage, and it may very well cause them.

Shaming the Parents

Authoritarians not only promote shaming children, but their teachings also have a shaming tone toward parents. If a parent does not teach a child to obey the first time a command is given, the child may be hit by a car or be bitten by a poisonous spider. This fear tactic insults both parent and child, who understand the difference of importance and tone between "Time for bed" and "STOP!" (The Pearls advocate no change in voice tones or emotion for different commands.) The point is well taken that parents often give too many warnings, but this authoritarian approach becomes manipulation of another sort, where every command is a crisis by definition.

The Pearls also tell parents, "Fail to use the rod on [a disobedient, bullying child] and you are creating a 'Nazi.'"[28] Fear of producing a Nazi may compel parents to use a "rod" even when their intuition tells them there is a better option in a particular situation. The Dedricks shame parents with, "It is disgraceful to hear a grown man putting on his 'I'm afraid you're not going to like me' voice when negotiating with a two-year-old."[29] They also state, "The parent who neglects or refuses to discipline his child [according to their idea of discipline] is himself undisciplined and disobedient to God."[30]

CULTURE CONFUSION

Authoritarianism and isolationism are often married. Christian isolationism endorses a "godly" subculture, encouraging separation even from other Christians who do not conform to the ideals of that subculture. Isolationist Steve Schlissel states, "The naiveté of modern Christians concerning the religious character of the so-called Culture War is astonishing. Culture, Henry Van Til taught us, is simply religion externalized and made explicit…We have been raised to believe that culture is religiously neutral rather than religiously determined."[31] Religion certainly does influence culture, but this all-or-nothing view sees nearly *every expression* of culture as a religious statement, either Christian or non-Christian.

There are, however, other approaches to understanding how Christians relate, or don't relate, to the culture in which they find themselves. Professor and author Michael Horton draws from H.

Richard Niebuhr's *Christ and Culture* to explain five different approaches: First, *Christ against culture* holds that "the world is evil, but the realm of the Spirit is good; earthly things are inherently sinful, while heavenly things are inherently virtuous."[32]

Second, *Christ of culture* views Christianity as an extension of culture. Niebuhr states, "The movement that identifies obedience to Jesus Christ with the practices of prohibition, and with the maintenance of early American social organization, is a type of cultural Christianity...Christ is identified with what men conceive to be their finest ideals, their noblest institutions, and their best philosophy."[33]

Third, *Christ above culture* "suggests neither antagonism nor assimilation."[34] This is an attempt at neutrality toward culture and is directly opposite Schlissel's view.

Fourth, *Christ and culture in paradox* sees the kingdom of God and the kingdom of humankind as "different spheres with different purposes...Culture can never be an avenue of finding God...But neither can culture be an object of disgust, since culture never promises to save or redeem."[35] In this view, while not all pleasurable aspects of life are spiritual in the salvific or godly sense, God is still present in them.

Fifth, *Christ the transformer of culture* is distinct from the *Christ against culture* and the *Christ of culture* views by holding that, "The problem is not the world, but the willful opposition of the world to God and His Christ. This frees the believer to participate in the world as a full-fledged citizen and to view it not as inherently wicked [or as an expression of false religions], but as a theater in which both God's glory and human sin are displayed."[36]

Isolationists embrace the *Christ against culture* and also the *Christ of culture* views to create their own culture, often based on ancient cultural practices found in the Bible. Horton explains that "there is great danger in mixing a 'Christ against culture' and a 'Christ of culture' paradigm...this mixture leads us to simply replace one culture with another and confuse the latter with God's will and kingdom."[37] *Christ against culture* and *Christ of culture* are two sides of the same coin. A true transformer of culture does not seek to create a separate culture; rather, he seeks to transform the existing culture.

Biblical Support for Isolation?

A look at Old Testament theocracy shows how covenants between a ruler and his people found in ancient Near Eastern *culture* were used as a pattern for God's covenant with Israel. Theologians Gordon Fee and Douglas Stuart state, "God constructed the Old Testament law on the analogy of these ancient covenants."[38] Even the God-given Mosaic laws were not entirely divorced from the culture in which they were given.

Horton argues that, "Scripture admonishes us, [with Christ's words 'my kingdom is from another place'] to avoid either the tendency to confuse the kingdom of God with an earthly nation (Israel, America, etc.) or, on the other hand, to view citizenship in one kingdom as completely antithetical to citizenship and participation in the other."[39]

There certainly are cultures that adopt God's priorities more closely than others, such as those that abolish slavery or ban the exploitation of children; nevertheless, like the once-godly Pharisee sect, there are dangers from within once we've "arrived." Jesus neither endorsed, nor participated in, a separatist lifestyle (such as that of His contemporaries, the Essenes); rather, He took positive illustrations from, and participated in, His culture. His prayer to the Father for believers was "not that you take them out of the world but that you protect them from the evil one" (John 17:15 NIV).

Fee and Stuart argue that "there is no such thing as a divinely ordained culture; cultures are in fact different, not only from the first to the twentieth century, but in every conceivable way in the twentieth century itself."[40] They caution against applying a biblical passage to a present-day situation when particulars in the passage are not comparable to the present-day situation. Even if a biblical *principle* is evident, they counsel, "the 'principle' does not now become timeless to be applied at random on whim to any and every kind of situation. We would argue that it must be applied to *genuinely comparable situations*" (emphasis in original). [41]

Isolationists' belief that God has a particular culture in mind for His people influences how they interpret the Bible. Schlissel, for example, addresses the cultural craze over body piercing. He uses Leviticus 19:28—"Ye shall not make any cuttings in your flesh for the dead, nor print any marks upon you" (KJV)—to conclude that (male) body piercing is scripturally wrong.[42] To apply this verse to today, however, would also mean we should not wear clothes made of two fabrics, since the same passage also instructs, "Do not wear clothing woven of two kinds of material" (19:19 NIV).

Schlissel also points to ancient practices of piercing slaves for subordination purposes (Exod. 21:6; Deut. 15:17) to argue that body piercing should not be practiced today.[43] Mosaic laws concerning the treatment of slaves, however, fail as bases for transcultural principles about body piercing. Fee and Stuart address the pierced-slave passage (Deut. 15:12–17), calling it a casuistic law. "Such casuistic or case-by-case laws," they say, "constitute a large portion of the more than six hundred commandments found in the Old Testament pentateuchal law...Because such laws apply specifically to Israel's civil, religious, and ethical life, they are by their very nature limited in their applicability and therefore unlikely to apply to the Christian."[44] Today, bondage is not in the piercing of a body part but in making such cultural issues absolutes. Paul warned regarding such bondage to the Mosaic Law, "It is for freedom that Christ has set us free. Stand firm, then, and do not let yourselves be burdened again by a yoke of slavery" (Gal. 5:1 NIV).

Isolationists also draw universal principles from biblical narratives. One area in which they do this is courtship/betrothal. From biblical accounts of betrothal Thompson concludes, "Biblical courtship isn't simply an option, it's an obligation...God established the courtship approach to marriage as trans-cultural, and thus normative for all people in all cultures and in all times."[45]

Fee and Stuart, however, also sound a warning against drawing universal moral principles from each biblical narrative: "The fallacy of this approach is that it ignores the fact that the [biblical] narratives were written to show the progress of God's history of redemption, not to illustrate principles. They are historical narratives, not illustrative narratives."[46] Confusion concerning what is or is not universal can result in creating a subculture based on ancient culture. The goal should rather be a transformed community acting as salt and light within the larger culture, based on the culturally transcendent message of the Scriptures (Rom. 12:2; cf. Matt. 5:13–16).

Finally, we might ask what was Jesus' view concerning the role of the family. Consider His radical "anti-family" statements, such as: "I have come to turn a man against his father, a daughter against her mother....Anyone who loves his father or mother more than me is not worthy of me; anyone who loves his son or daughter more than me is not worthy of me" (Matt. 10:35, 37 NIV). Jesus also said, "Whoever does the will of my Father in heaven is my brother and sister and mother" (Matt. 12:50 NIV). Jesus often used hyperbole to make His points. He was not discounting the value of family; yet, we can gather from these statements that He did not view the biological family as the center of Christianity, but rather *Himself* and His kingdom.

What about Homeschoolers?

Is homeschooling a form of isolationism? It is true that considerable questionable material is directed to homeschoolers, and isolationists often homeschool; yet, this does not make all homeschoolers isolationists. It would be inaccurate to view all homeschoolers, or even all Christian homeschoolers, as being on the same side of this issue. A growing segment of home educators question isolationist tendencies. Probably the most prominent evangelical homeschool curriculum company that rejects isolationism is Sonlight Curriculum Ltd. Sonlight's general manager Wayne Griess states that their philosophy is "to educate, not indoctrinate. We wish to grow learners aware of the world around them."[47] Sonlight owner John Holzmann plainly states that parents may *not* want to purchase Sonlight materials if "they want to shield their children as much as possible from contact with the world and the world system."[48] Home education is a viable philosophy in its own right and is not necessarily an expression of isolationism.

CONCERN FOR EVANGELISM

The issues of authoritarianism and isolationism carry grave implications concerning evangelism. First, to what do they convert people? The yoke of Christ is easy and His burden is light (Matt. 11:28–30). Authoritarianism and isolationism create an environment that is heavy and burdensome.

Second, isolationism is not the agent for evangelism it may claim to be but is busy converting people from one culture to another. Lacking interaction with current culture, isolationism creates a closed system, where, as author John Fischer points out, "a separatist Christian monologue has replaced meaningful dialogue with the world around us."[49]

In contrast, viewing culture as a theater where God's glory interacts with humanity, both sinful and needy, and where Jesus stepped into a broken world to eat, drink, and *abide* with us, *is* biblical (Luke 7:34; John 1:14). Fischer sums up an alternative to isolationism: "I would suggest that we as Christians need to learn to *embrace* the danger of living in a dangerous world and trust not a safe subculture to protect us, but a praying Savior."[50]

For notes, see Appendix F.

Introduction

I loved being homeschooled. If I had children, it's likely they'd be homeschooled, too—in part because of the hands on education I received from my parents. (Surely it must be more than a little mystifying to have a ten-year-old child sobbing over math books, and yet I appreciate the freedom I did have to sob over them—something that I suspect wouldn't go over well elsewhere.) Thanks to the patience and conviction of my mother and father, we got through it together—and I remain extremely grateful for their choice of my childhood education.

When they started schooling me in the early eighties, homeschooling was still a grassroots movement among those considered freethinkers and hippies. It has grown steadily, and as of 2007, over 1.5 million children were reported homeschooled in the United States.[1] In these findings, parents offered many reasons for choosing to home educate, but number one was to provide religious or moral instruction.[2] Today, the homeschooling movement continues to advance worldwide, and with it, new trends emerge.

Most conservative families are aware of Bill Gothard and his *Institute in Basic Life Principles.* Of less renown but making swift headway over the last several years is another trend among homeschooling advocates; considered "God's way" or "God's plan" for true believers, the Christian patriarchy movement calls for a return

---

[1] Planty, M., Hussar, W., Snyder, T., Kena, G., KewalRamani, A., Kemp, J., Bianco, K., Dinkes, R. (2009).The Condition of Education 2009 (NCES 2009-081). National Center for Education Statistics, Institute of Education Sciences, U.S. Department of Education. Washington, DC.

Author's Note: Since many who choose home education value privacy, we can safely attest that the actual numbers are higher than those documented.

[2] Ibid, Figure 6-2.

to biblical culture and teaches that since education of children by the parents is mandated by God, faithful Christians will consider nothing else.[3] Among other conservative values, it promotes the Quiverfull family, which is considered part of the dominion mandate in Genesis 1:28 and allows God to determine family size without human intervention.[4] Many who affirm patriarchal doctrine also emphasize familial hierarchy, gender roles, biblical living, and biblical womanhood.

Because of these tenets and more, patriarchal literature has flooded the homeschooling market. Actually, we can think of homeschooling as a gateway, for while not all homeschoolers are patriarchalists, all patriarchal families homeschool.[5] The numbers rise annually—both for new families who choose to educate at home, and for those who perpetuate the patriocentric lifestyle.

My primary concern is not necessarily with each tenet taught by patriarchal leaders, parents, or organizations. I fully acknowledge that those who preach biblical patriarchy sincerely believe they do so in obedience to God, and that some of the beliefs can be good, solidly backed by Scripture. However, I am deeply concerned with the manner this doctrine is carried out in the home. And as many daughters of patriarchy emerge from childhood carrying scars of soul and spirit inflicted in the name of "biblical" doctrine, where can they turn for gentle, Bible-based healing and support?

My intention is not to malign those who live as they believe the Lord has called them, but to offer a gentle alternative for the ones He calls differently. In obedience to His will for me, I've written the book I wish was available over ten years ago—not that the content itself is exhaustive or that I am worthy to write it, but because the body of Christ is too silent and perhaps somewhat uninformed regarding these issues. Those who have graciously exposed their hearts in these pages believe that it's important to share their stories so others might realize they are not alone, and find courage to do the same.

Please note that the letters and stories in this book are real and represent only a tiny fraction of what I've observed. Names and identifying details have been altered to preserve anonymity; journal

---

[3] Vision Forum Ministries. "The Tenets of Biblical Patriarchy." Vision Forum Ministries www.visionforumministries.org (11 December 2009)

[4] www.quiverfull.com

[5] If by chance they don't currently have children of schooling age, home education is still preached and encouraged.

entries are excerpts from the author's childhood journals. This leads me to an important topic that I don't cover extensively within my book, but want to acknowledge here. Unfortunately, it's about a heartbreaking subject hiding in more conservative homes than many are comfortable enough to admit. And I want to illustrate it through the words of a quivering daughter.

My name is Valerie. While I was growing up, if you met my family you would stand there counting all of us, and we'd see your lips moving even though you didn't know it—*"Six, seven, eight, nine..."*—before turning to my parents and exclaiming, "Are they all yours?"

Yes.

No, we're not Catholic.

Yes, we know what causes that.

And then you would pat my little brother on the head, smile at my parents and say, "They are all so well behaved! So polite! You've done a great job."

And Mom and Dad would beam with pride.

I'm number four out of ten; I have two older brothers and an older sister. I just turned twenty-one. That sometimes confuses people, because they look into my eyes and see an old woman looking back; but then they look at *me* and think I'm still fifteen.

In our town, my parents run our local homeschool group. We kids help out with printing newsletters and organizing meetings and get-togethers. New families often join our group; young mothers who admire us and call my Mom for advice. She stays on the phone a lot. I guess you could say she's like a celebrity in our little world. She teaches a Bible study and wants to write a book. My older sister and I take care of the house and help homeschool the younger kids when Mom is busy; I always say I know everything about raising kids except actually giving birth. Well, probably not, but you know what I mean.

But there is something else, this secret, this *thing* I have to tell. I told it to my Mom a few years ago and she just sat there real quiet. Then she tightened her lips like she does when she is thinking, and sighed.

"It happens in families sometimes," she said. It looked like she wanted to say, *"But not in my family"* but instead she just added, "Don't worry about that anymore. We will take care of it."

But it didn't stop.

I kept thinking, *it's my fault because of that prayer. I'm so stupid. Why did I have to pray that?*

A prayer.

I saw a movie when I was six or seven. It was sweet and romantic; I don't remember what the name of it was but it had to be something really innocent because we didn't watch many movies. That night I lay in bed thinking about the love it portrayed—exactly what I wanted to have someday. I said, "Jesus, will you please send someone special for me to love?" It was so simple. Just a little girl hoping for a prince one day, and asking God for him.

And then he came.

Just a few days after that prayer. My brother came to me and my sister, and the abuse began. A few times we tried to make him stop. My sister and I felt guilty; she told Mom and it stopped for a while. But then he started coming back to me, and it went on for years. I thought it was my fault; I kept hearing a voice say, *"You prayed for it, and look what God gave you instead!"* Despite our secret, we tried to be normal, doing our regular routines like schoolwork and chores and the homeschool group. A neighbor lady even moved in down the road and she and her little boy let us ride their pony. Trotting around their yard I felt free—I could forget everything that happened, if only for a moment, and be a happy little girl. It was so fun and instilled in me a deep love for horses that continues to this day.

But as I got older, I began to struggle with pornography and masturbation. I hated myself for it, but I also felt powerless to stop. Desperately hoping rules and accountability would help, I told my father about it, wanting to assuage my guilt and find help. At first it was good, because it opened up communication between us; he was very kind and non-condemning, which surprised me. But then he started getting uncomfortable and made me talk to Mom instead.

That was horrible. She started asking me all kinds of questions and telling me about *their* sex life—I felt abused all over again! I couldn't handle it anymore. The incest, the emotional-sexual abuse, and the whole environment—seven out of my ten siblings were molested in one way or another—were so toxic. Yet we were so godly and popular! Something like this didn't happen to people like us. So we just kept going around like usual, trying to pretend some big awful thing didn't hide under the surface. We sang at church, my parents counseled people.

When I became depressed in my late teens, I thought having a mentor might help. I asked my parents, but they said Mom was the only mentor I needed. Since she made me so uncomfortable before—and actually made things worse for me—I knew I wasn't safe so I just withdrew more and more.

The final straw came when I started working at a Christian book store. I'd just turned twenty and it was my first real job. My manager was a godsend and when I found out that she'd been sexually abused as a child too, everything inside me burst. I told her everything. And when Mom found out, she exploded. "You need to ask before you go around telling people, Valerie!" she said. "Tell the wrong person, and it could ruin everything! If your boss was godly, she would have stopped you right away and called me. A godly person always sends children back to their parents, no matter how old you are."

It was like someone punched me and I couldn't breathe. Besides the pain and guilt from the incest itself, to have someone not care or believe you, or worry more about what people will think is brutal. After that, I totally shut down. I couldn't take it anymore. When some friends offered to let me live with them a couple months later, I knew it was time. I packed up the little I had and was gone.

Thank God it doesn't end there! The prayer I prayed as a little girl *was* answered shortly after. Turns out, the little neighbor boy with the pony—he's now my husband. And God has healed my relationship with my brother, too. But sadly, my parents—well, that is a different story.

If you can relate to Valerie's life in any way,
please tell someone safe. Please seek those who can help you
find wholeness and support as you take necessary steps to healing.

I am compelled to note that some are concerned with my use of terminology. Not *every* Quiverfull, patriarchal, or homeschooling family promotes what I address in this book, but this doesn't alter the truth that countless women have experienced deep bleeding wounds, neglect of living needs, and very real pain and abuse within this system. If you are not reflected in these pages, please extend grace and pray for those who are.

I hope and pray these words will encourage all my readers, I write not to those who perpetuate these philosophies but to those who have lived under them. The doctrine and lifestyle of this lesser-known faction of Christianity warrants careful, serious attention, for spiritual abuse is real, emotional abuse is real—and the Christian patriarchy movement is rife with both of these. Although I write about and to women, I do not think men are unaffected. I believe that the repercussions of patriarchy on them are quite staggering, but in *Quivering Daughters,* I keep with my own experience as a woman and follow God's calling to write to my sisters in the Faith.

I hope *Quivering Daughters* offers a glimpse of sanctuary to women brought up within the patriarchal subculture of Christianity. These words are not intended to tell anyone what to think or believe, but to share a portion of one woman's journey to discovering the grace of God. I hope you are drawn ever closer to Jesus, whether this book confirms your own convictions, or gently challenges them. Seek the guidance of the Holy Spirit and weigh what you find according to Scripture. Give yourself permission to acknowledge the truth about how you feel, about what your life was like—both good and bad. Perhaps as you read, record your thoughts in a journal. And regardless, I'd love to hear from you. Know that I pray for you, my readers, daily, for this book is a labor of love from my heart to yours. May you come to know the God of grace, and may His love embrace, comfort, and bring healing to your life.

In the shadow of His wings,

Hillary McFarland

quiv · ver · ing

1. *The act or state of trembling. Implies fear and trembling.*
2. *A twist on the word "Quiverfull."*
3. *Response to reverent fear of God.*
4. *Response to authoritarianism.*

daugh · ters

1. *Women created in the image of God.*
2. *Women who are the offspring of God.*
3. *Women who are the offspring of parents.*

Dear Mom and Dad,

Y ou trained me well. You should be proud of me. I'm good at hiding how I feel and maintaining a brave face for the world. I'm good at pretending things don't matter, and denying my pain. I'm there for others to lean on, even when it hurts. I'll keep a stiff upper lip, even if I'm breaking apart on the inside. Of course, you never saw me fall apart, did you? No, I was good at hiding that, too.

So here I am. You've raised a daughter who is broken on the inside, but perfect on the outside. Or, at least, close to perfect. We all know that I didn't quite reach your standards. And we all know that I never would. You could sit there and tell me to strive toward perfection. You held up all sorts of examples of people I should try to be like.

It's okay, though, because you don't have to see me like I am now. You don't have to experience my dark side. You can deny that it exists, and when you can't do that, you can turn your back on me. It makes your life easy. Anything you like about me you can congratulate yourselves for, and anything you don't like, well, that was me not obeying you like I should.

But that's an upside to having lots of kids. You've got more chances to do better. You screwed up with me; you've left me to work myself out on my own. Well, fine. Just don't make the same mistakes with my siblings. You've seen me, and even if you don't want to admit it, you know I'm not as okay as I pretend. Don't bring the same fate upon your other children. You brought them into the world; you have a responsibility to protect them, even if that means protecting them from yourselves.

I don't hate you. Yes, there's bitterness, yes, there's resentment, and yes, there's pain. You don't see how much it killed me to play "Mommy Two". You don't understand why there are a million other things I'd rather do than become a Mom now. Come on, Mom—an eleven-year-old can't play mommy. Or a twelve-, or thirteen-, or fourteen-year-old. I was so young; you should've known better than to lean on me.

Just don't do this to the others, please? It's too late to fix me now; just...don't ruin the others? It's too late to undo the damage already done, but you can stop it from going further. Don't lose your children because you were too stubborn to realize you were wrong. I may have hated playing Mom to my younger siblings, but I would do it again a thousand times over if I could protect them from what I went through. Just...love them, and *really* love them. Please? Not for me, not for you, but for them.

—*Julia, a quivering daughter*

Part One

The Little Girl

She is not dead; only sleeping.—Jesus

One

Burning

Will you keep to the old way
which wicked men have trod? (Job 22:15, NKJV)

It burned, dripping down my back, scathing tender flesh. The stench crept through my nostrils and landed on my tongue. My eyes watered. "Hold still," Mom ordered, one hand rooted in my scalp and the other poised above my head. The ivory walls of that old, claw-foot tub restrained my frantic writhing as I held my breath and braced for liquid pain.

"It will kill the lice," Mom said, swishing my hair in kerosene. She poured it slowly from a metal cup. I lay in it, drenched, my body on fire.

I know her hands burned, too.

Grandma Millie, our neighbor, said it worked because that's what they did in the old days. We wanted to live like they did back then, because that's when life was simple. When people walked uprightly and followed ancient paths, for the old ways taught values that our current world disdained—of sacrifice, hard work, and family. Of living frugally and biblically, which meant not relying on the conveniences of modern culture, but welcoming hardship—*"For in the sweat of your face you shall eat bread."* (Gen. 3:19)

An agrarian life became a holy life.

I remember our first little goat. We named her Nellie and when she gave birth one spring, we watched, horrified, awestruck. When those two little kids bleated and dashed around the pen, leaping and flinging arabesques off each other's backs, we shrieked with laughter and wondered why people needed television. We cuddled those soft vibrant creatures, barely the size of cats; we named them Jacob and Esau and wondered why people went to school "in the real world". We speculated how poor were they, while we were rich, for we witnessed things that could not be taught in any classroom.

Then came the sweat of summer. We killed those creatures, Jacob and Esau, and hung them from a tree. We hacked and ripped and shredded, covered in flies and blood; then we gathered acorns and put them in gigantic white buckets that used to hold peanut butter bought in bulk. Dad covered the acorns with a mysterious toxic liquid, and plunged the soft furry skins into murky depths to sit for weeks. He wanted to tan them, he said. That is what the Indians did. And then we could put them on the floor, so our feet wouldn't freeze in winter.

We divided flesh in pieces and wrapped them in white. Butcher paper, tape, and marker: *jacob, shoulder, Sept. '91.* "Organic," they said. "Hormone-free, all-natural," which meant we'd taken another step closer to being self-sustained. Back to the land, like Laura Ingalls. Independent of the System, and closer to God.

We took the fat and chopped it, trying not to retch. Grandma Millie had the cauldron, so we stood behind her trailer and stirred that slimy fat for hours. "Cook it down," she said. "It's gotta be smooth." Our arms grew tired. The coals glowed red and the pot went ashen. Steam? Smoke? Fog? What hovers over melting fat? The wind blew it in our faces, and our stomachs churned.

We mixed in lye—but Mom and Grandma Millie did that, for lye could burn. We added a little peppermint and poured it out in boxes—thick gooiness the color of oatmeal, but smooth in texture. We covered it so flies would not get stuck, and let it sit for days.

Then we put it on our faces.

"This is the best kind," said Grandma Millie.

"Hey! We just made soap!" said Mom. "Isn't that neat?"

When things like lice come to live, and when you live in a world where modern, traditional treatments are expensive and considered unnecessary, we remember those who have walked the old paths and can tell us about old-timey ways of doing things, like making lye soap. Or how to get rid of lice with kerosene.

And yet, it didn't. Kerosene didn't kill the lice.

Still, she tried. She meant well. My Mom's a good mother; she works hard and loves us. We were desperate. And we burned.

That's the funny thing about the ancient paths. Everyone talks about them like they are The Way to God, the biblical way; how to become righteous and holy, how to be a *true* Christian.

And yet, so many of us just get burned.

Sometimes we can see it—see the burning that leaves us nearly lifeless, with hardened skin and eyes, with toughened scars. Sometimes we feel it as our hearts ache with the weariness of trying to measure up but knowing it's never good enough. Or from wondering why we struggle to hear God and understand His love and grace, while secretly wondering if He's worth following because the burdens seem too great.

These wounds of soul and spirit run deep. Honestly, I never thought I'd write about them because I grew up writing love stories and poems from the word lists Mom tapped onto the blackboard with crumbly white chalk. She homeschooled all of us; our text books came with pictures of Mennonites wearing simple dresses, hair tucked into caps that, to my eight-year-old eyes, looked like coffee filters. And when I wasn't writing or doing school, I'd roll out sheets of paper from the big ends they threw away at the newspaper place and make my sister lie down, and draw around her. Then I'd cut her out and make dresses from the pattern. Sometimes we would chop out rectangle sheets and sew them together to make books, illustrated with Victorian women in colorful array—our dream gowns, full and elegant.

At first we could have all the paper we wanted for free, but later they made us pay so we didn't get them anymore.

Such was life.

Things are different now—for me, for my family. For all of us, things have changed over the years. But for some daughters, they have not. Some girls, like Sarah, struggle with guilt and exhaustion and worry. She writes,

> I have nine brothers and sisters, and as the firstborn, I was always so tired and desperately needed a break! But I could never leave; my friends always came over to our house because I had to help with the kids. Most of them were from Quiverfull families too, but their mothers weren't able to have as many kids as mine. They always said my siblings were "just the cutest things," and were jealous that I got to have so many! I wished I were

them. It was not that I didn't love my siblings—I did! I adored them; it was just so much responsibility on me that never, ever let up. I dreamed of waking in the morning and having my daily quiet time like I was supposed to do, religiously, instead of being awakened with a baby on my lap and being told I needed "to help." I apologized to God over and over for not reading my Bible and praying like I should, but I was so busy with the kids. When I tried to set my alarm early for Bible time, one of the kids would wake up five minutes later.

I can relate to Sarah. For I, too, was tired and yet I adored my brothers and sisters. I, too, apologized to God—agonizing because I'd grown weary in doing good and felt guilty and selfish for needing a break, a relief from responsibility.

Over thirty years ago, beneath a full December moon, this firstborn drew her first breath. I have ten siblings, all with their own eyes, their own perspectives on life. All with stories—and they can tell them if they wish. But the words I write are my own and the ones given to me by others. They are secrets spilled from hidden places, entrusted to me by trembling souls—because sometimes it hurts more to *tell* secrets than to keep them. It's hard to talk about the brokenness, the pain, and the messy parts of life we can't see. I've made mistakes, many of them. I have regrets. I've been accused of many things. And yet, acknowledging the truth of pain is the first step to healing from it.

Paul reminds us, *"Blessed be the God and Father of our Lord Jesus Christ, the Father of mercies and God of all comfort, who comforts us in all our tribulation, that we may be able to comfort those who are in any trouble, with the comfort with which we ourselves are comforted by God."* (2 Cor. 1:3-4) This is why I write, and why I write how it was for me, as I remember them, felt them, believed and understood them. I write about the secrets held within the hearts of women just like me, and I share what I've learned. My journey is told through the eyes of that moon-drenched child whose spirit burned and who desperately needed the promise of Jesus—"I have come," He said, "that they may have life." And as He-who-brings-life stood before me with outstretched arms, my spirit stirred. His voice pleaded, *Come. Come to Me and find rest for your soul.*

I needed life—but even more, I needed rest.

My hope and prayer is that somehow through these pages, a quivering, tired, ashamed daughter might find hope and healing as she follows Jesus on the new way—the narrow way that leads to life.

The night my journey began was the night I left home.

My family gathered around the old white Buick I'd bought with tips saved from my job at the café, watching every move as I stuffed a box beneath piles of books and dresses. When I shut the car door, its tired click was somehow very, very meaningful.

A little sister's lips trembled. "Are you coming back for my birthday?"

I bent to hug her four-year-old body, frail and yellow against the sallow porch light. "Of course! I'll come over all the time." Her eyes met mine with the contagious flash of disbelief, confusion, and grief reflected in those around us. My brothers and sisters watched in eerie silence as I, Judas, straightened to go.

"I don't know why you think you need to do this." Dad thrust his fists beneath his arms. "This is a Bad Idea." He said it like that always—you could see the words stamped across his thoughts like a brand.

Mom leaned against him; tears flowed from her lashes to my heart—burning, sizzling despite the shuddering chill. They looked old then, older than they'd ever been. I fought the spreading fog that choked me every time I faced disapproval or disappointment. I'd tried to explain this a hundred times, prepare them, and get them used to the idea. "It's not like I just *want* to move out. I *have* to. And I've prayed, *hard*."

My soul added, "For years," but I kept it in, flooded with sadness as my siblings huddled together against the enemy—me. Not Judas. Me. *Worse.* How could I do this? Doubt, guilt—they sunk scorching blades into my heart.

Although I wanted to collapse into the clumps of weeds that left sharp miniature daggers clustered in the frayed hem of my jeans, waiting to pierce my fingers and draw blood when I'd pick them out, I managed to keep standing. We hugged each other and it felt weird. Because it wasn't really goodbye, like the farewells you give to grandparents who live halfway across the country. But how to explain that to little ones? How to make them understand why a familiar face is absent from the pillow in her bed? Especially when everything looked fine and breaking up didn't make sense—but sure hurt a lot.

Just try to go on living after that.

Driving away sure hurt, too. Our long driveway seemed to last for miles. Clay stuck to my tires as though the earth itself clawed at me, begging me to stay. In my rearview mirror I watched my childhood home grow smaller; I watched my family slowly trickle towards the porch where we'd sat a thousand times.

Home.

My family.

Suddenly they looked lonely. Lost.

How could I do this? I loved them. Loved them all so much. I wanted to reach out, touch them like one touches a Thomas Kinkade painting—with reverence, with warmed-by-illusion awe towards scenes of peacefulness, perfection. I wanted to run back, pleading for forgiveness. To say I never meant it; that yes, it's a Bad Idea and I'll never leave again. I wanted to take them with me. I wanted to steer my car into an oak and end everything.

A still small voice restrained me, and I burst into tears.

The choice to leave my family and be "on my own" was made many years ago. I was nineteen. It was hard on all of us. Sometimes choices hurt, and we don't know whether to go forward and fight new struggles, or stay behind and face familiar ones. Sometimes things don't make sense at first. Sometimes we have to close our eyes and just keep moving forward, knowing in Whom we believe—He who calls and bids us, *Come.*

Because it's a journey, this faith we claim. Of becoming, obedience, and life. And love.

This really is a love story—just one I never thought I'd write.

God is surprising sometimes.

Two

Refuge

The floors of our house, they curve and undulate, worn by a hundred thousand footfalls; memoirs, pressed in oaken vein.—Luna

Behold, You desire truth in the inward parts,
And in the hidden part You will make me to know wisdom.
(Psalm 51:6)

Memories frame themselves like photographs in my mind. I sift through them and smile, for there are times of sweetness, like when Mom met me outside with freshly squeezed lemonade—just for me—after hours of labor in the sun. Or when Dad laughed, his eyes—amused and blue like summer sky—crinkled shut, and we kids laughed, too. Or when we piled into our van and went on trips, windows down and hair slapping against red faces, elbows poking and shoving and kids hollering, *"But Dad! I gotta go!"*

I remember running around the farm in my little rose-covered bonnet, pretending to be Laura Ingalls while planting herb gardens and inhaling springtime. I loved kissing baby sisters and feeling their little fingers gripped around my own. I remember smuggling kittens into bed at night; I remember spinning round in wildflowers, round and round till I was dizzy and drunk with sunshine, with strawberries and roses strewing in wild orbit around my waist. And I can still relive plunging into the woods, where cozy pines brushed the sky and velvet timbers stood warm and soft and silent.

Safe.

I cherish these memories. My childhood is rooted in the same earth I ran upon and planted in, which bore food for our table and the pattering of little feet after me. It was good. We worked hard and loved one another, standing in the sun and united against the storm.

And yet, and yet...

I have other memories, too. Other moments that shaped my heart, my flesh, and spirit. In my adult life, even as I struggle to understand complex nuances of pain and as David's prayer falls from my own lips—*God, You desire truth in the inward parts, and in the hidden part you will make me to know wisdom*—the cry *"Do You really love me?"* slips out too. I can't help it. In child-like whimpers, the questions come, and He gently leads me into hidden places.

———————

Our little farm house, propped on creaky and tired wooden beams, is unbelievably cold in winter. Sometimes my sisters and I can etch our names in ice inside our bedroom windows.

But it's August now, and I stand at the stove alternately flipping tortillas and rolling them by hand. I long for coolness but it's a luxury we can't afford. My mud-streaked legs drip as farm-grime slides down my skin with sweat; heat affects me badly. But what did they do back in the prairie days? I'm just supposed to be thankful I don't have to wear petticoats under layers of skirts.

But along with the heat and sweat comes smell and rank unfemininity that cannot be masked regardless of how many skirts I wear. I really hate to smell, but fragrances are unnecessary and worldly—not something we need. Sometimes I go almost two weeks without a bath so we can be frugal and conserve water; my sandy sheets are normal and I don't really think about them.

I can't remember when our toilet worked. We just have one and with so many of us, it's always broken. The stench, the smell of unflushed waste permeates the house, especially since it's summer. And the flies, oh the flies—I hate whenever people come to visit and ask to use the restroom. It's so embarrassing, but all we hear is, "You shouldn't be embarrassed." We keep a bucket in the tub to flush it when it gets real bad, and if your tissue isn't that messy you throw it in the trash—don't flush it because it clogs up the pipes and we'll have to pump the septic tank again.

Later, I try to get ready for a wedding. I love this dress. It touches the floor and is black and white and beautiful. Mom bought it for me from Sears with money Nana sent her for her birthday.

I'm starting to feel overwhelmed, as I stand at the mirror and brush my hair, because my legs keep sliding together—the sweat makes them slippery. My beautiful dress sticks to me as I raise my arms, comb in hand. It's hard to move like this, and hard to breathe—I'm baking! The sweat is dripping! And there's nothing I can do. No matter what, even when I try to look elegant for an evening wedding, I—now my face is getting red. I just want to cry. But even more I want to find something and stab, stab, stab my stupid fat legs and the sweat that makes them slide around. My hair is hot, and it frizzes, and I can't do anything with it.

But I hear the reply: God calls us to live like this. We must bring conviction to people. To make people think. To be different—a peculiar people. To do without. I don't need comfort. I need to learn sacrifice, to embrace the hard way because it separates us from the world. To bear these burdens for righteousness' sake, regardless of the cost to my flesh. For it's selfish to seek comfort. To "feel good", to smell good. Relief is unnecessary. I am bad for wanting it. I am like the world, ungodly and bad, bad, bad...

And I'm surprised. I've never felt this burning, killing rage before. I want to kill something—the heat, the sweat, my hair, the fact that it's always like this and probably always will be. No end. I want it to end, and the only way I know it will end is if I kill it. But that's stupid. I can't kill these things. The only thing I have control of is myself.

But I can't tell anyone I feel like this. It's not safe because they wouldn't understand. They'd say I just wanted attention, that I am too dramatic, and haven't read my Bible enough. They'd tell me I needed to learn to be content, that all I want is to be comfortable.

Like the world.

Dad gave me my very first journal for my twelfth birthday. I love him very much, and his thoughtfulness in this gesture is one of the reasons. I still have it, tucked away, and it remains the best gift anyone—besides God or my husband—has ever given me. I endeavored daily to keep it from the hands of sly little siblings, and wrote in it laments that could not be trusted anywhere else.

It was safe.

"Safe" is a word I use a lot. If you know a safe person, you are blessed. This means you can trust them with your heart. You can spill your deepest secrets, your hardest struggles again and again without fear of reaction, shame, criticism, retaliation, embarrassment, or emotional blackmail. You can share your feelings without rejection, without wondering if they will be labeled "sinful" or "fleshly." You can question, doubt, engage, and wrestle with deep spiritual issues without concern that you will be considered rebellious, fallen, worldly, feminist, or apostate.

And safety brings relief, like spring.

April 6. Day before yesterday was pretty rotten. I hurt Mom's feelings—what's new—and cried off and on all afternoon. Got really depressed. Today Dad—who's been pretty frustrated—hurt my feelings bad. He said "I get so much resistance from you."

I don't feel resistant; where did that come from? I didn't know I was exuding resistance. How's that for discouragement? I try so hard to be calm and compliant but never am. I always make waves especially when I don't want to, or am unaware of them. I'm hopeless. I'm a terrible person. Nothing anyone can say will change that. I'm so frustrated with myself!

July 17. I'm having a hard time dealing with what Dad calls my defensiveness. I try to let it go when he gets frustrated, but it's like, he is always getting onto me for how I react to something he says. I sincerely try not to be defensive. But even if I try to explain why I may have said something a certain way or reacted in a certain manner—he shuts me off as being defensive. I am trying to be patient. But it makes me cry and grit my teeth and sometimes long for when I can be out on my own and not have to deal with it. Wrong attitude I know. But it's getting so that I don't know how to say anything without it "sounding defensive", or is taken as being defensive. And even if the total concept of self-defense never even occurs to me, sometimes Dad still often perceives and treats me like I've reacted defensively. It hurts and is discouraging and is really unfair of him. I can't avoid talking to him—I don't want to not talk to him. But sometimes casual conversation even is difficult because I'm just waiting for him to pounce on something and label it defensive. It's like he expects it, is looking for it. I don't know what to do. Just be very patient and continue trying to watch myself and let things go. He's probably under a lot of stress and is taking it out on me or something. I hope I can get better, be better. God, help.

Aug. 10. Last night I was dragged into yet another fiery battle over clothes. Dragged is the word. I was reading a book and Mom and Dad were talking about my poet shirt I made. I was hardly paying attention to Dad's remarks about clothes when Mom said to me, "Somebody's looking at you." I looked up to see Dad looking back and forth between me, Sarah, and Mom with a stern gaze. I was dressed decently, and somebody started Dad going. Dad's all, "Well, I am so tired of talking about stuff that I'm ready to make everyone dresses that when you sit down come halfway between your ankle and knee, sleeves that at least come between your shoulder and elbow, and veils…" He said that way, there'd be no hassle with clothes and we wouldn't have anything form fitting, etc. He kept (and has been for a while) harping on how I'd made him misunderstand about the poet shirt I'd made, how he thought it was supposed to be untucked when I had it tucked in. "So you were out running around the fair, shirt tucked in, showing your crotch and butt." Dad kept going on about clothes, getting raped, and guys staring at one's crotch and butt. I just sat quietly. I figured when he got to heaven and listened to all the conversations, (because the Bible says there is nothing hidden that will not be known) he'd hear the one I had with Sylvia about not wanting to be a stumbling block to any guy and wanting to be very careful of what I wore.

With Dad, I felt like I was being attacked. I tried to keep mostly quiet and listen to it all, though I have heard it before and know all about wearing stuff that's modest, etc. Mom assures me I and my clothes aren't a problem; but if they weren't a problem why would Dad keep bringing it up? Mom said, and I realize, I really, seriously, honestly do, that Dad is really frustrated and is trying so hard to keep us from utter poverty.

I wish I could make Mom and Dad so happy and proud of me. I pray and pray that I'll be a good kid and help them out and make them glad to have me. I know I help around the house and Mom says I'm a blessing...BUT. I wish I was perfect. I wish our family was perfect and loving like some other families I know. I wish Dad's back didn't hurt and all our bills were paid. I wish everyone was happy. I wish we were in Heaven.

Quiverfull is a lifestyle in which parents keep an "open womb" and view children as a blessing, welcoming as many as God wants to send. Many consider this 'letting God plan the family' or 'giving God control of our fertility' instead of usurping His place through human intervention.[6] This way of life is based on Psalm 127, where David writes,

> Behold, children are a heritage from the LORD, The fruit of the womb is a reward. Like arrows in the hand of a warrior, so are the children of one's youth. Happy is the man who has his quiver full of them; they shall not be ashamed but shall speak with their enemies in the gate. (Ps. 127:2-5)

Some families have only two or three, while others have a dozen or more. I'm the oldest arrow in a quiver of eleven. My parents said I should be thankful, because I'm the only one who got their undivided attention—for nearly two years!—before my sister was born. A sister whom, I'm told, I smacked on the head before promptly bursting into tears. I have a picture of that moment, of a wry Nana looking at the

---

[6] Duggar, Michelle and Jim Bob. *The Duggars: 20 and Counting!: Raising One of America's Largest Families—How they Do It* (West Monroe, LA: Howard Books, 2008). Houghton, Craig *Family UNplanning* (Xulon, 2009). Pride, Mary *The Way Home—Beyond Feminism, Back to Reality* (Wheaton, IL: Crossway Books, 1985) et al.

camera while attempting to console a red-faced, sobbing toddler trying to grasp this new phenomenon.

Somehow I learned at an early age that love wouldn't come easily. That love is a relationship reward, not a relationship default, and I had to earn it, to work hard for it. While Quiverfull teaching exalts children as supreme blessings, it doesn't reveal its grim underside—the silent reality that takes place in hundreds of homes every day and of which I learned: *I am only a blessing when I'm useful, helpful, obedient, cheerful, kind, unselfish, submissive, compliant, and responsible.* And only these kinds of blessings deserve love—at least, love as we understand it, the kind that busy parents have time for and use to curb behavior.

And that's what I ultimately learned about God, too.

At fourteen, I wrote:

> *July 7.* I'm trying to think of something I can do to make Dad love me for reasons other than the fact that I'm just his daughter. There is nothing about me, other than me being his child, that he would love me more than say, if Jane Doe was his daughter. It'd be the same. There's nothing extraordinary or uniquely loveable about me.
>
> But lately I've caused too much stress. I am so immature, I stink. I want to do better. I pray and pray but I don't change. I'm so fat. I'm so immature. There's nothing outstanding about me. I'm so ugly inside. At least God loves me. And I know Mom and Dad do, it's just that other than the fact I'm their daughter, I haven't given them any reason to love me.

> *Sept. 9.* I'm having a bad day today. I'm just so tired! I'm so tired of working—there is always something that needs to be done and Dad is never satisfied. I'm tired of washing dishes every night, I wish that the house would stay clean for 2-3 days—the kids are always cutting up paper, getting out toys, splashing water all over the bathroom sink, getting mud and sand all over the bathroom floor. I'm tired of doing laundry—there are mountains of it daily and I am tired of putting clothes away. Lately I have been doing some self-analyzing, or examining—I'm trash…I'm sick of disappointing God.

I know feeling this way displeases God which now makes me feel bad and guilty, which makes me even more depressed. It makes me mad that I'm not satisfied with the way I am, but legs like mine are downright embarrassing! I know people say I am pretty (my sister said I am the "prettiest fat person she knows")— anyway, I'm just embarrassed to be like this sometimes! And we don't have enough money to get more fruits and vegetables, and I'm so tired of everything!

Another thing is, Mom will want to lose weight [from the pregnancy] once she gets back on her feet, and so I asked her if we could go to the track together for an hour 3 times a week, but she said "That takes time." Well I never have Mom to myself! There's always a baby somewhere or brothers and sisters or things to be done or dinner to be made or we don't have enough money—but the track is free! All I want is 1 hour, 3 times a week, with me. But Mom's too busy. I wish we could even get up real early in the morning and do it, but she never gets enough sleep so I guess that wouldn't work.

My sisters and I loved the woods and gardens in spring. Our feet always headed to the luscious Bridal Path, a dark, verdant knoll plush with ferns waist-high and surrounded by delicious groves of Dogwoods. Their veils of white blossoms gently streamed in soft, green, loving air, untainted by the summer's heat which brought sharp, spiky yucca and poison ivy to grassy fields—a yearly war with sweat and bone, watermelon, tomatoes, and corn.

Once, we discovered a hill: steep, long, and perfect for flying down on bikes. We rose at dawn and fought dewy webs—the spiders wove through the night a magical corridor which caught our faces as we rode through. And after we dashed back to the frantic calls of parents who woke to find us gone, the spiders sighed, shook their heads, and set to work.

But in summer, my saving grace came anchored in the earth. Serene and lofty, the strong, silent pines emanated warmth like an old familiar friend. The whippoorwills lived there—my enchanting twilight orchestra and the mournful greeters of the summer-night moon—and the locust, the cicada, and the who-whooing owl.

We swayed in unison, these timbers and I, feet sunk beneath soft, fragrant needles, our heads wrapped in clouds. We were dreamy, ethereal, old and young, reaching high for other places. Lush branches with flowing velvet tresses hid me with love, and invited me to stay the afternoon. To rest, to be, without restraint, without price. Like sentinels, they regally stood guard while child-fingers scratched a thousand pages in little books. They asked no questions, kept all secrets glimpsed over my shoulder.

Those days, I turned and returned to that safe place; I lay in peace, tranquility. Wind brushed hair with languid strokes. My evergreen elbows, a pine-etched map on skin, ached from leaning on the ground. The sky, that flirty sapphire pool, winked through needled lashes, reminding me with jealous twinge how close she was to God.

I picked up my journal. Eyes drifted up there; I scribbled. *God, why did I have to be born? I just want to die!*

Three |

Unspoken

*I do not pray that You should take them out of the world,
but that You should keep them from the evil one. (John 17:15)*

Cognitive dissonance arises when something we observe does not line up with what we're told. This happens when words contradict a lifetime of subtle, unspoken messages; a common example is a mother saying "I love you," then turning away in disgust. The ensuing mental and emotional disorientation creates dissonance in the brain as it seeks to make sense of what occurred. It also describes the conflict arising from inconsistent behavior, attitudes, beliefs, or facts, and often results in confusion, shame, guilt, anxiety, and fear.

Much like a formulaic religious lifestyle which promises we will be more Christ-like, more peaceful, more righteous and godly if we adhere to everything it teaches—and do it the right way, just as it prescribes—but in reality leaves us depressed, sad, suicidal, and exhausted.

In families like mine, girls just don't move out; rather, they stay home and learn how to be good helpmeets and mothers until they begin to court and marry. In this lifestyle, women who choose stay-at-home-daughterhood follow stretched interpretations of biblical passages such as Numbers 30[7] and live "God's way" as defined by many patriarchal homeschooling advocates. Perhaps there is nothing wrong with this, in and of itself, except that those who do otherwise are considered

---

[7] Botkin, Anna Sophia, and Elizabeth Botkin, *So Much More* (San Antonio, TX: Vision Forum, October 2005) et al.

rebellious, drawn away by fleshly desires, feminism and the world—not by God, who loves them.

So why did I? It's complicated, yet furiously simple.

God led me to.

"You aren't held by chains," my parents said to me. They sat together on our old sofa, frustrated and sad and stern. Disappointed, again. "Do what you want. If you want to just leave, *leave.*"

The room swirled. Overhead, bugs kept running into the wobbly ceiling fan and slamming into the wall. Dirty yellow light from bare bulbs cast everyone in a weird shade of saffron. I knew that the older kids, the ones not in bed and who sat in various nooks around us, hung on every word but gripped their books, pretending to be fascinated by the text. Even after dark it was one hundred degrees in that living room—but all I felt was cold, clammy sweat.

"But it's not like that! It's not like I want to just *leave,*" I protested, recalling labels like *selfish* and *of the flesh* used to describe "worldly" people who made similar choices. Besides, I loved them. "Just wanting to leave" sounded so callous and flippant—*not* what was in my heart. Desperate, I pressed on. "Will you be mad at me?"

"Hillary, what do you want us to say? It's what the world does. We are to be a peculiar people. Simple; different from the world. But if it's what you *want* to do…"

The meaningful trailing-off was leading—suggestive, without actual verbal commitment. The significance of it lay in a message understood for years: *if you* want *to do it, it's probably bad.* Because the flesh only wants bad things. Worldly things. Sin.

> *Oct. 21.* I feel so inadequate as far as my parents are concerned. I hope I am not a disappointment to them. I'll compare myself to my sister just to show, although I'm not at all bitter or jealous or anything. She likes goats and I hate them. I read novels; she'll spend days in a history book. I want to be a makeup artist; she wants to be a veterinarian. Just look at me: I hate goats and chickens. I just feel I'm not their "ideal" child. I've tried to like goats and chickens. But I can't; I hate them! And they are always talking about, "We'll get that one bred; keep him away from her because they can't breed together; alright we'll sell this one; how much milk are we getting; we need to get a milk stand; do you want to

go to the goat show; it's time to de-bud the goat; we need to get him castrated…" And I'm sitting there like a leftover pancake, feeling left out—I know by my choice—and bored and disgusted by some of the things they bring up—especially at meals.

Maybe one day I will be more like someone they— whatever, I can't think. Today my sister is at a goat show. And here I am, they talk about goats and I talk about dresses I like and characters in a book, and Dad says, "Are these people we know?" I have a Sweetheart Calendar and Dad says, (sarcastically) "Oh, do we know these people?" I have posters of cute little kids and Dad says "Do we know these people?" I told Mom what I wanted to do and she's like, "Well, that wouldn't be a very important thing if the economy ever collapses. Who will need it?"

Maybe I should, but I don't want to base my life on whether the economy collapses or not. Well—Mom said that everyone is "different" so I shouldn't worry about it. She says she loves me. I feel better.

"Come out from among them."

Mom reminded us often that we were to be separate. Peculiar. It was us against the System—that's what we called modern convenience, government, the way of the world. How 'normal' people lived.

As homeschoolers, during weekdays we hid when cars drove by or played behind the house. We didn't want anyone to see us and call Child Protective Services. Not that we knew who they were, except that they took kids away and ruined families and made children go to real school and get vaccines, which were made from aborted babies.

We definitely didn't want to get taken away or have aborted babies in our arms.

Whenever CPS visited homeschooling families, stories flew up and down the grapevine. "Always in other people's business!" Dad ranted, bristling. "A child doesn't need protection from their parents; *we* need protection from the government! We have the right to school our kids in peace. Why should the state get involved? They just want to control and spy on people!"

Especially people living God's Way.

I tried not to notice when people stopped in their tracks and openly counted our heads when we walked by. I tried not to be embarrassed when Dad and I took the youngest to the store to give Mom a break, and people gushed over "our" baby. I tried not to feel tired when baby after baby was placed into my arms, or ashamed when they tried to nurse or lift my shirt or grope me because I felt like Mom to them— even as young as eleven or twelve, thanks to fullness inherited from my grandmother.

I tried not to be embarrassed because I loved them. I wanted to help. I wanted to lay down my life daily for God, to take up my cross—and could not understand the growing heartache and depression. One day I wrote,

> *April 19.* Mom's been over at Carol's all day. Carol said, *"Thank you for taking care of things so your Mom could be at my house all day."* I'm glad Mom can help her. But it is so entirely stressful. And aside from God, I have absolutely no one to talk to. I hate it that I feel this way, but it must be nice to have someone's undivided care and attention, like Mom for Carol.
>
> I feel lonely. Mom and Dad are wrapped up somewhat with Carol and believe me, I am all for it— and so I am trying to keep up with the kids (bad job today; I've been stressed, and so reacted badly most of the time—wish I could be Christ like under stress!) but there's no one to be wrapped up in me. Oh boy, I'm so selfish and sinful.

From a very young age, I was terrified of several things. Death. Hell. Loss of salvation. The "mark of the beast." One thing was certain: indulging in the System eventually led to all of these.

Only those who lack faith and disdain hardship and suffering succumb to the lures and conveniences of the world. We are a peculiar people, and we trust God to provide without selling our souls to the System. As a child, I knew these messages innately, just as I knew how to make twenty-four loaves of bread at a time, or rock a little brother to sleep in my arms. Simply, this was my reality. And to take a step towards the world, to embrace it, to join the System, meant one thing: *"Adulterers and adulteresses! Do you not know that friendship with the world is enmity with God? Whoever therefore wants to be a friend of the world makes himself an enemy of God."* (Jm. 4:4)

I did not want to be an adulteress. And I definitely did not want to be considered an enemy of God! But did the System really mean all that? What about Christians in the System—our beleaguered friends who Dad berated for defending their bank accounts or for having Internet? What about Mom and Dad—they had driver's licenses. Were they going to hell? Ambiguous reassurance that there was a clause of sorts for "prior ignorance" created only temporary pause. "Plus, we didn't get to choose," my parents told us. "We want all of our children to have a choice. An option. Because once you're in, you can't get out."

There is no doubt that a "peculiar" lifestyle is based on faith. But sometimes the daily mechanics of this life bear testimony not to faith, but to fear. Fear of the world, of the System, of rebellious children, of the "appearance of evil." (1 Thess. 5:22, KJV) Thus cognitive, and perhaps spiritual, dissonance establishes the urgency for totalitarian family control. So between babies and sewing and cooking and my school books from Rod and Staff, I began to grapple with growing up, truth, revelation, depression, and fear—and the deepest, darkest facts of life, my future, and God.

Four |

I thank You, Father, Lord of heaven and earth,
that You have hidden these things from the wise and prudent
and have revealed them to babes. (Matthew 11:25)

A few years ago, I found an old family picture taken when I was thirteen. I stared at myself, at my shapeless face, awkward body, weird clothes, frizzy hair, and red cheeks. I couldn't stop the thought—it lurched from some deep, raw place and assaulted her, the girl in the photo, with a lifetime's accumulation of disgust.

You. Are. So. Ugly!

This unexpected reaction jolted me. Startled, I began to cry. And then sob, uncontrollably, with inexplicable grief. My initial response—*why did you say that?*—dissolved into shrieking screams from a broken spirit. *Why wasn't I good enough for you? I'm the only bad one, the only fat one. The one who is nothing but a disappointing failure. The stupid one who keeps causing problems and making life hard. I'm so sorry...I should have died. I should die; I should've never been born; I'm sorry I was born! I was so sad as a baby...so sad as a baby...so sad...*

At thirteen, I would've liked the adult me. Still creative and dreamy, in my mid-twenties I worked as an artist and relished the love of my handsome, funny, beloved husband. The young me would wonder why I didn't have kids, and where I lived. We'd laugh, share hidden sorrows, and compare childhoods. But if I'd known that I'd be ashamed of whom I was then, perhaps my devastation would have lent courage to deadly desires.

That experience stays with me even now, years after seeing the photo. That girl—she stays with me, too. I remember her well. She hated herself; she thought she could never do anything right, that she was a terrible disappointment to God and a burden to her parents. She considered herself ugly in face and heart; she poked herself with needles, bit her tongue till it bled, pulled hair till eyes watered with pain, dug nails into skin, pounded her obese thighs and clutched her face with hatred. And although she often wept, many times she shook with turbulent sadness because there was no truly acceptable way to release what she felt, except "to pray," and sometimes that didn't help.

A photo freezes time, frames and captures an event, a glimpse of life, a memory—and she, the desperate, hungry-for-love, exhausted little-girl-me, is forever paused in that family shot. Stuck, she is, immortalized; carved in ink at thirteen. As her young face smiled at my aging one, I couldn't stop the flurry of *I'm so sorrys* tumbling out between sobs. My fingers traced her reflection and I yearned to snatch her away, the girl in the photo, to hold her close and make everything okay. To listen to her and teach her the truth about God. To help her see how beautiful she was, how valuable and worthy. To show her that she's not alone. That she was wanted, and infinitely loved; that God loves her and is glad she was born.

There are other photos. Boxes of them, in fact, from all ages, all points in my life. Memories. Glimpses; frozen moments. They string like pearl after delicate pearl on the strand of life, separated knot by knot, intricate, unique, and shaped in darkness. Each one tells a story. They are little fragments of soul, heart, body and spirit crying out for redemption, for wholeness and healing.

They are *my* fragments. She is still there, within me, and aching. What to do with her? I can't abandon this child whom Jesus loves, the little girl who writes,

> *Feb. 26.* I did it again—just said something that hurt Mom's feelings and made her cry. I hate myself for that. I do it constantly. I try so hard to say the right things, edifying things, and I pray so hard, but I don't succeed. I love Mom so much but she still "wonders what I think of her." I wish I could die. No, I wish I was never born so I wouldn't make her unhappy. I wish she was always happy. But rarely am I the source of her happiness. If I was never born she'd never know the sorrow I bring her. I pray that God will reward her greatly because she's wonderful. I'd be content to just be in heaven; God could take my reward and give it to Mom.

Lord, show her I love her and I'm so sorry I ever hurt her. I really am. Help me Lord, help me please. I'm a sorry excuse for a daughter.

March 5. I have come to a place of such self-loathing. I pass up so many chances to be unselfish and giving to my brothers and sisters. Or I've got a bad attitude about whatever I do for them. Why can't I be happy and cheerful? I get impatient with them and I know I'm a jerk. But I am so tired of trying to be good. I pray so much, I try so hard. There has got to be a breaking point.

Something needs to change. Today Mom and I got into an argument. Why can't I be gentle and sweet? I'm getting to a place of detachment, almost numbness. I want to give up but I can't. What is the point of my life? Day passes after day, and every day is the same. I don't seem to be learning anything or changing for the better. I have this heaviness surrounding me. I hate myself this way.

I failed...hurt Mom's feelings and made her cry. Ugh! I hate myself for that! Cried myself for thirty minutes afterwards.

P.S. *Just did it again!* The morning I wake up dead will be a blessing to the world. I'm so hopeless! I can't believe how awful I can be. One of the only good things to come out of this is that I'll always remember that I need God. I'll never be able to forget it! But still, sometimes I just can't believe I say and do some things. I hate myself for it. Like now. Mom and Dad are pretty stressed out, financially and otherwise. Why do I have to make waves? I cannot forgive myself for saying what I do. I feel rotten to the core. One of my new daily goals is to get through the day without making Mom cry.

She wrote those things so long ago, and shut them up inside. Then she grew up and grew away—but there is something my little girl needs, something she knows, and something she has that *I* need.

If she will give it to me...

She towers over me, a smile stretched across her face. "Would you like some candy? You can pick whichever one you want!" She is mama's friend; she helps run this store. It's my favorite store. There are many fun things to see and there's still that faint cedar smell from the floors which creak a little when we walk on them. There's tools and things on the walls and lots of colors peeking out of baskets. I want to look in them—especially those barrels! So full, they are, with sweet, tantalizing shapes and colors—they wink and watch me eye them longingly.

I look at Mommy, who nods.

"Okay," I whisper. But which? So many to choose!

They sit and chat. I'm glad my dress has pockets! I love pockets! They are my favorite. I can barely see over the top of this barrel but I manage, and pockets bulge.

"Just one," calls mama.

Oh!

I hope I put the right ones back where they go. It takes time, but I unload them and pick the one I want to keep. It looks like a strawberry; its red and green wrapper crinkles in my hand, almost too pretty to eat.

Almost.

It's later, much later, and we sit at the table, my mama and daddy, baby sister and me. But wait—my pocket feels lumpy. That's weird. My hand enters, and I am shocked. Oh no! "Mama, look what I found! I forgot one." Out comes a wayward delight, hidden away in a stubborn corner-fold.

Why do mommy and daddy look at me like that?

"You stole the candy?" Eyes wide, they stare, shocked, angry. "Stealing is wrong!"

"I didn't steal it," I say, confused and small and all of three years old. "I thought I put it back." They look at me like they've never looked before. It scares me. How do I explain? "It got stuck in my pocket at the store. I didn't know it was there."

"You took it and stealing is wrong."

I start to cry. I didn't mean to do anything wrong; I really thought I put them all back.

They spank me.

We drive to the store.

"Tell them what you did." She pushes me forward to her friends, who look at me with serious eyes, somber faces.

I sob, embarrassed, confused. I am shaking. Ashamed. It was an accident, right? Did I steal it? They say I did. I must confess. "I'm sorry." I choke on tears. I hold out my hand, a sweaty little piece clutched within. "I stole the candy."

They look so sad. So grieved, mama, her friend, the owner lady. I want to fall through the floor. To be invisible.

"We forgive you," they say.

I really didn't mean to take it. I promise. But they don't believe me. I cry and cry. I'm such a bad little girl. I've hurt mama, her friends, and Jesus. And I'm so confused, now.

I named her Luna, the girl in the photographs. The little girl carved in mind-ink, who aches within; the secret-keeper, the pearl-child of frozen moments and journals. It helps to give her identity, because once upon a time, she lived. She existed; she had hurts and feelings, experiences and ideas. Jesus loved her. God *made* her. She is part of me. She *is* me. And if I want to be made well, if I want to be made whole, I must bring all of me to Jesus. All the broken pieces, stuck moments, hidden parts that cry out for the life and light of Christ, I must bring—bring *her,* Luna—to the narrow way that leads to life. I must bid her listen to the voice of He who says Come.

I must be her safe place.

So I've immersed myself into her world, to listen, to hear what she wants to say, to feel what she wants me to feel. "I don't know how to uncover roots of pain," she says, "but I'll try." And they come, the captured moments and stuck places; they come from Luna—strands of questions, memories, hurts, separated knot by knot:

> Why do I hurt all the time? Why do I want to cry and cry and never stop?
>
> Why do I say I'm sorry all the time? Why is everything my fault, even if it isn't?
>
> Is it really bad to have feelings? They said the heart is deceptively wicked. Is my heart wicked? I thought Jesus lived in my heart.
>
> Is it normal to feel this guilty just for living?
>
> I wanna be invisible. They used to stare at me *down there* to see if I was presentable or not, if my clothes were too tight. Because we had to be modest so guys won't get stumbled or defrauded or want to rape us. What is rape?

I don't like to smell bad on my body but they said little girls don't need to smell pretty. It's just so embarrassing to stink all the time! What can I do?

I haven't read my Bible in—I don't want to say how long. All I hear are the words in Dad's voice. I can't focus on anything except that voice. I open my Bible, and there is Dad. Where is God? Is He really like this?

I burned the beans today and Mom yelled at me. I know we're poor but I'm such a bad, stupid cook! I can never do anything right. I mean, anyone can cook beans.

I thought God told me to do something but Dad said no. Will God not talk to me just because I'm a girl?

If I was a good daughter, I would think all the same things they think, and like all the same things they like, but I can't! And I pray for God to change me but I'm not changed! What is wrong with me? I don't want to be filled with such worldly desires. I try not to like pretty things. God, please take away all the things I'm interested in and replace them with Your interests.

I can't make any decisions. This is ridiculous. I just want to go back to bed. I should've never been born.

I hate myself for not liking chickens and goats. If I were a good Christian girl I would *like* living on a farm, because it's a good way to live and makes us trust God more. Sigh.

I should be doing so many things right now but I cannot get motivated. I pray and pray, but I'm so tired. I can't finish anything I start. Since Jesus is coming back in the next few years, why bother? It's more important to save souls—but I'm not even doing that!

I'm tired of trying. But does that mean I'm rebellious? I'm probably rebellious. But that means witchcraft! Am I of the devil?

Why do we always have to be a "responsibility?" I wish it was fun for parents to have kids.

There are so many things I'm *not* doing that I *should*. The Bible says to him who knows to do good but doesn't, to him it's sin. *I.Have.So.Much.Sin.* Sometimes I don't care anymore. I'm sorry God, I mean I do. I just can't keep this up, this trying so hard. Please let me die.

Because I am so worldly and headed for the world, I get lectures that seem to last all night! But if I do something right, they don't want me to be puffed up, so they don't really say much. This makes me tired and is really discouraging.

Even if I think God is showing me something—the woman was deceived so how can I know what is true? But even though Eve was deceived, Adam willingly disobeyed, so how is that better? UGH! This is so confusing! What if I'm wrong on *everything?*

I hope it counts that we do all this stuff and live this way. I know we're poor but even if we weren't, we'd still do without. We still wouldn't have things that are comfortable, like air-conditioning. Because then we would get distracted and forget about God.

I shouldn't be sitting here enjoying this novel. This movie. This cappuccino with cinnamon on top. I should be productive. There's a lot that needs to be done. I should be getting stuff accomplished. I shouldn't buy this new shirt. They have used ones, just as good, even if they aren't as pretty. Lots of people don't even have money for food, and here I am buying a new shirt. Please forgive me, Lord.

Is it bad I hid in the closet to read a book today? I just wanted to read for a while. But every day is exactly the same! What is the point of my life? I'm useless to everyone. Even if I get all my jobs done, I still mess up and yell at my brothers or sisters. Or get impatient, even if I try not to.

Nothing ever changes. They say I just want things to be exciting. That I'm only interested in frivolous things. They say I'm not content. But I'm just tired of everything being so hard all the time. If we do anything fun, I feel guilty about it. I've started losing all hope! I mean, I do hope for the day Jesus comes back and takes me away from this life.

Nothing is free. I can't enjoy anything without feeling guilty. I can't do anything without thinking I should be doing something else. I disappoint everyone. I never have energy. Even my heart feels tired. It never changes. All I want to do is sleep and cry all the time.

It feels selfish, Luna says. This focus on me. Because we are supposed to die to ourselves. To lay down our lives daily, to sacrifice and help others, to love. Jesus said to love others as we love ourselves; I guess I don't know how since I hate myself so much. And it makes more sense to love others *by* hating myself. Because then I can focus on them and what they need. I can hate myself and all the sin I commit every day and deny my flesh, and by doing so, show others love—because instead of focusing on loving *me* I can love *them.* That's how my brain works, anyway.

But you know what the real reason is? I need pain. If I didn't have it, then how would I learn to be like Jesus? Suffering, even little hurts others might laugh at refines me, sanctifies me. I think I'm afraid *not* to hurt, you know? Because the more we suffer in this life, the more we go through that refining fire, the closer we are to the Lord. That's right, isn't it?

But until you have knelt for hours in a field like my mommy, scrubbing out thousands of cloth diapers by hand because you are trying to do what is best for your children, until you wear your simple clothes till they are stained and shredded and patched and patched again, till you cry with guilt when someone buys you something new and you try to take it back to the store because you could use that money to buy groceries or pay a bill—and yet, with your own birthday money you buy your daughter a new dress so that her father will be happy with her appropriate clothes—till you grow your hair so long you have to hold it so it doesn't fall into the toilet; till you school your children all day, bake twenty loaves of bread by hand, and then stay up all night because one of the goats has birth complications; till you believe so strongly in natural remedies that instead of simple medication you spend hours preparing poultices made with freshly ground herbs or seeds; till you have no close friends; till you have experienced many pregnancies and still get in trouble about your weight—

Until then, you won't understand.

That's my mama. I wish I could be like her. She helps me learn that yes, this life is hard. But that's okay. Because in the harshness of it, we learn holiness. She's as holy as they come while still here on earth. And then I go and make her life miserable. I make her cry all the time and it makes me want to kill myself. If I wasn't afraid of going to hell, I would. My mama's been through a lot. She almost died giving birth when I was three. I accepted Jesus that year but did it again when I was six because I didn't remember and thought it didn't count and I'd go to hell.

Always so preoccupied with hell.

Sometimes people judge us but they don't know. They don't understand and they don't want to know truth! It makes me mad when people say we're like a cult out here in the woods. Just because we want to live separate from the world and homeschool. My parents shelter us because they want us to be innocent and pure; they had worldly childhoods and want it to be different for us. They are doing what God wants.

Dad works hard too. Nobody understands him; everyone criticizes him. That's why I try so hard to communicate right, and be obedient and respectful—and then I go and get "defensive" or "resistant." I hate myself for that too. Why can't I be just like them, to like what they like, and make them happy and proud? God, help!

So yeah, I have some little pains sometimes, but they make me more like Jesus. I wish I had more.

"It's not that I wanted to be comfortable,"
whispered Luna.
"I just wanted to be comforted."

Five

The Old Way

Who among you fears the LORD? Who obeys the voice of His Servant?
Who walks in darkness and has no light?
Let him trust in the name of the LORD and rely upon his God.
Look, all you who kindle a fire,
Who encircle yourselves with sparks:
Walk in the light of your fire and in the sparks you have kindled—
This you shall have from My hand:
You shall lie down in torment. (Isaiah 50:10-11)

Hillary, may you come to know the love of God in your grown up life." I always shrugged at these words, penned on the inside cover of my little New Testament. They sounded nice, but we kids came out of the womb singing "Jesus Loves Me" and already knew about God's love. It was basic—the skeleton of our faith. *"For God so loved the world..."*

Yet I came to cling to this simple prayer, written by the pastor at my dedication service as a child. Turns out, the love of God is a mysterious thing. And for those of us who teethed on the leather flaps of our mama's Bible, knowing, believing, and understanding His love can be one of the most difficult challenges we girls face.

Especially for those of us raised in the old ways, on the ancient trails carved for us.

> There is a way that seems right to a man,
> but in the end it leads to death. (Pr. 14:12)

We all have stories. We all have frozen moments in our lives that linger and ache. It's quite disconcerting to continually wander in confusion and guilt, not knowing exactly what troubles us or how to make it stop. In desperation, we do more—more prayer, Bible study, service—but often reap the fruits of burnout and spiritual exhaustion.

The fruits of the Old Way.

I'd been married a few years before really trying to address them. But as guilt increased and depression tightened its chains, as futility—*why bother?*—and thoughts of death overwhelmed me, one particularly haggard day I stumbled across a flicker of hope on a blog called *A Study in Brown*. Life-laced words swelled and tears flowed as I read:

> Part of redefining normal for ourselves is also realizing that God has created each of us uniquely. Just as the horse and the turtle both reflect God's glory though they are wholly different, so each of us can reflect God's glory by being who we are without apology. For a long time I have thought I must hide my peace and mercy loving ways; their incarnation in my heart seems so different from others' and I have been told I am naive and foolish (oh, if you knew how I have struggled inside against those labels!) but the turtle gains no glory by attempting to be the horse and vice versa. I have learned to respond to the Holy Spirit's promptings in my own heart and follow Him down the path that is right for me. I pray each of you will do the same. It is a joyful, beautiful thing.

Reflect God's glory by being who we are without apology. If only! In desperation I pounded a reply to the author.

> "Each of us can reflect God's glory by being who we are without apology..." How beautifully and simply written, and how tortuous the doing! I am known as the one "who walks into walls and apologizes." I say I'm sorry for everything. I don't know why. I question things that I probably shouldn't, from a rigorous "question everything" upbringing. But that leaves me questioning myself on each little tiny detail in life, dissecting the thoughts and feelings that tiptoe into my path; shredding apart the Spirit-breathed wisdom I have been given from He who is Eternal. Once it is broken down, analyzed, mulled over, and rebuilt, much of the sweetness and

beauty have crept sadly away. I am left with a very mathematical approach to all things lovely which strips the joy out of making my own way through life. I would LOVE to follow the path that is right for me, but I still struggle with the day to day religious voices that were hammered into me from the time I was a young seedling, stretching towards the light. "There is a way that seems right to a man, yet the end thereof is death." Therefore I do not trust anything—least of all, myself. What you describe is like the first sweet breath of fragrant spring air after the harshest, coldest of winters. This probably seems stupid to people who read these words. I'm nearly thirty and love the Lord. I am still coming to grips with things in life. I want to be me without apology. I want I want I want. (And then I hear in my head *"I want starts with 'I' which means it is selfish. We must not be focused on ourselves."*) So I hang my head in guilt and shame and withdraw into the blackest of darkness.

Jesus said, *"Enter by the narrow gate; for wide is the gate and broad is the way that leads to destruction, and there are many who go in by it. Because narrow is the gate and difficult is the way which leads to life, and there are few who find it."* (Mt. 7:13-14) I used to accept without question that "narrow way" meant the Christian faith. And it is—it's following Jesus, as opposed to another religion or person. Yet He also says that *"few will find it."* Christianity is one of the largest religions in the world. So what could He mean?

"You need to choose," says Sara. She is my soul friend and I cling to her words like parched lips crave water. "What is it that you want?'

A whimpering mess, I shake as I cradle the phone. "It doesn't matter what I want; wants are bad. My spirit wars with my flesh." Years of denying myself teach me this—*"I want" starts with 'I' and what's in the middle of s-i-n?*

"Hillary, wants are God-given choices."

My ears hear blasphemy. "No no no. If we listen to what we want, it's our flesh. Our carnal nature fights against the spirit."

Her voice is patient. "What is it that your carnal nature tells you to do?"

I close my eyes, head pounding. "I don't want to feel guilty anymore. I just want to rest. *To be,* without pressure."

"You mean like Jesus said? Come to Me and rest?"

I hesitate. "Well…" It not that simple. "The Bible says to not grow weary while doing good, but I *am* weary! I've spent my whole life trying to do what's right, but I'm nowhere near where I should be. I still struggle with the same old problems I had when I was fifteen—I'm depressed, I'm sick, I can't think, even the old suicidal feelings are coming back. It's one big cycle that never ends. I don't want to hear any more voices telling me what I *should* do; I'm tired of it."

Sara stops me. "Whose voices do you hear, telling you what you should do?"

Overwhelmed, I nearly laugh. "Whose do I not? My parents—I hear Mom's disapproval if I just sit down for a minute because 'there's still things that need to be done.' I hear Dad reading the Bible in my head or arguing about everything. I hear my own self screaming how I've failed."

"It sounds pretty destructive," she says.

"Yes, but we are to die daily."

"Hillary." She speaks firmly but with kindness. "The old way is broad. Old voices, old burdens, old Pharisees telling you what you should do. Do you always want to listen to the old ways?"

"If I know what is good and do not do it, the Bible says I sin. So I can't give up. I'm just so tired, but I can't give up. I have no other choice. No other way." I fight tears.

"There is the way you do not know."

The way I do not know. She speaks with love and I pause. The way I do not know—unfamiliar terrain, uncertain paths, unforeseen steps. A different way.

A new way.

One thing's for sure—I've walked old paths until I've grown dizzy, spinning in the same old circles of doing and trying. Futile effort, while *"the evil days come and the years draw near when you will say, 'I have no delight in them…'"* (Ecc. 12:1) And yet—*"Therefore, if anyone is in Christ, he is a new creation; old things have passed away; behold, all things have become new."* (2 Cor. 5:17) My head whirls. "Come to Me," Jesus says. His words whirl through my head. *"Broad is the way of destruction and there are many who go in by it…"* (Mt. 7:13-14) *"I am the Way, Truth, and Life…"* (Jn. 14:6) *"I have come that they may have life, and that, more abundantly…"* (Jn. 10:10) *"Take My yoke upon you and learn from Me, for I am gentle and lowly in heart, and you will find rest for your souls. For My yoke is easy, and My burden is light."* (Mt. 11:28-30)

Life. I close my eyes. I need life. I crave life. Something must change, for the fruit born on the way in which I tread, even as a believer, is killing me. The burdens I bear are heavy. *Come to Me and rest...*

"Our wants are God-given choices," said Sara. Is it possible for our wants to line up with His? What if, all along, my spirit *did* war with my flesh—the flesh of going the broad way of earning righteousness? Earning love? Is it possible that instead, He was wooing me to follow Him? He, the One who's Spirit dwells inside of us, who writes His laws into our hearts and minds, wanted me to come to life? Me *and* Luna? Did the Spirit of God, who indwelt me even as a believing child, whisper to her, *"This is the way, walk in it?"* Did I then quench the Spirit, listening to what I thought was right, things cloaked in righteousness, having the form of godliness?

"Difficult is the way which leads to life," God says. Perhaps because we go by faith and not by the maps of Pharisees, the burdens of man's *shoulds* and *oughts,* or old voices shrilling in our ears. Perhaps because we do not rely on the light of fires built *by* us or *for* us, but, like Moses, in faith obey God and set out in darkness following a mysterious flame upon the way we do not know.

For our God is a consuming fire.

Without Apology

She didn't know it, but the author of that blog spoke healing straight from the Father's heart as she discerned my cries and answered,

> Hillary,
>
> Dear girl, I wish I could take that weight right off you...the first thing to remember is God does not give us fear. If you are feeling fear—it's NOT the Holy Spirit. He brings gentle, loving conviction and it is not hard to follow Him. He is so much bigger and broader and more patient than we give Him credit for. Religion has a loud, urgent voice that will continue to screech at you (it screeches at me daily) but He can teach you to hear His own gentler voice and ignore the other. Just know that if the voices bring shame, guilt, blackness— that is not your Lord.
>
> I encourage you to take one piece at a time, hold it up to His light and ask Him if it is right for you or not...then just sit back and wait. He always, *always*

answers the heart that is seeking to do His will. Everything you lack you can request from Him: wisdom, direction and courage to walk out your own path. He will provide for you.

I have often had to shut out other voices—even people who are doing good and right things that are just different from my own calling—in order to gain courage to go forward. Get around people (even people online) who are going in the direction you feel God is calling you and stay open to His leading.

Even the Christian world is widely diverse and it is okay to not be a part of—or even in agreement—with every aspect of it. (Just keep loving them!) I have had several times where I started getting interested in something that God did not have for me. I read blogs, daydreamed about it, started changing my actions, and then the Lord came in and gently turned me away. I want to really emphasize that part of it: God is so gentle to the heart that is soft towards Him. You WANT to do right and He will not be harsh with you. You can trust the Lord to treat you as a loving, good Father should treat His child.

I will be praying for you in this area, Hillary. One day you are going to break through the blackness and confusion and find yourself rejoicing and free on the other side. Keep moving forward, sister!!

With love,

Tonia

The New Way

Coming to understand this, to know it deeply, is not like simply asserting a truth. It takes time to transform. It is a journey. It is a life lived in response to the words of Jesus: *follow me.* Not a burden—an invitation. *Come, rest. Enter in the narrow gate. Love the Lord with all your heart, soul, mind and strength; love one another.* It is the willingness to step into the unknown—truly, a narrow way that few find. It is, as Tonia says, breaking through the blackness and confusion to find joy and freedom on the other side.

And it is the response of the little girl to Jesus' voice: *"Arise."*

Part Two

A Maiden's Lament

Behold, You desire truth in the inward parts,
And in the hidden part you will make me to know wisdom.
(Psalm 51:6)

It is a grave disservice
to the heart, soul, body, and spirit of a woman
when she is given the subtle message
that the truth of her own pain
is not as important
as the reputation of the ones who inflict it.

—Luna

40

Dear Mom and Dad,

I know you wanted the best for all of us. You have always tried hard to put God first and be Scriptural. But somehow, in the mess of things, you forgot that each of us are individuals. You also forgot that we were children. You raised our souls and lost our hearts. We need to be great men and women of God, but we cannot be frail, sinful humans. You are continuing down the same path with the younger ones. I have tried to speak out, but it has fallen on deaf ears.

Daddy: I don't know why you did what you did. I wanted to pretend nothing ever happened, but I could not forget. Not the years of pain and issues, and not your arrogant pride. You have never really been sorry for what you did, and I cannot respect you until you face yourself and acknowledge what happened. I will live with your legacy for the rest of my life—in my temperament, in my character, and in the scars on my heart. Because of you, I cannot seem to trust the man I want to marry.

Mommy: I could always sense your disappointment in me. I have always tried to make you proud of me, but somehow I could never be good enough. Thank you for teaching me and homeschooling me. I am using what you taught me to stand on. It is my launching point to fly. You taught me to know what I believe and to swim against the current.

—*Stella, a quivering daughter*

Six

The Rise of Neo-Patriarchy

"I thought it made solid families and was a guarantee of non-divorce."—A divorced mother

I didn't know I could be jealous of a baby. No, not those long, dark eyelashes or that luscious smile. Or his dimples and happy coos. No, Sara's Andy had something else I wanted, although I didn't know it yet.

"He is too hot!" Sara fretted, bouncing up to twist the vents for maximum cool.

"This is Texas. It's always hot." I tickled his toes; Andy lay on my knees and smiled at me like I was an angel.

"But he has to stay comfortable!" Sara bent to kiss his cheek and curled up beside me. I think I glared at her.

"What? He's fine." *I should know; I have ten brothers and sisters. I know about babies!* "It's just 'cause you're a new Mom. Wait till your next one. They'll learn to adjust. They're just babies."

Just babies? Where did that come from? Whatever she said faded away as I chewed the words still lingering on my tongue. I love babies. Of course they should be comfortable. What was I thinking?

She never mentioned the envy on my face as I watched her hold, cuddle, nurture him. And never did he earn the title "just a baby." As she ministered to this precious soul, the startled pang that lurched out of nowhere began to germinate, and I tucked it away in a secret place.

Unfortunately, I am not a mother. But I have been a child. I'm friends with parents and have spoken to both young and old who have offspring of their own. And while I do not know the joy of holding one called "mine" within my arms, there is something I can state with surety: parenting is hard. Rewarding, yes; a blessing, yes, but one that brings inherent challenges. To see that sweet, newborn face is truly a gift, a miracle which no doubt fills every new parent with utter happiness—followed by gripping throes of fear, because truth is, it's an evil world out there. As reality hits—*it's up to me to keep this little one safe, to raise her in the Lord*—many parents seek ways to protect and train their little ones that offer reassurance, Scriptural principles, and godly, faithful offspring. In this quest, some find comfort in the promises of what is known as biblical patriarchy. I will refer to it, instead, as neo-patriarchy.[8]

A Biblical Solution?

Karen Campbell, founder of "That Mom," a ministry for homeschooling mothers, describes this movement in a series known as *Patriarchy & Patriocentricity.* Because it can be difficult to understand, she discusses how those in the patriarchy think. She notes that adherents believe:

> ...that God has given fathers a calling that encompasses the entire family, and that others in the family are there to support and maintain that calling as they have no calling of their own apart from his. Some have called this viewpoint 'hyper-patriarchy,' 'uber- patriarchy,' or 'patriarchy-on-steroids.' I have chosen to call it 'patriocentricity,' which means that the father is central to all things in the home. ...[I]t was derived from the word *ecclesiocentricity,* which means the local church or their (sic) leadership is central to all things. It should not be confused with the sociological term *patricentricity,* which has a similar meaning but is outside the context of the evangelical world.
>
> There's a parallel between *ecclesiocentricity* and *patriocentricity. Ecclesiocentricity* teaches that the church leadership—a pastor or an elder—represents the congregants to God, and God to the congregants.

---

[8] While sincere Christians argue that true biblical patriarchy exists, I believe that what is currently promoted in the conservative homeschooling movement is new and extra-Biblical, therefore I've chosen to make this distinction in my writing. I will use the terms 'patriarchy,' 'patriocentricity,' 'biblical patriarchy' and 'neo-patriarchy' interchangeably. True biblical patriarchy is outside the scope of this discussion.

Patriocentricity teaches that the father represents his wife and children to God, and God to his wife and children. We are examining a religious teaching, a new theology, a modern view that has no historic roots in true New Testament Christianity.

In his book, *Family Man, Family Leader,* Phil Lancaster uses the true biblical concept of Jesus being "prophet, priest, and king"[9] as a word picture of the roles of fathers in their homes. Although he states that the father is not the mediator between Christ and his family, but rather is a representative as defined above, the impression that I get from reading this book and the writing of other patriarchs is that there is a fine line between being a representative and being a mediator.[10]

Families desiring to live God's way and to bring their children up in the fear and admonition of the Lord can find in this neo-patriarchy a strong ally against feminism, immorality, and secular culture. Because the principles of "biblical patriarchy" are by very definition derived from Scripture and provide clear guidelines for those desiring a "biblical family", it naturally appeals to many homeschooling Christian parents. As previously mentioned, while not all homeschoolers are patriarchal, those who preach the doctrines of neo-patriarchy both homeschool and advocate many alternatives to secular and evangelical culture. This patriocentricity, in fact, often seems like the only valid option for those seeking an alternative both to the world and what many consider to be watered-down Christianity. An adult daughter familiar with this lifestyle explains its attraction:

It has everything to do with promises: the promise of a perfect, God-honoring life wherein you shall be blessed abundantly, your children will grow up to be good people, you and your spouse will be happy, fruitful, loving God and others, and therein inherit the abundant life promised by Jesus. On the outside, for those whose hearts are longing to live pleasing to God and longing

---

[9] Lancaster, Phillip *Family Man, Family Leader* (San Antonio, TX: Vision Forum, 2003) p. 139

[10] Campbell, Karen "The Patriarchy & Patriocentricity Series, Part 1" That Mom—Real Encouragement for Real Homeschool Moms. 7 September 2007. www.thatmom.com

for an abundant life, the patriarchy package looks heaven-sent.

That's why my parents got into Gothardism *[the teachings of Bill Gothard—H.M.]*. They were afraid of their kids rebelling and doing what they did as teens; their marriage was struggling, and suddenly here came a program that promised the life they so desperately wanted. And with it, people whose lives looked perfect. There was just enough good teaching to keep them coming back, keep them trying harder, and keep them sucked in. When we rebelled anyway, they were told it was because of our bad hearts, or that they didn't follow the program well enough, or because they didn't protect us from bad influences—any reason BUT that the promises and the program were flawed.

A wife and mother who supported these beliefs in her own family agrees:

One huge attraction to patriarchy is that Everything Will Work Out Wonderfully (if you just do x, y, and z). Boy was that ever attractive—and I've seen that same lure pull in so many others!

In a similar vein, the teaching that This Is God's Way, and that you are outside of His protection and covering if you are not following it—versus inside His protection and covering if you are—is highly attractive if you love God.

So, if you believe it is God's way *and* you love God, then you don't feel like you have any other choice but to follow it. The teachings become all wrapped up with your concept of God, and you begin to believe that you can't have the one without the other.

Biblical Roles

The doctrine of biblical patriarchy asserts itself as true and God-ordained, rising in part as an urgent response to what leaders consider false ideology and the subversion of society and family.[11] Explicit delineation of gender roles is essential, for as family is considered the

---

[11] Vision Forum Ministries. "The Tenets of Biblical Patriarchy." www.visionforumministries.org (11 December 2009)

basic foundation of society and begins with *male* and *female,* living and growing "God's way" requires faithfulness to its tenets.

Understanding patriarchal interpretation of gender roles is precluded by grasping other Christian views. Many evangelicals are divided between complementarianism[12] and egalitarianism.[13] Because Christians can disagree over these precepts and can equally find support for their positions in Scripture, it is not my aim to debate this matter but to provide a brief, cursory overview.[14]

A complementarian view of manhood and womanhood maintains that while men and women are created equal before God, they have distinctive roles and responsibilities in the home and church. Adherents teach that Scripture prohibits women from leadership positions in ministry, and that husbands have authority over their wives as long as they do not lead them into sin.[15]

Egalitarianism also teaches the equality of men and women, but differs from complementarianism by affirming that Galatians 3:28 covers everything pertaining to life, ministry, and society; and therefore one's gift, not gender, fits an individual for their role. Egalitarian husbands and wives practice one-anothering submission, to the chagrin of patriarchy which denounces egalitarianism as heresy on par with humanism and feminism—perhaps even more so, for many Christians support and teach its tenets within evangelical churches.

In agreement with the others, biblical patriarchy officially affirms that men and women are equal before God in personhood. But, adding to the complementarian view of gender roles in the home and church, patriarchy asserts that when women assume positions within the community alongside men—much less *over* men—regardless of matrimonial status, they step outside the "ordinary and fitting" place designed for her by God.[16]

Patriarchal documents exhort husbands and fathers to lead as Christ, with sacrifice, love, and grace, bounded by Theonomy and civic law. The literature is exhaustive, in fact, and provides overarching

---

[12] The Council on Biblical Manhood and Womanhood. www.cbmw.org

[13] Christians for Biblical Equality International. www.cbeinternational.org

[14] While such a debate holds value, in my humble observation it often distracts from helping those who are truly hurting individuals.

[15] The Council on Biblical Manhood and Womanhood "Core Beliefs: The Danvers Statement on Biblical Manhood and Womanhood" November 1988 www.cbmw.org. (27 May 2010)

[16] Vision Forum Ministries. "The Tenets of Biblical Patriarchy." www.visionforumministries.org (11 December 2009)

instruction and guidance for all of life for those who embrace its doctrine—which in addition to gender roles, includes claiming dominion through the womb (Gen.1:28) and other presuppositions.

Unfortunately, there is little accountability within many patriocentric homes, and grave opportunity for the abuse of authority. And while many, no doubt, succeed leading their families well, there is a growing under-culture of pain and tragedy within this branch of conservative Christianity. And in the effort to follow formulaic teaching, many families experience the serious fruits of a father-centric system.

Reflection

Seeking to raise one's family using strong, confident, biblical precepts is not an unworthy desire. How it is carried out is another matter. How the Bible is interpreted is another matter. For when well-meaning yet imperfect humans attribute beliefs, behavior, and personal values to Scripture, and ultimately to God, they bear a solemn role as ambassadors to others, even to very young children. This *can* be a good thing. Unfortunately, it isn't always—and what then?

In the patriocentric family, many times emphasis is placed on doctrine over person, where practically—and sometimes literally—one's secondary doctrines are considered more important than flesh and blood, and therefore more important than our Friend and Brother, Jesus Christ. (Mt. 25:40) In the patriocentric family, we see time and again judgment promoted over mercy, law over grace, and shame over love. And in the patriocentric family, all too often we see what happens when stumbling blocks are placed in the way of earnest children seeking Christ.

However, Jesus showed us something altogether different. He emphasized through His life, death, and resurrection that our relationship with God is about person over doctrine. We, the children of God, are more valuable than the law, and because of this, the progression of neo-patriarchy and its formulaic nature misrepresents the true nature of God. He's written His laws on our hearts. He sent the Holy Spirit to guide us as we learn to walk in the Spirit. As adults, we can seek our heavenly Father as we search for truth and healing; shifting our focus is essential if we want to be set free.

"Follow Me," Jesus said.

Consider this your invitation to life.

Seven |

Abba, Father

"My parents said it was my fault that my extended family, grandfathers specifically, weren't saved, because I was ruining the witness I should have as a submissive daughter."—Mary R.

My friend Steph has four little girls, bundles of energy, constantly clamoring for stuff—toys, books, trips. "Ask your Dad!" she often proclaims. "It puts the burden on him," she confides with a smile. It gets Dad involved, Mom's job is easier, and the girls experience the boundaries of authority. And kids need that—children need to know their limits, not only for themselves, but also for the parent, and later, for others in positions of power.

A godly father is a valuable asset to the strength and growth of his wife and children. A gift. Within any system comprised of humans, there is natural potential for selfishness, dysfunction, and for honest but hurtful mistakes—but hearts surrendered to the transforming power of Christ can seize the opportunities which arise from sin, through them demonstrating the humility, love, faith and sacrifice of Jesus. A parent who humbles himself before his child, admits sin, and asks forgiveness show that child the truth of what he's taught her all her life. For a mother or father to openly acknowledge false doctrines, hurtful standards, a lack of lovingkindness or other mistakes reminds children how important it is to keep their eyes on the Lord and seek truth. If anything, this helps them to have compassion and respect their parents *because* of their humanity, not in spite of it. In these ways and more, despite our frailty, God is glorified, relationships are strengthened, and growth is sustained.

Sadly there is very little of this in a patriocentric family. A patriocentric family instead focuses its attention on the shortcomings of the children, and this makes it very difficult for them to be at peace with their parents.

Godly Authority

As Christians, we know that our Heavenly Father is the perfect parent and has ultimate authority over all of creation. We find our final standard as parents in the parenthood of God. Not only does knowing Him and His nature reveal the boundaries of godly authority, but He daily gives us wisdom for all parenting issues in our lives, including those as imperfect daughters of imperfect people.

Authority has the potential to be abused, like any other gift. To understand how neo-patriarchy derives and understands authority, I want to contrast two particular parenting styles.

First, when earthly parents derive their authority from their Heavenly Parent, we call this *authoritative parenting*—as the influence of the living God is alive and well within a family. The fruits of this kind of parenting lead to life and growth. Let's look at some of the characteristics of our Father God:

- He chastens whom He loves. (Heb. 12:5-7) The Greek word for "chasten" is also used for "nurture" (Eph. 6:4, KJV), "instruction" (2 Tim. 3:16), and "chastisement." (Heb. 12:8)
- He is merciful, compassionate, longsuffering. (Ps. 86:15, Mic. 7:18)
- He is appropriately angry—which also means appropriately not angry. (Dt. 7:4, 32:16; Jer. 25:6-7)
- He is our Helper. (Ps. 121:2, Is. 41:13, Heb.13:6)
- He meets all our needs. (Phil 4:19)
- He is gentle and comforts us. (Ps. 18:35, Rm. 15:5, Is. 66:13, 2 Cor. 1:4, 7:6)
- He finds joy in His children. (Zeph. 3:17)
- He has reasonable expectations in keeping with His character and relationship with us. (Mic. 6:8, Mk. 12:29-31, 1 Jn. 3:24, 1 Jn. 5:21)
- He is love. (1 Jn. 4:8) Love suffers long and is kind; it does not envy; it does not parade itself, is not puffed up; does not behave

rudely, does not seek its own, is not provoked, thinks no evil; does not rejoice in iniquity, but rejoices in the truth; bears all things, believes all things, hopes all things, endures all things. (1 Cor.13)

Note that while our Heavenly Father wants us to obey, as our patient Helper, He *helps* us obey. He knows we can't do it without Him. He doesn't sit back and tempt us as some parenting 'experts' do,[17] but He actively loves, draws in, and strengthens His children. He is angered and grieved by rebellion, but a biblical study of anger and rebellion reveals a primary context of perverse idolatry and worshiping false gods, or of those completely degenerate.

This is not an accurate portrayal of many quivering daughters.

Totalitarianism

Authoritarian parenting, on the other hand, differs greatly from *authoritative.* While godly authority seeks to parent after the heart of God, submitting their authority to His own, authoritarian parents derive power from status—a runaway version of: *I am the mom. I am the dad. Obey without question.* We see cognitive dissonance as "blessings" essentially become "property" to be manipulated and controlled. While this certainly may not be intentional, an authoritarianism environment grievously injures children and misrepresents our Heavenly Father to the souls He's created.

Many in favor of authoritarian parenting argue that it's necessary because we need to learn blind obedience to God. But true obedience is never blind, even when it doesn't understand fully. A study of the heart of God and reflection on His merciful nature reveals that He is tender towards us. He is not threatened by our questions, our mistakes, our misunderstandings. He wants us to obey from the heart, because we *want* to. But authoritarianism coerces children to satisfy the immediate, temporal desires of parents, to obey only because they *have* to. This is ineffective for addressing hidden and eternal issues which are more important.

Let's contrast these two styles in light of how they might appear within the family:

---

[17] "Try it yourself. Place an appealing object where they can reach it...When they spy it...say, "No, don't touch it.".Remember, you are not disciplining, you are training...It may take several times, but if you are consistent, they will learn to consistently obey, even in your absence." Pearl, Michael and Debi. *To Train up a Child.* (Pleasantville, TN: No Greater Joy Ministries, Inc. 1994) p. 5

Authoritative Parents / Parenting	Authoritarian Parents / Parenting
Responds to the child; sensitive to her needs; through example shows her the heart of God; "person over doctrine"	Reacts to the child; emphasis on requirements of the parent, lifestyle or conviction; "doctrine over person"
Communicates reasonable expectations, is humble and helps the child obey; more concerned with truth than being right; respects the child's thoughts and her feelings; demonstrates unconditional love; quick to forgive	Is highly demanding and proud; more concerned with being right than truth; invalidates and disrespects the child's thoughts and feelings; withholds love, approval, and acceptance; quick to condemn and shame
Encourages responsible decision-making while still at home; appropriately loosens the reins throughout maturity; views mistakes as necessary for learning and opportunities to teach grace	Exerts extreme levels of control—physical, mental, spiritual, and emotional—over all aspects of life into adulthood; emotionally abandons or wounds the child; treats mistakes as proof of innate badness
Discipline is nurturing, with an ultimate goal of directing the child to the Lord and the influence of the Holy Spirit	Discipline is intimidating and power-motivated, reminding the child that the parent is "the boss"
Points to Christ; steps out of the way of the Holy Spirit; shows that faith trusts in God	Points to the father; stands in the way of the Holy Spirit; shows that faith trusts in "methods" (works)
Teaches healthy, age-appropriate physical and emotional boundaries; is "safe"	Highly enmeshed; physically, spiritually, emotionally and psychologically destructive; is "not safe"
Values the relationship with the child; encourages personhood, mercy and grace; communicates love	Emphasizes first-time obedience, performance, law; utilizes fear and shame

Jesus and Authority

Authoritarianism is a form of government that assumes complete and total control—like that of a dictator with absolute sovereignty within his realm. As King of kings and Lord of lords, Jesus came to serve and to pour Himself out for the world. His words and example establish the clear scope of godly authoritative power and govern every potential gender, marriage, or parental "role."

> And He sat down, called the twelve, and said to them, "If anyone desires to be first, he shall be last of all and servant of all." Then He took a little child and set him in the midst of them. And when He had taken him in His arms, He said to them, "Whoever receives one of these little children in My name receives Me; and whoever receives Me, receives not Me but Him who sent Me."
>
> (Mk. 9:35-37)

The following passage carries it the extra mile:

> The scribes and the Pharisees sit in Moses' seat. Therefore whatever they tell you to observe, that observe and do, but do not do according to their works; for they say, and do not do. For they bind heavy burdens, hard to bear, and lay them on men's shoulders; but they themselves will not move them with one of their fingers. ...They love the best places at feasts, the best seats in the synagogues, greetings in the marketplaces, and to be called by men, 'Rabbi, Rabbi.' But you, do not be called 'Rabbi'; for One is your Teacher, the Christ, **and you are all brethren. Do not call anyone on earth your father; for One is your Father, He who is in heaven. And do not be called teachers; for One is your Teacher, the Christ. But he who is greatest among you shall be your servant.** And whoever exalts himself will be humbled, and he who humbles himself will be exalted. (Mt. 23:1-13, emphasis added)

With these words, Jesus contrasts *what authority often looks like* and *what it should be.* He challenged scribes and Pharisees, teachers and fathers—men whose core identities carried power, authority, dominion—to become humble. To lay aside their rights to assert this power and instead, present themselves as servants. And worse, as slaves, for culturally, slaves were the scum of the earth. In doing so, Paul issued a plea to be like Jesus:

> ...who, being in the form of God, did not consider it robbery to be equal with God, but made Himself of no reputation, taking the form of a bondservant, and coming in the likeness of men. And being found in appearance as a man, He humbled Himself and became obedient to the point of death, even the death of the cross... (Phil. 2:5-11)

Reflection

Consider that we are on loan to our mothers and fathers. We came into their world so they could minister to us the compassion, mercy, and love of Christ—to be His hands, His feet, and through the authority vested in them by the Most High, lead us and then release us to Him. To care for us until we are able to care for ourselves and others. Contrary to what some may insist, this does not promote an ungodly form of autonomy. Actually it requires us to cling all the more to our Heavenly Father and be dependent upon Him while He heals us and our relationships.

Many of us struggle with feeling that we never measure up to the standards or expectations of our parents. But in reality, it's not a question about how we measure up as daughters, for in the end, our parents will be accountable to the Lord for how *they* measure up. They will answer to God. Just as "Salvation belongs to the LORD. Your blessing is upon Your people," (Ps. 3:8) we as daughters are gifts from the Lord—but we still belong to Him and will answer to Him alone at the end of our days. Salvation and faith may be taught and influenced by our parents, but just as they answer to God, we will answer to Him as well and are responsible for working out our own salvation with fear and trembling.

An understanding of patriocentricity and authoritarianism will prove invaluable when we discuss the effects they have on womanhood. But it's important to understand that regardless of your view on roles, the answer to becoming a healthy, growing, and truly biblical family is not to be father-centered or even family-centered, but to center on the Rock, Jesus. Because when everything else falls away, what you're centered on will be all that's left. And sometimes that is nothing.

Eight |

Womanhood

> *"I was told that because I felt as though God was speaking to me personally and calling me in a direction my Mom and Dad didn't authorize, that it really couldn't be Him, and therefore I was committing 'parental adultery.'"*—Charis

> *...In the day that God created man,*
> *He made him in the likeness of God.*
> *He created them male and female, and blessed them*
> *and called them Mankind*
> *in the day they were created. (Genesis 5:1-2)*

My father loved to quote a line from an old Henry Bogart movie, *The African Queen:* "Human nature, Mr. Allnut, is what we were put on this earth to overcome."

Human nature—the propensity for sin that haunts all of us. As a sensitive, dreamy child, my nature responded most to sensory or emotional experience and was often condemned by others. I wondered: had God made me this way so that I could learn to overcome myself?

Now that I'm a woman, according to complementarian interpretation of 1 Timothy 2:14 I am by nature particularly prone to deception: *And Adam was not deceived, but the woman being deceived, fell into transgression.* But if the Lord writes His laws into my heart and mind, can't He help me know truth and avoid deception?

These questions and the natures of personhood and womanhood are very convoluted—even controversial—subjects among Christians; especially in neo-patriarchy which emphasizes the roles of men and women in the home and family and uses the Bible as a list of proof-texts to support their claims. These spheres of dominion and domesticity become layered, confusing, and complex as sincere believers wrestle with what they've been taught, what the Bible says, what others tell them—while simply wanting to live faithfully.

While this chapter is by no means exhaustive, I hope that it provides a comforting place to pause and rest while we seek the Lord for truth regarding His precious creation.

True Biblical Womanhood

In Paul's second letter to the church—comprising both men and women—at Corinth, he writes, *"But I fear, lest somehow, as the serpent deceived Eve by his craftiness, so your minds may be corrupted from the simplicity that is in Christ."* (2 Cor. 11:3) This verse reveals two things: that even though Paul used the well-known example of Eve and the serpent, the concern of deception is not limited to gender; and that the simplicity of Christ is something to value.

While life is not always simple, Jesus is. At least for us, He should be. He is the Son of God. He is the way, truth, and life. He came to heal the brokenhearted and to set the captives free. Jesus is all about obedience, truth, love, freedom, and eternal life. A woman pursuing Christ-like living will concern herself with all of these—and so will a man. We are all mankind, reflecting God's image as female or male. (Gen. 5:1-2) We are called with a heavenly calling (Heb. 3:1) and there are no roles in heaven for believers other than sons of God, equal to the angels who neither marry nor are given in marriage (Luke 20:34-36). Christ defines us (Gal. 3:28), and our highest calling is from God *"who has saved us and called us with a holy calling, not according to our works, [what we do] but according to His own purpose and grace which was given to us in Christ Jesus before time began* (2 Tim. 1:9)."

But for those of us still confined to this earth and reflecting God's likeness as female creatures, modern patriarchy tries to interpret for us what this should look like. It reduces personhood to a matter of what we do, not who we are. It takes beautiful attributes given by God and strips them of their mystery and pristineness by making them universal for all women, all cultures, all time. But what God makes unique, patriarchy makes normative. What God makes blessings, patriarchy makes commands. What God makes secondary, patriarchy makes primary. What God makes for some, patriarchy makes for all. God is a God of order, and as God, exceptions—miracles, the supernatural, or anything that He wills—are a part of His order.

Since only women can be mothers, patriarchy asserts that motherhood is our highest calling, and that godly women will aim for it.[18] Yet Scripture records instances when the Lord closed the womb (1 Sam. 1:5) and even when barrenness is cause for rejoicing (Is. 54:1). True, motherhood is precious, but the Lord cautions us against drawing our worth, value, and identity from anything other than Him. Paul writes,

> For we do not commend ourselves again to you, but give you opportunity to boast on our behalf, that you may have an answer for **those who boast in appearance and not in heart**...and He died for all, that those who live should live no longer for themselves, but for Him who died for them and rose again. Therefore, **from now on, we regard no one according to the flesh.** Even though we have known Christ according to the flesh, yet now we know Him thus no longer. Therefore, if anyone is in Christ, he is a new creation; old things have passed away; behold, all things have become new.
>
> (2 Cor. 5:12-17, emphasis added)

Let us be women who serve the Lord Jesus first, and naturally we will do and be whatever He asks of us, whether that is to be a mother, a missionary, a wife, an artist, a mechanic, a doctor. Let us abide in Him, and He in us, and we will bear His fruit—whatever that may be for our lives. (Jn. 15:4-6)

Unfortunately, for quivering daughters, it isn't that simple.

Older Daughters at Home

Many patriarchal families stress stay-at-home daughterhood—adult daughters[19] remaining under the command of their fathers at home until marriage, continuing to learn homemaking skills and how to be a "keeper at home" until they have families of their own. Such

---

[18] Campbell, Nancy *Be Fruitful and Multiply* (San Antonio, TX: Vision Forum Ministries, 2003) et al.

[19] I want to emphasize that I do not presume to address minors, or situations regarding minors, on the subject of authority. My remarks are intended towards, and apply to, adults only.

arrangements extend beyond practicality, which might be when a daughter who is involved in animal husbandry needs space on the family farm; or others who choose to stay home while furthering education, saving money, or enjoying companionship.

In neo-patriarchy, fear of feminism drives many to demand a controlled femininity, and through misinterpretation of Scripture, elevates the father to priest-like status as he mediates between—or represents, or answers for—his wife or daughter and God. In patriocentricity, it is taught that women who move out, take jobs within a man's "public sphere of dominion" (including industry and commerce)[20] are outside of God's will, and consequently, His blessing and fruitful growth in the faith. A popular article among courtship advocates suggests that God essentially takes a back seat in the relationship between a father and his "property"—his daughter.[21]

Carolyn is in her mid-thirties and recently married. She explains the difficulty she faced trying to listen to the Lord while growing up in her childhood home:

> They told me I was "deceived" because I am a woman. That God would only speak to me through Dad. At one point I cried out and said, "I just want you to acknowledge that I can legitimately be led by God myself!" Dad answered me, "That is an oxymoron! You cannot be led by God yourself!" Dad even said I would never be his equal before God. When he said that, I tried to leave the room but Mom grabbed me and tried to physically force me to stay. Over the next four months, they tried many things. They withheld love. Refused to hug me. Told me I didn't love them. Had "discussions" that were 2 to 3 hours in length. Told me I was "making people in my family sick."
>
> They blamed me for any problems, saying that since I'd never told them I had these thoughts, it was my fault. When I tried to explain that I was too afraid to share, they said they never did anything to make me afraid. Anything I told them about pain in my upbringing was called "family-bashing."

---

[20] Vision Forum Ministries. "The Tenets of Biblical Patriarchy." www.visionforumministries.org (11 December 2009)

[21] Schlissel, Sarah. "Daddy's Girl: Courtship and a Father's Rights." Bible Topics. www.bibletopics.com (10 February 2010)

Another woman who left home as an adult writes,

> I grew up under the influence of Bill Gothard and all
> related thinkers, although my parents were not as
> militant as some. Throughout my adulthood—I'm in my
> thirties now—I have always felt dogged by guilt. The
> whole large family, courtship, no college education
> thing still makes me feel so trapped and guilty despite
> not actually being a part of it anymore. In a moment of
> great depression I read about "visionary" daughters and
> seriously thought about returning home—that maybe
> God would bless me then, and I would feel "right". My
> one sister married a man totally "free" in his Christianity
> and my other sister has struggled with same-sex
> attraction and anorexia. My parents admit they had
> moments of "weirdness" and have struggled with guilt
> now that they know we have not turned out "perfect."

Bill Gothard, who founded the Institute in Basic Life Principles,
promotes the "umbrella of authority" philosophy which teaches that
there is essentially a mystical, divinely-ordained patriarchal protection
for women who remain beneath a father's protection, which is defined
by his headship and bounded by the walls of his home (see Job 1:9–
10).[22] This is loosely based on the verse, *"Honor your father and
mother," which is the first commandment with promise: "that it may be
well with you and you may live long on the earth."* (Eph. 6:2-3)
However, parental honor is not determined by one's living quarters or
even by obedience, which we discuss in a later chapter. Yes, there are
daughters who have enjoyed the protection their fathers provide; yet as
evidenced by the story of Tamar, who at her father's request—with his
blessing—obediently went to her brother's house and was raped by him
(2 Sam. 13:7-14), we know there is danger in placing faith in our
principles and teachings. We need to each seek the Lord for His
wisdom and will for our lives.

But since women supposedly cannot hear from God apart from their
fathers or husbands, this teaching continues to confuse father-
centeredness with Christ-centeredness. These are commandments of
men presented as sound doctrine.

---

[22] Gothard, Bill *Institute in Basic Youth Conflicts: Research in Principles of Life*
(Oak Brook, IL: Institute of Basic Life Principals, 1987) et al.

The Daughters of Patriarchy

Besides crippling a daughter's direct relationship with God, those who seek to reinstate conditions of biblical patriarchy (father-centered neo-patriarchy) and who essentially "keep their virgins" (1 Cor. 7:36-38) inadvertently often delay fulfillment of a crucial goal: a legacy of many faithful offspring to carry on the values, convictions, and visions of neo-patriarchs throughout future generations.[23] For in a sad ironic twist, increasing numbers of women in their late twenties and thirties remain "safely" at home, patiently waiting for husbands to find them. As unmarried adult daughters continue to perfect the art of homemaking, help to mother and school young siblings, and learn to be a godly helpmeet, many through spiritual discipline strain to cauterize wounds made tender with disappointment. This explains why for both stay-at-home adult daughters and those who leave the home, the issue of a father's authority is a complex and delicate matter.

Diana is the oldest daughter in a homeschooling family of ten and writes,

> Because my parents wanted to follow God, they tried to follow the standards listed in the Biblical Patriarchy articles. They controlled me to such a degree that I could not do anything on my own. My entire future was laid out for me—I would stay at home and care for my younger brothers, make meals, garden, sew, play music, and have some type of home business until "Mr. Right" came along. We would have the perfect courtship and then get married and start having children of our own. In fact, they taught that if you weren't ready to have children as soon as you were married, you shouldn't marry!
>
> But I kept failing all the time. My cooking never measured up to what it "should". My older brother teased me about making the same meal again and again, but that was the only meal I could actually make taste right! I was only fourteen and still had to cook at least half the week's meals, so I did what I could. But when I turned fifteen I began thinking that maybe I didn't want to marry. Not out of rebellion; I just felt so exhausted and couldn't handle the possibility of being this tired,

---

[23] Einwechter, William "A Biblical Vision for Multi-Generational Faithfulness" (Audio CD; San Antonio, Texas: Vision Forum Ministries, Inc. 2005) et al.

misunderstood and controlled my whole life. I also wanted to pursue interests that God had given me—not sewing, playing music or cooking. But then this made me feel guilty again, like I was being selfish.

At fifteen I told my parents that I did not agree with a lot of things that they believed—like wearing long skirts all the time, even to swim. I did not believe that rock music would send someone to hell. And most of all, I did not believe that Jesus loved us any less if we did not stay at home to be homemakers. I told them exactly what I wanted to do with my life…but then the next few days were miserable! My dad went and talked to the elder of our church about me. I felt so wicked and depressed.

My guilt just grew and grew; I finally wrote my parents a letter, telling them I was terribly sorry, that God convicted me, that I would be a homemaker—that I *wanted* to do that. I felt ashamed that I'd dared be so selfish, thinking about what *I* wanted, instead of having children or caring for children. I apologized and cried.

While I felt disappointed being such an awful Christian, at the same time I thought I might be okay—not good, but okay—enough for God because I was still wearing my long skirts every day. I started wearing a head covering for a short time, thinking that would help me; I listened to classical music and hymns—never anything with a beat! I grew my hair really long and told everyone that I wanted to have lots of children too, one day.

The worst part is I never felt good enough. If I was praised by someone at church, they would be told that "she still has far to go." In our lifestyle, it's an unwritten rule that adults shouldn't give a child too much praise or they would become proud and puffed up. So, I received very little. But I heard lots of negative. Lots of "God says this or that," "We are WORMS," and "He would not like that attitude."

My parents tried so hard. They did what they knew to be best, they followed the "standards" for doing things God's way and thought it would turn out picture perfect as Quiverfull or conservative books suggest. But those books forget about reality sometimes, the complications in life, the things that come up that you can't plan for. That's why it's so important to trust God, have faith, and learn that it's not about all these extra things we do that matters, but our hearts.

As we sort through the mixed messages we receive regarding womanhood, it helps to study how God sees and interacts with us. Writer Adele Hebert, who contributed to Katharine Bushnell's book *"God's Word to Women,"* reminds us that:

> ...Jesus never got angry with the women. Jesus corrected five women. They were definitely not rebuked as some commentators/preachers have alleged. Jesus only rebuked the wind, sea, demons, unclean spirits, fever and men.
>
> Jesus was more severe with his male disciples than anyone else. He rebuked Peter, calling him Satan (Matthew 16:23). He rebuked James and John for wanting to call down fire from heaven to burn up the Samaritan village (Luke 9:55). And He rebuked the eleven male disciples for not believing the women's testimony (Mark 16:14). However, Jesus never rebuked women.
>
> Let us examine the verses pertaining to women. Notice how Jesus leads them ever so gently, no names, and no harsh critical words. In fact, Jesus always uplifts them, guarding their honor, hearing them, blessing them...[24]

In neo-patriarchy, *who we are* as women becomes lost in the frantic quest of *what we do*. Roles and responsibilities become as dry as mathematics. This culture stifles grace through pressures cloaked in Titus 2 type language—to be "more submissive," to be "keepers *at* home," (complete with emphasis), to "have a gentle spirit," and others. Perhaps some of these exhortations are needed, but we must remember that Jesus advocated balance—

---

[24] Hebert, Adele. "Jesus was Angry." God's Word to Women. www.godswordtowomen.org (13 April 2010)

> Woe to you, scribes and Pharisees, hypocrites! For you pay tithe of mint and anise and cummin, and have neglected the weightier matters of the law: justice and mercy and faith. These you ought to have done, without leaving the others undone. (Mt. 23:23)

Patriarchy is never balanced. And through lack of balance, we lose sight of the heart and will of God, who is more concerned with our *being* than our *doing*. God seeks those whose hearts will follow Him, who respond with obedience (1 Sam. 15:22)—regardless of the cost, regardless of cultural norms, regardless even of family.

> Do not think that I came to bring peace on earth. I did not come to bring peace but a sword. For I have come to *'set a man against his father, a daughter against her mother, and a daughter-in-law against her mother-in-law';* and *'a man's enemies will be those of his own household.'* He who loves father or mother more than Me is not worthy of Me. And he who loves son or daughter more than Me is not worthy of Me. And he who does not take his cross and follow after Me is not worthy of Me. He who finds his life will lose it, and he who loses his life for My sake will find it.
>
> (Mt. 10:34-39)

Reflection

In Scripture, we find the example of Mary who submitted to the call of God independently (Lk. 1:26-38) and was immeasurably blessed for her obedience. After His resurrection, Jesus first appeared to Mary Magdalene (Mk. 16:9-11). But one of the most moving passages in the New Testament reveals a precious glimpse of God's tenderness through the stricken lament of His Son:

> O Jerusalem, Jerusalem, the one who kills the prophets and stones those who are sent to her! How often I wanted to gather your children together, as a hen gathers her brood under her wings, but you were not willing!
>
> (Lk. 13:34)

What an emotional outpouring! It is this same Jesus, made known to you and me, who transformed the life of one broken, desperate soul while His feet walked upon this earth. *"And suddenly, a woman who had a flow of blood for twelve years came from behind and touched the hem of His garment. For she said to herself, 'If only I may touch His garment I shall be made well.'"* (Matt. 9:20-21)

Consider this Jewish woman. Twelve years of uncleanness. Twelve years of sorrow. Twelve years of loneliness and isolation; likely without even the comfort of a human touch. Twelve years of lost wages, dwindling hope, and despair. Twelve years of enduring the requirements of the law:

> If a woman has a discharge, and the discharge from her body is blood, she shall be set apart seven days; and whoever touches her shall be unclean until evening. Everything that she lies on during her impurity shall be unclean; also everything that she sits on shall be unclean...If a woman has a discharge of blood for many days, other than at the time of her customary impurity, or if it runs beyond her usual time of impurity, all the days of her unclean discharge shall be as the days of her customary impurity. She shall be unclean.
>
> (Lev. 15:19-25)

Into this world walked Jesus. Imagine this woman's fear—yet also the desperation that drove her to grasp the hem of his robe! For even that small touch would render Him unclean, according to the law, and yet twelve years of agony drove her to seek a new way, the narrow way of life, which few find. *"But Jesus turned around, and when He saw her He said, "Be of good cheer, daughter; your faith has made you well." And the woman was made well from that hour."* (Mt. 9:22)

Other translations quote Jesus as saying, *Take heart! Have courage!* For in addition to the healing of her body, consider the impact on her soul. Instead of disdain, she was welcomed into the presence of God. Instead of turning away, He made her whole. He looked at her—oh, imagine the love in His eyes! He received her in her shame, when all others would have turned away or recoiled from her touch. He commended her for walking in faith. He comforted her, for she still felt trepidation, despite her faith. In one moment, He took away her uncleanness. He brought life to her body and healing to her heart. She was touched by God in the midst of her impurity, while all others in the name of God rejected her.

It is this Jesus who wants to heal and restore the womanhood that has been so convoluted for us. While others may argue over roles and definitions, may we instead be like Mary, the sister of Martha, who sat at the feet of Jesus, drank in His words, and discovered a better way. May we be like Mary Magdalene, who saw the Lord and proclaimed Him, even when those around her did not believe. Let us be like Mary, the mother of Christ, who said *"Yes!"* to the Lord's calling, even though it challenged religious, cultural, and physical norms. Even though she was afraid.

As you step into the new way, the unknown, the way you do not know which leads to life, know without a doubt that Jesus looks at you with love in His eyes and says, *"Come. Rest. Have courage. Take heart, daughter. Your faith has made you well."*

Nine

Valley of the Shadow

"But it's not just the Quiverfull daughters who are depressed. So are the parents. I could tell countless stories of the shame, guilt and legalism my mom endured under this movement. There is so much pressure to conform, to pretend we're all so incredibly happy. We aren't. But we think doing it for God is right, so we do. We smile and act like everything's okay, that we want this lifestyle; in fact, we want ten more children if God would only send them."—Leanne

I was 6 when I saw that old 70's movie, *Thief in the Night*. Tucked into a musty pew at a local church, I watched a nightmare splash to life. You mean people are gonna disappear? That I might wake up, alone, next to a pile of clothes?

My poor Dad. Terrified of waking up abandoned, I didn't want to go to sleep after that and kept him up many nights, crying and asking questions about Revelation, end times, and the mark of the beast. His tenderness and patience—no brusque *"you need to go to bed"*—eventually paid off and my fears were stilled.

I write about fear a lot. Along with a twist on the word "Quiverfull," it's the basis for "quivering" daughters. It's important, because in a religious, neo-patriarchal, authoritarian system, fear is what gets you what you want. I wince—it sounds callous that way. Without the emotional element of fear, the patriocentric structure remains skeletal. With fear, it pulses with climatic urgency.

It hardly needs stating that there is growing spiritual darkness, cultural apathy and immorality in our society. Our families, our children, and our future are in danger and it is natural to want to protect our loved ones. But God is not surprised by evil, nor is He powerless against it. He calls Christians to trust in Him, and not to fear the schemes of man (Ps. 56). How we react to danger shapes our victory over it, and it shapes our faith.

Ironically, fear tends to run in circles. When we fear something, we naturally react to protect. Sometimes we hide and defend, or become compelled by revolution. A crisis demands response, change. But with change, how do you maintain momentum, commitment, loyalty? How can you ensure that future generations will remain faithful? By cultivating a fear-based environment, you perpetuate the cycle. Furthermore, if you use the Bible and add God's name to justify and motivate, fear takes on a whole new dynamic.

But there is no real victory in fear, only a misplaced faith.

Fear is a Verb

Fear moves. It motivates and speeds us up, or slows us down to a halt. For Christians who struggle to know how or what to fight, fear has a radical power. It tempts many Christians who are ruled by it to place their faith in a system of rules, rather than in God:

- When you are afraid of the System, withdraw.
- When you are afraid of the devil, pray.
- When you are afraid of the world, hide.
- When you are afraid of wrong behavior, manipulate.
- When you are afraid of making mistakes, add more rules.
- When you are afraid of the government, go off the grid.
- When you are afraid of embarrassment, shame.

While some of these things are good to do—we are commanded to pray, in fact—it's important to note that the only biblically-endorsed fear is the fear of the Lord. In this context, fear denotes reverence, respect, and awe. Scripture tells us that to fear God is wisdom (Job 28:28, Prov. 3:7). But note: fear of any kind induced by others is not godly, helpful, or righteous. *You,* fear the Lord, is the command. This is self-controlled, healthy fear. But toxic fear seeks to control others.

- When you are afraid of chaos, control.
- When you are afraid of worldliness, control.
- When you are afraid of sin, control.

- When you are afraid of temptation, control.
- When you are afraid of being too permissive, control.
- When you are afraid of your children failing, control.
- When you are afraid of failing as a parent, control.
- When you are afraid of having rebellious children…*you control.*

Now imagine being a little girl, born and raised within this environment.

Sheltered by Fear

Fear-based totalitarianism manifests in many ways. Some families fear the government; others fear the world and secular institutions. Some fear evil. While not limited to patriocentricity, fear-rooted behavior employs characteristics that are inappropriate for faithful Christians. A secular document, The BITE Model, identifies many areas high demand groups seek control of members, and this is eerily similar to how women from authoritarian families experience life.[25] Yet unfortunately, when they seek amelioration, concerns are often considered reflective of rebellious attitudes towards authority and a disdain for "godly" sheltering.

There are various degrees of it, of course. I remember Christian magazines snatched mid-air by Dad as friends would hand them over. We grew up without television or internet. When they had time, Mom and Dad liked to read books before we did; many times we just ended up reading the same ones over and over. Personally, I appreciate that my parents cared about me and wanted to protect us. I sympathize with those who desire to keep their children from sin, even when their methods may be unorthodox. But does this always make it right?

When I was twelve, we began hosting a home-church with a few other likeminded families. A single bachelor came sometimes; he was about forty and kept saying how he couldn't believe I was only twelve, that I looked "at least sixteen" to him despite my modest clothes and lack of any sort of cosmetics or style. I always felt that he watched me when I walked away, although I was actually kind of tomboyish. It embarrassed me, but I didn't say anything. What if I was wrong? To me at twelve, that would've been even more embarrassing, inviting questions I didn't know how to answer.

---

[25] Hassan, Steven "Mind Control: The BITE Model." Freedom of Mind Center. www.freedomofmind.com (12 January 2010)

This man was popular and jovial, always giving hugs, making people laugh, and rubbing our shoulders. One day in our family's living room, he made inappropriate sexual advances towards me. I froze, shocked and startled. Then he casually remarked that "we" would get in trouble if anyone knew, because, *"I forgot you aren't sixteen."*

As if.

For months I writhed in guilt. I wondered if I'd led him on somehow. And I worried that others would accuse me of being immoral or immodest when I wasn't—and I couldn't bear to risk accusation. I should have spoken up, but I didn't; maybe I was afraid my parents wouldn't let anyone come over after that and we'd be even more isolated than we were before. And in fact, I never said anything about this until I was married, years later.

I'm not resentful and don't blame anyone other than him for what happened. But as we children continued to be sheltered and monitored regarding things like books, activities, even the news we listened to or the "ungodly" neighbor kids, I remember thinking quietly to myself, *"all this control over relatively insignificant things, but you have no idea what happened in broad daylight in our very own living room."* It goes to show that despite the best intentions and careful work of parents, sometimes things still happen. As previously mentioned, Tamar the daughter of King David obeyed her father and went to her brother's house—which is a perfectly reasonable and respectable thing for any young woman—and we see the tragedy that followed.

Obviously this doesn't negate efforts to protect children from harmful influences. Many parents do what they can, and may God bless them for that. And as adults, we can address the fruits of these things and more without dishonoring them in the process. Is it possible to over-shelter? Is it possible to cultivate an environment of fear? Yes. And is it healthy, good, and helpful to examine the effects of them, to untangle sordid roots? Also yes. We can scrutinize all the ramifications that fear-based living drilled into our framework and take them before God for healing—and we can do this without fear ourselves.

In the midst of a dangerous storm, Jesus asked His disciples, *"Why is it that you are so fearful? How is it that you have no faith?"* (Mk. 4:40) And Paul reminds us that whatever is not from faith is sin. (Rom. 14:23)

The Fruit of Fear

We are repeatedly cautioned in Scripture to look not at appearance, but at heart. As Jesus taught, washing the outside of the cup—keeping busy focused on externals—has little effect when the inside remains unclean. He said, *"Do you not perceive that whatever enters a man from outside cannot defile him, because it does not enter his heart but his stomach, and is eliminated...What comes out of a man, that defiles a man. For from within, out of the heart of men, proceed evil thoughts, adulteries, fornications, murders, thefts, covetousness, wickedness, deceit, lewdness, an evil eye, blasphemy, pride, foolishness. All these evil things come from within and defile a man."* (Mk. 7:16-23)

The concept of child sheltering exists as a responsible endeavor to bar the effects of these defiled men from tainting vulnerable children. Certainly, age-appropriate cautions need to be in place. But Christian daughters who have left behind the milk and who chew on the meat of the Word need room for the Holy Spirit and faith to work and grow. And when a consistent, urgent milieu of fear governs every move a family makes, this is counter-productive to quiet, steady, faithful living. Whereas faith can move mountains, fear grows and *builds* mountains. We fear:

- what others might think
- labels
- pain
- neglect and abandonment
- that God will not intervene
- walking in the flesh
- being disobedient
- hurtful words and accusations
- failure

A fear-based environment shifts scenery from time to time, but unless the root is eradicated, it never really goes away. The overwhelming emphasis on fear-based control within religious families affects every part of life.

The reason why it's so effective has to do with a common little psychological wonder we call *the human mind.*

Bounded Thinking

When someone seeks to affect behavior apart from God, controlling the mind is the most effective method for coercing change. For example, if someone can make you *think* a certain activity is ungodly (and perhaps it is) then a woman seeking godliness would naturally refrain from this activity. But this can be dangerous when it's based on extra-biblical applications and gravely increases the potential for spiritual and psychological abuse.

Perhaps these words will sound familiar: *"We are teaching you to think for yourself." "I just want you to think." "You're not thinking, are you!" "You need to learn to use your brain."* Many families, homeschooling ones especially, strongly encourage independent thinking. There is nothing wrong with this; it's important to stand strong against the dumbing-down so prevalent in our culture. It's good and biblical to develop intellectual prowess. Scripture tells us how to guard, mature, and strengthen our thought life and mental capabilities. Unfortunately, patriocentric families hold true free thinking captive to a more controlling system of thought I call "bounded thinking." [26]

This happens within many kinds of close relationships—parent-child, husband-wife, employer-employee, and sometimes even within codependent friendships. And it's a prime example of cognitive dissonance. Within such conditions, freethinking quickly mirrors the dominant pattern of thought controlling the environment. Instead of giving others the tools to come to godly conclusions via Scripture and the Holy Spirit, those who—intentionally or not—promote bounded thinking for all practical purposes *become* "Scripture and the Holy Spirit," or the arbiters of truth and wisdom that reveal God's will. In this case, dependents are encouraged, "think, use your mind." Then they are conditioned to intuit what types of thinking are satisfactory and acceptable—thus demonstrating the bounds of independent thinking.

But Paul tells us, *"And do not be conformed to this world, but be transformed by the renewing of your mind, that you may prove what is that good and acceptable and perfect will of God."* (Rom. 12:2) To be conformed is to be squeezed from the outside, whereas transformation comes from within—and with it, we discover God's "good and acceptable and perfect will" for all of life. This includes our minds, but bounded thinking is ultimately all about control.

A young newlywed named Emily shows how it can gradually develop:

> Sunday used to be 'family council' day—a fun, family routine, initially facilitating discussion and

---

[26] Janja Lalich, author of *Take Back Your Life: Recovering from Cults and Abusive Relationships* with Madeleine Tobias, coined the term "bounded choice" to describe how one's options are constrained by their environment. This is the foundation for my use of the phrase "bounded thinking."

communication. But as Mom and Dad began adopting many new philosophies and ideas, it became an 'announcement ceremony' where we really couldn't have any input or ask questions. And then it phased out of existence. At one of the last ones we had, Dad told us that from now on, he and Mom had to oversee all our books from the library, and look at our mail before we could read it. It seemed like we replaced communication and relationship with rules and control.

Laura is in her thirties and affirms the type of control many parents seek to have upon their adult daughters:

My sister and I were not allowed to have any jobs except those we could do at home. I found teaching piano to be enough for me. God made me love kids and love teaching and music. But my sister did not like either. Still, she was forced into it because it was the only thing she could do. She had very few students. From the time she graduated high school until age twenty-nine, she mostly sat at the computer playing games. She suffered terribly with hating herself and thinking she would never amount to anything. My parents picked on her about "not having ambition." They didn't get that she wasn't created to do what they were forcing her to do. The control was so strong at one point (she was twenty-eight) that they were chiding her when she came downstairs with her hair naturally curly because they thought she should do it straight. She still had to ask if she could get a haircut.

When someone seeks to affect behavior apart from God, controlling the mind is the most effective method for coercing change. For example, if someone can make you *think* a certain activity is ungodly then a woman seeking godliness would naturally refrain from this activity. This can be dangerous when it's based on extra-biblical applications and gravely increases the potential for spiritual and psychological abuse.

How do we distinguish when control is called for, and when it's unhealthy or too much? Others may help guide and train us, but for Christian adults, self-control is a fruit of walking in the Spirit. While there are times that control is necessary, such as the legal restraint of criminals or those who intend to inflict harm on themselves or others, this only becomes necessary after they have ceased to control themselves. The only biblically-endorsed control of any human being is limited to that of yourself.

Reflection

> …Woe to the shepherds of Israel who feed themselves! Should not the shepherds feed the flocks? You eat the fat and clothe yourselves with the wool; you slaughter the fatlings, but you do not feed the flock. The weak you have not strengthened, nor have you healed those who were sick, nor bound up the broken, nor brought back what was driven away, nor sought what was lost; but with force and cruelty you have ruled them. (Ez. 34:2-4)

Authoritarianism, ungodly coercion, and debilitating levels of control never have a place in a godly home. When your earthly shepherds have not fed you, strengthened you, healed you, or sought what was lost, but have instead weakened you, broken your spirit and your heart, and driven you away—there are inexorable wounds crying out for the grace and mercy of Christ. While many abuses are committed in Jesus' name, *He does not condone them.* Repeatedly He reminds us that He is the Good Shepherd who lays down His life for His sheep. Many adult daughters, exhausted and desperate to serve the true Shepherd and seek a better way, are like those of whom Jesus says: *"Yet they will by no means follow a stranger, but will flee from him, for they do not know the voice of strangers."* (Jn. 10:5) As neo-patriarchal parents demand, control, withhold love, and serve the law, consider that perhaps the troubled spirits of their quivering daughters wisely do not recognize this voice.

Ten |

Flesh

"Inside I was suffering. I was so tired. I just wanted to do something for me. But what a selfish, ungodly thought! I had to not matter, while everyone else did. But I was a little rebellious; I snuck off with a baby on my hip, to read for a few minutes sometimes. But then I'd be reprimanded for not getting enough done. And the guilt would just increase—a heavy, never-ending cycle."—Kelly

"Eventually I developed a deep longing for a good relationship with my mom. But I felt so ashamed of myself and how I didn't measure up. I coveted how the "best" Christian daughters always claimed their mom was their best friend. My mom didn't have enough time in her day. By the end of the day, when the children were finally all sleeping, there was no time left to spend with her, and I was too tired anyway. She did try. Once in a while we had a special night when we crafted together. But those were rare."—Faith Davis

As the oldest of 11 children, if you asked me which of my brothers or sisters I could part with, without hesitation I'd say, "Not one. Not a single one." They are all precious to me; like a vibrant bouquet, if one stem went missing the whole gathering would not be the same. I thank God He gave me my family and I cherish the moments I've had with each beloved brother and sister.

I struggled, however, for years, straining to correlate the very real love I felt for them with reality. The depression, perfectionism, suicidal fantasy and emotional, spiritual, and physical exhaustion made it very difficult. I've heard many girls add to this: "If I so much as suggested how tired I felt, all anyone would say is, *"then imagine how your mother must feel."* You can't say anything after that. So I just shriveled up inside."

And it's true. As deeply committed Christians, most of us grew up on the milk and meat of the Word. When we'd wish we spent more time with Mom and Dad, we'd remember to be thankful in all things. If we felt overcome with tiredness at the news of a new baby coming, we'd remember how we loved babies and that we are called to love and serve one another—and then feel guilty for feeling tired in the first place. But we missed the point. We slowly became buried in pain—lamenting, like Elizabeth, who writes:

> I was never patient or perfect enough. But I was 12, 13, 14 years old, and watching children all day! I was so tired, and no matter how hard I tried, I could never measure up to this girl or that girl at church—girls who had maybe one or two siblings around their own age, not ten, mostly younger, who they had to care for. I started to feel angry being compared to a girl with one sibling, held up as my role model. I began asking all my friends to "pray for me, I need more patience." No one ever told me that I was already more patient than seventy-five percent of mothers—and I was just a young teenager! I cried into my pillow at night, but no one saw. What made it worse was that I was always so tired. And people thought I was looking for an excuse to be lazy. But I wasn't—I just never felt rested or that I ever got the sleep I needed. But having this hanging over my head made me feel terribly ungodly!

It's hard to admit being heart-and-soul, flesh-and-bone weary. That deep exhaustion which means we have nothing left seems so unchristian, for this tiredness seems to prove that we've failed, that we've let everyone down—including God. Daring to whisper the truth seems like blasphemy. Yet for many of us, what is the truth? The words—they are nearly impossible for a woman seeking godliness to say.

"I'm tired."

When I finally collapsed, it was after nine years of avoiding the truth that my body tried to tell me. And even then, the overwhelming thunder of *shoulds, oughts,* and a thousand memorized verses roared without mercy in my ears, rendering me incapacitated with guilt—"He who knows to do good and does not do it, to him it is sin." "Do not grow weary in doing good, for in due time you shall reap if you do not lose heart." "Press on towards the prize." "The Bereans searched the Scriptures daily."

As a sinner who had lost heart, too exhausted to press on, and without the mental stamina of a Berean, my shortcomings pounded my brain until it turned to mush. I could not think. I'd stare at a page, words swimming before me, and re-read a single paragraph ten times before it sank in. I'd pop my vitamins, consume massive amounts of Verona from Starbucks and still have no energy to complete simple household tasks. Prayers consisted of fuzzy thoughts—*"Lord, help!"*—wafting heavenward. Lack of motivation and extreme lethargy seemed to freeze my muscles while hours passed and I accomplished nothing. "This is my thorn," I'd sigh, and beg God to make His strength perfect in my weakness.

I was depressed, but depression is too clinical an explanation. It was more than that. I'd been in this place before, throughout my life, fighting differing degrees of fog that never went away for good. I felt burned out. Stuck. Useless. For a while, I think I went a little crazy. But I was desperate. It was only when I began to observe the connection between my fatigue and guilt that light began to dawn—at last, I found something that made sense.

Shame.

Like identical twins with opposite personalities, guilt and shame often mimic one another but they have radically different effects on a woman's heart, soul, mind, and body.

Understanding Shame vs. Guilt

The definitions are simple enough. *Guilt* is the result of a sinful choice or action, an externalized feeling of regret over a committed wrong. *I did a bad thing and I regret it.* Guilt is designed by a loving God to bring us to repentance, restoration, and growth—necessary qualities in the life of a believer. But *shame* is an emotion caused by an overwhelming sense of worthlessness. It is a feeling of perceived wrong internalized through negative thoughts: *I am bad. I always do bad things. I never say the right thing. I am worthless, disgraceful, a failure who should have never been born.* The problem is that shame often masquerades as guilt—but it is false guilt. When we're raised in an environment that judges our worth based upon our actions, we learn to filter what we think, what we do, and everything said to us through a screen of disgrace that shapes how we view the world, ourselves, and ultimately, God. While Jesus can miraculously cure everything that ails us, most often learning the truth is part of our healing journey—tailored with love to meet the deepest cries of our souls as we walk with Him.

Here are a few examples of the differences between guilt and shame, and how they affect our thinking:

Shame	Guilt
Makes us want to run away from God: "I am wicked and God cannot look upon sin. I am a filthy rag, a worm, a wretch. I wish I were never born."	Makes us want to run to God, and His kindness leads us to repentance. "Forgive me Father for I have sinned. Create in me a clean heart."
There is something wrong with me.	I have done something wrong.
I'm no good.	What I did was not good.
I am a mistake.	I made a mistake.
I am depressed, exhausted.	I need to make it right.
I feel shame for who I am.	I feel guilty for what I do.
I feel sorry for who I am.	I feel sorry for what I did.
Tool of abuse, a weapon, used by those who wish to manipulate and control. Brings humiliation.	Gift from God to restore us to fellowship with Him and others. Brings humility.
I'm not good enough and can never measure up to what I should be.	I trust the One who justifies the ungodly.

Earlier I mentioned that "depression" is too clinical, too sterile a diagnosis to explain the nag of shameful exhaustion. However, the Lord has given us tools in clinical psychology to help us understand complex problems in human thoughts and behavior, and these tools are incredibly useful.

Boundaries

As a result of living in a shame-filled environment, many women struggle to distinguish between their needs, feelings, wants and ideas and those of another—and they feel guilty when they try. We've all known people who seem "extra clingy" and "extra needy" or who always want to fix someone. In psychological parlance that's known as being codependent—when someone's boundaries get blurred and they are no longer self-controlled, but are mentally and emotionally exploited by another person's needs.[27]

We all have and need boundaries; they are the lines that say, *"Here you stop, and I begin."* While we would never agree that violation of body or sexuality is okay, many people run wild with emotions, time, resources, minds, hearts, and souls—or allow this behavior from others. When a child (even an adult child) is used to meet the emotional or religious needs of a parent, spouse, etc., the child is taken advantage of. This results in enabling sin and irresponsible behavior in the loved one. Scripture tells us to exhort one another to good works, but we can't do someone else's good works for them. Being over-responsible is not conducive to helping others become strong, mature individuals. Placing someone in a position of inappropriate responsibility is to take advantage and cause them to stumble. "Love your neighbor as yourself" is the second greatest commandment, suggesting a beautiful balance between selfishness and selflessness. Unfortunately, within many patriarchal families, boundaries are not only confused, they are often condemned. Labels like "selfish" or dire warnings of evil autonomy serve to keep the lines blurred. But the consistent violation of boundaries is abuse—mishandling, misuse, causing hurt or injury. Here are just a few of the many ways they can be breached:

- *Physical boundaries:* lack of adequate privacy, inappropriate expectations and over-responsibility, incest or any form of sexual abuse, slapping.
- *Emotional boundaries:* denying or belittling the feelings of another—*"You shouldn't feel that way," "You shouldn't let that bother you!"*—as well as redefining and reinterpreting: *"You aren't sad; you're just mad you didn't get your way," "You're too old to feel like that; you're just being foolish."*

---

[27] I highly recommend "Boundaries" by Cloud, Henry and Townsend, John. (Grand Rapids, Michigan: Zondervan, 1995)

- *Psychological boundaries:* Telling another person what or how to think—*"You shouldn't think like that," "Use the brain God gave you."* Judging one's intellectual capacity—*"That's stupid," "If you were smart, you would..."*

Violating the boundary of another—the personhood of one made in the image of God—is highly disrespectful, sending the shameful message of unworthiness. As Christians, we know the importance of service and having a humble heart. But when a young woman is given the subtle message that she doesn't matter—often through use of Scriptures that encourage her to "die daily," to "take up the cross," or "to consider all others better" than herself—she learns that she is here for the *use* of others. These beautiful, sacrificial exhortations from our Lord become twisted theological barbs to wound, stab and confuse.

We must retrain our minds to understand truth when we have been scarred by lies. Protecting our God-ordained boundaries helps us recharge, refresh, and maintain the health we need—physically as well as emotionally and spiritually—so we can serve and help others in our lives. Even Jesus knew the value of boundaries when He sent away multitudes of needy, desperate people so He could spend time alone in prayer. Discovering our boundaries and enforcing them can be difficult, especially when others aren't supportive, but one thing that helps is listening to what we need and want—and realizing that these are actually choices that we can make.

Choices

Sara stuck with me as I struggled to comprehend this. "Your wants are God-given choices," she said, words lingering in mental grayness, mind savoring the aroma but unsure of the taste. But as guilt, malaise, and exhaustion compounded, I finally "rebelled." I gave up, gave in to my "God-given choices." Long after this, I wrote the following letter:

> My upbringing was drenched in Scripture. I read and memorized the Bible on my own, daily, sometimes two or even three times a day—in addition to family Bible time. I printed pages and pages of verses and taped them to the wall by my bed so I could read and memorize while waking or drifting off to sleep. I am grateful for this, for the words are written deeply on my soul which benefits me greatly even now.

However, as an adult I began to question and wrestle with my upbringing. I experienced loads of shame and guilt in the process, down to hearing my father's voice while I read the Bible, hearing it when others prayed, seeing my mother's disapproving or disappointed face in my mind and hearing *my own conscience* speak to me in her voice—I became desperate.

I stopped everything. I withdrew from society, from everyone really except for my husband and one or two trusted friends and mentors. I stopped reading my Bible. The truth is, I didn't want to view the Bible or God as hurtful; I still loved God with all my heart and knew that beneath it all, the god I thought I knew was not the true God. But when something inherently good—like the Bible—has been used as a tool for abusive control, it is necessary to distance from this and heal. In a sense, I went under a spiritual 'de-tox'. It's not unlike a de-programming regime for those who exit cultic groups.

During this time, which lasted nearly a year for me, I determined to decide what to believe for myself, and not because I was told that it was true. I became willing to let go of everything I'd ever been taught. I still clung to Jesus and His work on the cross, for I knew deep within that He is the Way, Truth, and Life—but anything besides Him I shed off me like a fur coat on a summer day.

Without sanctuary and rejuvenation of spirit and flesh, treading the old way of religious "doing," trying to measure up, to please others who drain us while we can't say no, and when our shame-charged environment and the fear-based control in our upbringing takes its toll, a very real and serious infirmity can take place, proving the Scripture true: *"For he who sows to his flesh will of the flesh reap corruption..."* (Gal. 6:8) And often our flesh reaped, and still reaps, the corruptive fruits of shame.

Reflection
Sometimes as adults we find it extremely difficult to say "no" even when it's a healthy response. Often we feel empty and drained as others take advantage of us—which perpetuates our exhaustion and guilt because we know from Scripture that we are to serve others. But it's

important to understand that we need balance, just like Jesus who frequently sought solitude during His ministry.

This leads us to a very important heart issue commonly associated with an authoritarian environment. As we follow the tangles that trip us, emotionally and physically, something that nearly all of us face is overwhelming, unrelenting self-condemnation.

Near the beginning of my healing journey, I wrote the following in my journal—

> *"By your words you will be condemned."* As I consider the impact of this, reflecting on how that which is my Flesh is so wicked, bad, evil, how-can-God-even-look-at-me sinful, I stop to think: *flesh.*
>
> What is flesh but bone and blood and skin? And as we casually toss words like this around with righteous self-deprecation, what, even now, are the fruits that I reap? I am plagued with boils. I am infertile. I feel as hairy as a man. I am fat. I grew up seething with hatred towards my "flesh", and look at the sickness, disease, and horror that is wreaked upon it.

An authoritarian, performance-based family who trains through coercion—such as withholding love, affection, acceptance, or approval to manipulate behavior—creates an environment that can't help but keep household members at a heightened state of stress. A demanding or fear-based atmosphere requires constant adrenaline for survival mode, keeping one perpetually "on edge" through fight-or-flight syndrome. For some, the effects of chronic stress remain dormant for years and flare up without warning. When compounded over a lifetime with little to no relief, this overworks the adrenal glands, rendering adults exhausted without any logical reason why.

We closely identify with the words Isaiah used to describe Jesus, conveying His suffering and shame—*like one from whom men hide their faces He was despised*—and yet, most of the despising comes from ourselves. We see our mistakes and shortcomings more clearly than anyone. Yet as we seek to retrain our minds and discover truth in the hidden places (Ps. 51:6), it's essential that we understand that there is truly no condemnation for those who are in Christ Jesus. (Rom. 8:1) We may *feel* condemnation towards ourselves, but these feelings are rooted in shame rather than truth. Meditate on these Scriptures and ask God to fill you with wisdom:

For if our heart condemns us, God is greater than our heart, and knows all things. Beloved, if our heart does not condemn us, we have confidence toward God.

(1 Jn. 3:20, 21)

Eleven |

This Holy Wanting

"My Mom told me, "'If I miscarry after all this stress you've caused us, it will be your fault."'" —Jeri

"I experienced more problems from this lifestyle than I wish to admit, more than I can share. Serious emotional issues, depression, thoughts of suicide. But I couldn't tell anyone, because we were told depression is sin and I couldn't bear to face that. Yet it never went away. I bore so much pain inside. It still isn't all out. I have so much shame, so much guilt and depression to this day."—Bethany

It's not limited to neo-patriarchy, of course. Nor to women. But emotional abuse is a common tool of choice for those who feel the need to control and manipulate those within their care. It can break the spirit faster than any other method of discipline because it uses the number one element that cuts deepest and quickest to the heart and personhood: *shame.*

Emotional abuse can be overt: verbal destruction aimed to intimidate, coerce, or subdue another person. It can be subtle: withholding love, attention, affection and approval to compel someone to change, perform, or behave as desired. It can be so covert that perhaps neither party is really cognizant of what's occurred until devastating truth is revealed through traumatic measures such as self-injury—which is also associated with sexual abuse[28]—thoughts of or attempted suicide, and depression. They are bad fruits from bad roots.

Janelle, a wife and mother who struggles with the effects of childhood emotional abuse, writes

> The worst thing that happened was right after we moved to our farm. We brought our dogs with us, and they'd been used to living in town so of course now they thought they were in heaven! To keep them from wandering off, we had to keep them tied up a lot, and when we let them loose it could be only one at a time.
>
> One day I let Elsie loose, and only later found out Honey was loose. They went off together to our neighbor Bill's and killed ten of his chickens—and maimed most of the 24 he had left. So he took a shotgun and shot Honey dead. He thought Elsie was another neighbor's dog (who was a troublemaker; otherwise he would have not shot to kill). So he called Mom who came out of her room sniffing and told everyone to get in the van. My oldest brother Caleb was nineteen and she held him back to tell him what happened. Then we all went over to Bill's. Since I was the one who let Elsie loose, Mom kept blaming it on me and yelling at me on the way over and even while we were there, which was very embarrassing in front of Bill. And even more so when I started crying, which I always do when Mom yells at me.
>
> Before we knew for sure that Honey was dead— although I had a hunch—Bill said, "I'm sorry, but…" And Mom kept interrupting him, saying stuff like, "Now he had to do what he had to do. It's our fault." After he told us what happened Bill put his hand on my shoulder and said, "I'm sorry, Janelle," because I was crying. I tried to smile, but then Mom said, "Now don't go comforting her, it's her fault." Mom told Bill that Honey was the family dog, but Elsie was mine and should've

---

[28] Romans, SE Martin, JL Anderson, JC Herbison, GP and Mullen, PE. "Sexual Abuse in Childhood and Deliberate Self-harm." Dunedin, New Zealand Department of Psychological Medicine, Otago Medical School (Am. Journal of Psych. September 1995)

been the one to die so I'd be the only one grieving. That would have been good because it was all my fault. Mom said, "Now Honey will have to die anyway because she's a chicken killer"—she went on and on about how it would've been better if it was Elsie, or both dead instead of Honey. And so finally, trying to say it with authority but instead, crying, I said, "Kill Elsie, then." So Mom asked Bill if he'd shoot Elsie, but Bill didn't want to.

Caleb and Bill put Honey in a trashy, metal bucket and covered her with a rag. My older sister Kendra had stayed with the little kids in the van when we got out to talk to Bill, but Mom decided she wanted all of them to see what dogs can do to chickens. She told me to go get the little kids, so I went into the van and started bawling.

I just wanted to get out of there. I almost walked away down the hill but Mom made me get back in the van. She was so angry that several times she nearly crashed into trees on the way back home. Of course, I was angry too. I knew it wasn't my fault—at least, to the degree she heaped upon me. Things like this made me feel like I could do nothing right. It reinforced that I ought to double-check before I did *anything* so I didn't end up with the responsibility and overblown repercussions if something went wrong.

There were a lot of emotions that Mom wanted me to have. Blame, shame, self-hate, confusion, guilt, depression, a sort of false meekness, self-deprecation. Yet when I'd start to grieve or express the natural effects of what happened Mom got angry. It was okay for her to react, to be emotional, to express her emotions, but it was not okay for me. Her expectations of me were nothing like how she lived or what she expected of herself.

The day the dogs got out also taught me a great deal of fear. Fear of how close we came to a dangerous accident because Mom would not control her temper. Fear of what she would do as punishment—kill my dog?

Nothing was safe. Cruel and unusual punishment was around the corner of every least infraction or accident. We just learned to shut up, behave, keep everything inside, and stay in line.

Verbal Assault / Criticism

It's no secret that words are among the most powerful forms of influence. Through words God created the world. Through words we have God's will, nature, and heart as revealed through Scripture. Jesus Himself is the Word made flesh which dwelt among us (Jn. 1:1). A word fitly spoken has the power to heal, nurture, encourage, teach, exhort, and to bring life (Jn. 6:63, 68).

Alternatively, words can steal, kill and destroy. Jesus said, "Out of the abundance of the heart, the mouth speaks." And when words come from a heart that seeks its own, that exalts itself, and that is not surrendered in humility before God, they can crush the spirit and bring death. *"Can you believe what he said to me?" "I never forgot what she told me." "How can you say such a thing?"* Some of our best and worst memories involve words. Not only the phrases themselves, but tone, facial expressions, and poignant silence all effectively communicate a message.

Labeling is one common way the daughters of patriarchy are verbally manipulated. To hear things like, "You are rebellious," or "foolish," "defensive," "not thinking," "leading your brothers and sisters astray" works to coerce change while not encouraging life or growth. Who wants to be considered rebellious? Stupid? Evil? Yet just as effective, what is left unsaid also bears consequences of its own. "We heard a lot about what we should and shouldn't do," writes Catherine, "but never "good job," "I'm proud of you," or really even "I love you." Just what we could've done better, and what was wrong with us."

> Death and life are in the power of the tongue, and those who love it will eat its fruit. (Pr. 18:21)

Emotionally abusive tactics can be subtle. Sometimes parents, spouses, friends, and teachers justify criticism and verbal shaming as Christian exhortation. *"If you were more obedient, respectful, serious, righteous, mature, godly, humble, patient, kind"* or, *"If you were less sensitive, emotional, imaginative, impulsive"* all communicate shame because they convey fault and sin in the view of another person—who may or may not be correct—without true, compassionate help or grace.

While we can agree that as Scripture states, "There is none righteous, no not one," the focus is different. The kindness of the Lord leads us to repentance. Pointing out flaws, sharing disappointment that your daughter or wife is not all she "could" or "should" be, and other shaming ignores the crucial issues—relationship and personhood—creating a screen through which all thoughts, feelings, and actions are filtered. It literally *becomes* us. This screen effectively shuts out truth, which is that God values us, loves us and sent His Son to redeem us. He has made us worthy. Shameful messages communicate that we are worthless and unlovable as we are. That we must change, do better, and measure up. These lies quench life.

Within neo-patriarchy, emotional-verbal abuse is especially convoluted because it's often mixed with spiritual abuse. *"God isn't pleased with you!" "If you wanted to be a good Christian, you should _____."* It's all about manipulation, coercion, dos and don'ts, and control. *"How can you call yourself a Christian when you do that!" "Godly, biblical, feminine, Christian women don't _____."* Sometimes there are messages of truth that we need to hear, but the Bible is clear that truth needs to be spoken in love for the edification of others (Ephesians 4). As women who crave life-giving validation, support, and nurture from parents, husbands, and even our friends, when words are wielded as weapons we experience deep, often life-lasting scars.

Abuse of any kind is never okay in God's eyes.

Asceticism and Emotional Abuse

All humans need to feel appreciated, validated, loved, safe. To feel worthy, that we matter to someone. And when feelings or emotions are *consistently* denied, devalued, neglected, belittled, or shamed, this is abusive because it perpetuates toxicity and withholds that which is healthy and necessary for life by a primary caregiver. Refusing to be pleased, an environment of disapproval, accusation, intimidation, criticism and manipulation are subtler forms but equally as devastating, if not more so.

One way some families do this is through what I call "emotional asceticism." In and of itself, asceticism is rigorous self-denial for religious or spiritual reasons—a common value among many agrarian patriarchal families, especially the more isolated ones. But as women with minds, bodies, hearts and souls, we're created with basic needs in every area of our lives. Parents may not realize that when they teach their girls, without balance and context, to lay down their lives for others and "die daily" (1 Cor. 15:31), true needs often become overlooked in the process. Sadly, this includes denial, neglect, and rejection of essential emotional needs, too.

A social worker who has spent most of his adult life working with suicidal teenagers, Steve Hein observes the effects of emotionally abusive behavior:

> Emotional abuse is like brain washing in that it systematically wears away at the victim's self-confidence, sense of self-worth, trust in their own perceptions, and self-concept. Whether it is done by constant berating and belittling, by intimidation, or under the guise of "guidance", "teaching", or "advice",[29] the results are similar. Eventually, the recipient of the abuse loses all sense of self and remnants of personal value. Emotional abuse cuts to the very core of a person, creating scars that may be far deeper and more lasting that physical ones. In fact there is research to this effect. With emotional abuse, the insults, insinuations, criticism and accusations slowly eat away at the victim's self-esteem until she is incapable of judging the situation realistically. She has become so beaten down emotionally that she blames *herself* for the abuse. Her self-esteem is so low that she clings to the abuser.[30]

In most patriarchal Christian families, heavy emphasis is placed on self-denial, guarding the heart, controlling emotions, and feeling only "right" things. This is where confusion generally sets in for many daughters. We *do* need to guard the heart. We need to be self-controlled, to practice self-denial. But to guard the heart is to protect its worth, not to ignore it.

On the other hand, addressing issues of low-self-esteem and emotional pain often draws fire for being "selfish", "focusing on self" or having a "victim mentality". These accusations serve to stop-thought and keep the light of God from shining truth into darkness. But truth is,

---

[29] Author's note: Manipulators—spousal, parental, or others—often 'teach', 'guide' and give advice within emotionally unsafe relationships. This is not to be confused with counsel or wisdom from godly, healthy people in our lives.

[30] Hein, Steve "Emotional Abuse." Eqi.org. www.eqi.org (2 March 2010) Used by permission.

emotional asceticism creates wounds that run so deep that it is only *when* God's light and truth embrace them, they will begin to heal.

Quenching Grace

Emotional asceticism has especially tender effects in Quiverfull families. Here, children are embraced as blessings but many times struggle with the cognitive dissonance of *hearing* "blessing" but knowing this means "a blessing only when..." One of the most common spiritual repercussions from a lifestyle like this is the quenching of grace. I've heard many stories from daughters who know all too well the bitter sting of feeling not good enough and not measuring up. Not accepted "as is" but always reminded that they could be better, be more holy, more righteous, more perfect. In its barest form, this is rejection and turns the beautiful, biblical concepts of blessings into what feels more like curses. Unfortunately, many parents intend these words as "exhortation" and "Christian encouragement" or "training in the admonition of the Lord" but often it only backfires by discouraging, exasperating, and reminding children that we are not welcome when we're messy. When we're sinners. When we make mistakes—and this can affect us for the rest of our lives. Moreover, when invalidation[31] and rejection become religious, justified with "the Bible says" or attached to God's name, this is serious and can lead to depression, even spiritual depression.

Taylor, one of five children in a homeschooling family, knows what this feels like. She writes,

> My Mom wrote a popular book, years ago in the eighties, when homeschooling first started getting popular. She still speaks at churches and events, teaching parents how to raise children to be godly adults. Hundreds of people look up to them, and they get lots of financial support for their ministry.
>
> Before I got married I fell into a long period of depression trying to sort out my beliefs about God and figure out my place in the world. My parents thought this must be related to demonic oppression; that my unhappiness with them and their teaching was a spiritual problem. For now, I still believe in God but the Bible and Christianity stuff is not looking so good. I've based

---

[31] http://eqi.org/invalid.htm

all my life decisions on what I "ought" to do and there has been a huge heart disconnect. I got married and had our daughters based on these principals, and recently had to come to terms with the fact that I didn't get to make these choices for myself. Here I am, five years later, wondering what I've done! So it's a bit messy right now.

Now that I'm a Mom, I parent so differently than how I was raised. I do attachment parenting and grace-based discipline for my kids. My Mom was—and is—really strict about spanking; people look up to her for that. She just sent all of us girls a book about how we're created to be helpmeets. My sister-in-law is into that stuff, but I'm just so different and they don't understand how I don't fawn over conservatism.

A few years ago, I tried to sort things out with my folks, with my Dad in particular. But it didn't go very far. They don't feel it's right for children to confront their parents or ask them to change, that we should just be thankful to them for raising us.

I only see them every few years, but it's always difficult and stressful for me. We communicate through blogs and telephone calls, and keep things pretty surface level. At this point, it's somewhat futile to try to come to a real understanding with them, since we don't fit in with their worldview. And that is all they really cared about.

One way rejection and depression manifest is through unhealthy self-esteem. This can be either too low or too high. For me, messages of self-denial coupled with personal, extreme self-hatred and struggle with weight contributed to a lifelong pattern of low-self-esteem. I remember feeling as though I did not deserve relief from pain; that I, as a sinner, deserved my headaches, depression, hormonal issues, and death. But Jesus reminded me of the second greatest commandment: *"Love your neighbor as yourself."* The issue of self-love is wrought with confusion among Christian women. Girls, taught from birth the external religious constraints to "do without", to be "set-apart" and to "die daily" inevitably struggle to correlate this message of Christ with a lifestyle of religion all too prevalent within these kinds of families.

A new wife, Marla confesses:

Sometimes it's hard for me just to brush my teeth every day. My husband wanted me to get a massage for my birthday, but I nearly passed out at the thought of it. Growing up, I learned that humility means to consider everyone else better than me. There are some really bad people out there—so believing I was worse than even a child molester made me hate myself. This affects me now, even though I know that isn't what the Bible meant. I never do anything for myself; even when my husband asks me to, I feel guilty. I'm afraid I'll get proud, and God won't be pleased.

Lack of self-care is the ultimate in self-hatred and as Marla continues to tussle with basic hygiene—much less "luxuries" as she sees the loving attempts of her husband—Paul addresses this astutely as he preaches, *"These things indeed have an appearance of wisdom in self-imposed religion, false humility, and neglect of the body, but are of no value against the indulgence of the flesh."* (Col. 2:23) Yet unfortunately, the feelings and beliefs she holds are often modeled and instilled in childhood.

Neglect
Besides clothing, food, and shelter, there are other things necessary for life. Yes, it's possible to do without for a while, and in some cases, like poverty, God gives the grace necessary to deal with extreme circumstances. But David writes, *"give me neither poverty nor riches"* for a reason (Pr.30:8). Many families seeking to live the "peculiar" life adopt a quasi-survivalist mentality—while claiming faith, often a study of underlying currents reveals a base of fear—that overlooks the living needs of their offspring. Some may provide physically, but underestimate the importance of meeting emotional needs. Some of these areas may include:

- Adequate medical or dental care
- Balance between alternative and traditional medicines or treatments
- Adequate nutrition on a per-child basis
- Physiological education, i.e., how the body works
- Personal attention—not just for reason of discipline or reward
- Encouragement and praise

- Healthy, age-appropriate intellectual stimulation
- Respect, as one values another human being fashioned in the likeness of God

In addition to these, rest is a need. Is it possible to over-esteem basic hard work? In an effort to curb "foolishness," many families create a lack of balance between work and leisure. Other, perhaps controversial, needs are healthy outside relationships, friendships. Many older daughters hear, *"You don't need friends; you have your sisters."* While godly companions are important and it's wise to choose close associates carefully, we need interaction with others in our real family, the broader family that makes up the body of Christ.

Besides cultivating healthy friendships, women also need a safe place, a sanctuary for solitude with the Lord—like Jesus, who enjoyed gardens and mountains. We need space and time to pursue hobbies and passions—gifts from God. We need complete nourishment of body, soul, heart, and mind, where personhood can flourish and develop according to God's unique designs. We need rest. And as adults, recognizing areas of childhood lack can help clue us in on our current struggles—so truth can be known, and healing begin.

Joy, a third-born daughter in a family of twelve children, remembers the guilt that always shadowed her need for rejuvenation.

> Inside I was suffering. I was so tired. I just wanted to do something for me. But what a selfish, ungodly thought! I had to *not* matter, while everyone else *did.* But I was a little rebellious; I snuck off with a baby on my hip to read for a few minutes sometimes. But then I'd be reprimanded for not getting enough done. And the guilt would just increase—a heavy, never-ending cycle.

Whenever a quest for holiness asks, *"How much can we do without and still survive?"* there will be wounds. Simple living, especially for many off-the-grid families within stringent religious homes, actually feels more like skeletal living. While flesh, heart, soul and spirit are affected, *"I have come that they may have life,"* says Jesus. "And that, more abundantly."

Reflection

As a woman who has been healed from deep emotional pain, I've learned that the only way to find freedom and healing from any kind of hurt is to first acknowledge the truth of it—the truth in the inward parts—rather than using Scripture as a bandage. It's what Jesus came for: "He heals the broken-hearted and binds up their wounds." (Ps. 147:3) And He longs to do so!

Do you have a pattern of discrediting your own emotions? Do you say things to yourself like,

- Physical abuse is worse than emotional abuse, so I shouldn't feel this bad.
- I am stupid for feeling like this; there is no reason for it.
- I just need to get over this—whatever it is.
- I am just under a spiritual attack.
- Others have it worse, so I should just be thankful and pray the depression goes away.
- I must not be reading my Bible enough.
- It's not like I am being beaten or going hungry or anything, so…

Discussing emotional abuse and matters of the heart does not mean relying solely on emotions or feelings to guide us. But in a healthy life there will be balance, for God created the heart and its propensity to feel. God, in whose image we are created, is Himself a feeling God, prone to anger and jealousy, love and wrath and grief, joy and hatred. Note this serious exhortation by Paul in Ephesians 4 which shows us how to find true holiness:

> …You should no longer walk as the rest of the Gentiles walk, in the futility of their mind…who, **being past feeling,** have given themselves over to lewdness, to work all uncleanness with greediness. But…the truth is in Jesus: that you put off, concerning your former conduct, the old man which grows corrupt according to the deceitful lusts, and be renewed in the spirit of your mind, and that you put on the new man which was created according to God, in true righteousness and holiness. (Eph. 4:17-24, emphasis added)

Emotions are a gift from God and help identify the condition of your heart and help provide an invaluable glimpse to motivation, roots, and areas that need the Lord's touch. Sometimes the Holy Spirit uses them to guide, teach, and convict us. Our conscience is often linked with our heart as godly sorrow leads us to repentance.

If you've been hurt by others condemning your redeemed, Christ-filled heart, take a moment to pray for wisdom, discernment, and balance, and meditate on these verses:

> I will bless the LORD who has given me counsel; my heart also instructs me in the night seasons. (Ps. 16:7) This is the covenant that I will make with them after those days, says the LORD: I will put My laws into their hearts, and in their minds I will write them. (Heb. 10:16)

Twelve |
Darkness

"As an adult, I was told by a church elder that if I moved out of my parents' home it would be like a wife leaving a marriage."—Erin

"It feels like they are pushing me down under water because God wants them to. And that He wants me to learn to not breathe while being happy about it." Heather

It's undeniable that extreme conservatism is hard. Due to expansive households and meticulous standards, living a patriocentric or Quiverfull lifestyle greatly increases parents' responsibility to their children and to God. It requires diligent oversight, calculated control of thoughts and behavior, and consistent discipline from arguably overwhelmed, preoccupied, and exhausted parents. For neo-patriarchalists, however, these challenges represent holy hardship and are often perceived as a path of sanctification. Yet what happens when little bundles of blessings grow into energetic, intelligent, emotional adults full of questions, desires, thoughts, and opinions? As many quivering daughters know, often parents' initial proclamation of faith slowly shifts to fear, which is then fleshed out by over-coercion. But there is another, more subtle and insidious way parents attempt to control: by appealing to something—and Someone—greater.

Appealing to the Lord who loves us should bring comfort and strength to a child. But sometimes parents use God as a weapon against their children, so that behavior, thoughts, attitudes and the heart can all be controlled, influenced, and changed. This happened to Cara, who is an atheist now and explains her experience.

As I got older, and especially after I graduated from homeschooling, I had a hard time keeping quiet about certain things. I did not want to wear dresses all the time, or see in the Bible that we had to. I cut my hair one spring which was a major cause for concern. I was, undoubtedly, a bad influence on my sisters and cousins and my parents needed to find a way to curb that behavior.

Enter George. George was my parents' solution to what they took to be "demonic influence" in my life— they said I was restless because I was not yet married. So George and I would court, get married, and all would be well.

Unfortunately things did not work like that. I did not like George. From the first week of our acquaintance it was obvious he had anger and self-image issues. He hated himself, but expected me to think he was the greatest thing ever and to be thrilled to be his darling submissive homeschooling housewife—who he said would "wear skirts and dresses in public, and preferably nothing at home."

I knew I had to get myself out of that before it went any further. So I told my parents I had no interest in George (which was scandalous—he was the "perfect Christian boy," studying to be a pastor).

The next thing I know, I was declared to be "under the power of Satan." My parents arranged several meetings with the pastor, who counseled me to submit to the authorities God gave. But I couldn't submit to anyone who decided I was demon possessed, or who thought I had anything to do with Satan. These meetings were torturous. I dreaded them, but my parents dragged me nonetheless.

Eventually everyone decided I was hopelessly backslidden, refusing to heed the word of God. So my membership in the church was revoked, and I was excommunicated.

Through all of this, I still believed in God; I prayed and read the Bible, and tried very hard to stand up for what I believed as truth about a God who loved me, who would not send me to hell over impossible standards of perfection that had little to do with morality or a relationship with Jesus.

But life continued to be miserable. The anger and yelling grew worse. My parents and I fought every time we spoke; I felt so out of place and hated in my own home. I couldn't say anything without Mom thinking I was disrespecting her. If I tried to ask my parents just to *listen* to my perspective, I was "being rebellious". They told me I was "corrupting" and "leading astray" the younger children and that all contact with them would cease unless I did what they asked. I had no intention of marrying George.

Instead, I decided to go to grad school and all communication ceased. If I called, they did not answer. If I emailed, they did not write back. Not for Christmas, not for New Year's, not for my birthday.

It's as if I no longer exist to them. My heart is broken. As hard as it was to be with them, my family had been my world till now. And I love them—especially my sisters and cousins, who in some ways, I helped raise. But now it's gone; my world has collapsed. I wonder if I've made the right choice, if I'm being selfish and prideful; if it would be better to go back. But I know I can't. It would be a lie if I did. I miss them so much—but it was too painful.

So I'm stuck in this awful place—alone.

Overt Abuse

Before we can understand the dynamics of what happened to Cara, lets begin with a more basic understanding of abuse. The United States Department of Justice states,

Domestic violence can be defined as a pattern of abusive behavior in any relationship that is used by one partner to gain or maintain power and control over another intimate partner. Domestic violence can be physical, sexual, emotional, economic, or psychological actions or threats of actions that influence another person. This includes any behaviors that intimidate, manipulate, humiliate, isolate, frighten, terrorize, coerce, threaten, blame, hurt, injure, or wound someone. [32]

Next, it describes violent behavior.

- **Physical Abuse:** Hitting, slapping, shoving, grabbing, pinching, biting, hair-pulling, biting, etc. Physical abuse also includes denying a partner medical care or forcing alcohol and/or drug use.
- **Sexual Abuse:** Coercing or attempting to coerce any sexual contact or behavior without consent. Sexual abuse includes, but is certainly not limited to marital rape, attacks on sexual parts of the body, forcing sex after physical violence has occurred, or treating one in a sexually demeaning manner.
- **Emotional Abuse:** Undermining an individual's sense of self-worth and/or self-esteem. This may include, but is not limited to constant criticism, diminishing one's abilities, name-calling, or damaging one's relationship with his or her children.
- **Economic Abuse:** Making or attempting to make an individual financially dependent by maintaining total control over financial resources, withholding one's access to money, or forbidding one's attendance at school or employment.
- **Psychological Abuse:** Causing fear by intimidation; threatening physical harm to self, partner, children, or partner's family or friends; destruction of pets and property; and forcing isolation from family, friends, or school and/or work. [33]

Miriam, a young wife and mother, tells about a tragic event that illustrates the pain of physical abuse. While it happened over twenty years ago, it still brings her to tears.

When my little brother Noah was one or two years old, he was still learning how to speak. The words "thank

---

[32] United States Department of Justice. "About Domestic Violence." www.ovw.usdoj.gov (6 January 2010)
[33] Ibid.

you" were recently added to his vocabulary, and one night we were all gathered in the family room. My sister Sharon brought him a bottle, and Mom told him to say "thank you." He didn't. We older kids saw that it was an issue of 'no comprehension' rather than rebellion—but rebellion is how Mom saw it. So she told Dad to start spanking him right away. After several series of spankings, with pauses in between to tell him to say thank you, he finally did...but then the spankings continued! Why? Two main things: *"He's still rebelling—I can see it in his eyes,"* said Mom. *"We need to break his spirit,"* said Dad.

Eventually they ordered us kids to leave the room while they wailed away on Noah but we stayed on the staircase, peering over the bannister. We were literally in shock and helpless at the brutality and detachment from reality as they beat him till his diaper started to shred and they took it off. Once Dad's hand became sore, they used a stick. We older kids felt so defiled yet unable to do anything. We knew that they would not listen if we asked, begged, or demanded that they stopped. We were absolutely shocked that Dad participated in this—we already knew Mom was crazy. The madness in her eyes freaked us out as she, in frenzy, kept telling Dad to spank. "He's still rebelling—his spirit isn't broken yet!"

I don't know what finally happened. Something along the lines of "his spirit" breaking. He'd do anything they'd say and had no spark of "life," of soul, anymore.

Mom claimed it as a victory. But for the next few days, whenever we kids changed his diaper, we cried.

Abuse is not only inflicting harm upon another person—it is also intentionally withholding things that are needed for life, health, and growth. There are times that finances and lack of knowledge bear negative ramifications in a family, and while of course this is not abuse, sometimes a child still faces these issues in adulthood—and because we live in a fallen world, everyone experiences dysfunction and pain. However, we can still seek the Lord's guidance, His loving help and healing—and then minister to others He brings along.

Most parents know there are limits to what they can do and lines that are not to be crossed. The obvious ones, of course, are sexual and physical abuse. Harmful behavior, age-inappropriate exposure. Extreme neglect. But what about subtle, confusing, iffy areas? What about when it looks godly and right? When others claim their actions are biblical, and because God said?

Jesus takes abuse seriously, especially when it is inflicted in His name and when it hurts His children.

> But whoever causes one of these little ones who believe in Me to stumble, it would be better for him if a millstone were hung around his neck, and he were thrown into the sea.
>
> (Mk. 9:42)

Domestic Spiritual Abuse

Professionals often associate spiritual abuse with organized religious groups, but it also characterizes the milieu within many patriarchal families. Using the name of God or the Bible to manipulate, control, isolate, frighten, coerce, threaten, or hurt is just as injurous, if not more so, than abuses universally condemned, such as rape. Sexual assault is the ultimate abuse of power over the powerless. Yet while physical rape assaults the sacred and leaves devastating scars on heart and flesh, spiritual rape violates the soul. One's spirituality is intensely intimate, personal, and of inestimable value. Even God does not coerce or seek to dominate others or manipulate hearts. He woos, yes. He loves. And He is gentle with the souls He's made. But when the name of God is used to plunder those created in His image, when He and His words are used against others with violence—"It would be better for him," warns Jesus, "to have a large millstone hung around his neck and to be drowned in the depths of the sea." While God is able to heal us from the most despicable of abuses, when we are devastated by what we think is God and therefore confused about God Himself, the search for truth and healing can be especially arduous.

Scripture is clear about some things, but there are other issues that require us to faithfully seek God for wisdom. Attaching God's name to something is serious. Even using the term "biblical" as a modifier or qualifying something with "the Bible says" carries solemn importance.[34] He desires an intimate, living relationship with us and will impress on our hearts certain values that may or may not apply to someone else. We call these "convictions". But in a neo-patriarchal culture, where a Christian worldview and having a biblical family are prime objectives, personal convictions are taught as doctrine. And unfortunately in many cases, spiritual abuse occurs.

According to David Henke, founder of Watchman Fellowship which is a Christian research and apologetics ministry, spiritual abuse has five distinct characteristics: *authoritarianism, image consciousness, suppression of criticism, perfectionistic standards, and imbalance.*[35] We've discussed many aspects of these traits in previous chapters but they warrant repeating, because spiritual abuse needs to be recognized and acknowledged for the evil that it is.

Authoritarianism and the Daughters of Neo-patriarchy

Authoritarians demand subjection to authority and dismiss freedom and autonomy. In families, this happens when a parent assumes absolute control over his children—for the scope of this book, adult children, although roots of it in childhood have significant, harmful effects, as the levels of control are exhaustive—encompassing not only one's physical reality but also thoughts, decisions, will, and future.

A common tactic used by patriarchal parents is choice binding.[36] "But she lives under my roof," a parent says. "My roof, my rules." This is a sticky situation. Technically—yes, and especially for minors. However, for adult children, this presents the phenomenon of bounded choice, where a person's options are constrained by his or her environment. While parents may insist, "She can do what she wants, we don't lock her up with chains," such an argument is a red herring and distracts from reality. In the neo-patriarchal family, a daughter is more than discouraged from seeking outside education or outside employment. She therefore has no viable alternative or means with which to choose any other course for her life; considering options outside her bounded choice is unthinkable for her.

Fear is powerful, and daughters from Christian patriarchal homes are groomed to fear—therefore avoid—anything autonomous. Hearing

---

[34] Sire, James *Scripture Twisting: 20 Ways the Cults Mis-read the Bible* (Downers Grove, IL: InterVarsity Press, 1980) p. 41

[35] Henke, David "Spiritual Abuse" Watchman Fellowship. www.watchman.org (2 May 2009) Used by Permission.

[36] Lalich, Janja *Bounded Choice: True Believers and Charismatic Cults* (Berkeley, CA: University of California Press, 2004) et al.

"worldly," "feminist," "rebellious," "prodigal," even *"loss of salvation," "God will do whatever He needs to get you right with Him,"* or *"if you are of the world, which is filled with homosexuals and prostitutes and immorality, we cannot have your influence on the younger children"* is reality for them.

Furthermore, when a daughter hears, "You are free to choose," but knows that if she does so, she...

- needs to repent,
- is in error,
- is selfish,
- is hurting her family,
- is deceived,
- is rebellious,
- is under delusion, believing a lie,
- is worldly, and seeking worldliness,
- is a disappointment,
- brings sorrow,
- is leading others astray,
- is foolish,
- is not hearing God...

. . . does she really have a choice?

Simply put, she is not allowed to leave the "roof" that serves as her physical and spiritual covering of protection. Given the rise in adults living at home and even in home churching, it's important to remember that all Christians, including one's family members, are members of Christ—and therefore part of church. Churching at home is not a way to dodge the issue. A father who makes himself prophet, priest and king is no less liable for his actions than a pastor for his flock. And what is done to the least of these is done also to the Lord of heaven and earth. Consider that:

- Jesus Christ is our only High Priest. (Heb. 3:1, 4:14)
- Christ is head of the church. (Jn. 5:26-27, Eph. 1:22-23, Col. 1:18).
- All authority in heaven and on earth belongs to Jesus. (Mt. 28:18)

- God does not permit Christians to control others. (Mt. 20:25-28, Mk. 10:42-45, Lk. 22:24-27, 1 Pet 5:3, Mt. 23:8-12)
- Christ is our only Master, and we are all brothers and sisters in Him. (Mt. 6:24, Mt. 23:8-12, Lk. 6:13)

Image Consciousness

Henke's second characteristic is also extremely prevalent within a spiritually abusive family. *"What will people think?"* *"What about your witness?"* The King James Version Bible tells us to "abstain from all appearance of evil." (1 Thess. 5:22) This translation is frequently proof-texted with detrimental results, because certainly we are to avoid sin. But the New King James reveals it's meaning with more clarity: *"Abstain from every form of evil."* So what happens when the Authorized Version Translation verse is misapplied?

Abstaining from the *appearance* of evil is widely encouraged within "biblical" households, but it is not Christ-like. In essence, patriarchy is the step-child of works-righteousness, where family members are right with God only if they obey patriarchal rules. Jesus, however, preached liberty and regularly met with prostitutes and sinners. He who was often alone with women and accused of gluttony and drunkenness concerned Himself with what was real, not how things looked. He promoted relationships, healing, and love over appearances. Truth, over what people might think. A daughter raised to be overly-concerned with what people will struggle with this all of her life until she is healed. Sadly, this sometimes serves to keep her from following Jesus.

Suppression of Criticism

Within an authoritarian family, it is impossible to raise legitimate concerns about beliefs, convictions, or way of life, and asking questions—or challenging long-held convictions and doctrines—without it being perceived as a threat to authority and family values. Adult children, urged to "learn to think," once again encounter cognitive dissonance as the act of thinking leads to dire consequences. The doctrine (to think for oneself) does not match what the unspoken rules of the family (conformity and suppression of criticism) require of adult children. In this environment, to question is to rebel, and biblically, rebellion is as the sin of witchcraft. (1 Sam. 15:23) I don't think parents realize just how severe, demeaning, dangerous and grievous it is to essentially accuse their children—who are crafted in the image of God and bear His name—of this, placing them on par with demonic behavior. Rather than blessing them, a frequent and casual reference to their "rebellion" is a curse.

Henke writes:

> Because the religious system is not based on the truth it cannot allow questions, dissent, or open discussions about issues. The person who dissents becomes the problem rather than the issue he raised. The truth about any issue is settled and handed down from the top of the hierarchy. Questioning anything is considered a challenge to authority. Thinking for oneself is suppressed by pointing out that it leads to doubts. This is portrayed as unbelief in God and His anointed leaders. Thus the follower controls his own thoughts by fear of doubting God.[37]

Looking at those who are Quiverfull and neo-patriarchal, we see why this is such a crucial issue to parents and why it is easily abused. Anyone who has spent time with children understands the serious impressionability of young ones, especially the influence of older siblings on younger brothers and sisters. In an authoritarian system, questioning threatens power. If seeds of doubt become implanted in the minds of his children, a parent's control and influence wavers. When this happens, whoever challenges the status quo *becomes the problem* by default. She is the black sheep, the prodigal child, and possibly unsaved; in some cases she is removed from the family.

This tenet of spiritual abuse, the suppression of criticism, relates directly to the manipulative, cyclic use of fear. No Christian wants to willfully sin or be considered in sin. If connoted with what wayward or ungodly people do, questioning authority is a quickly eliminated concern.

However, questioning is necessary to grow and discover what is righteous and true. But as we do, it's very important to remain humble before our perfect Authority, the Lord; otherwise, pride can sneak up and offer a counterfeit autonomy that is rooted in sin.

What does God tell us to do to avoid the appearance of evil? "Test all things; hold fast what is good." (1 Thess. 5:21) And parents shouldn't fear this, because if their values are rooted in truth, a child who seeks the Lord will arrive to godly conclusions.

---

[37] Henke, David "Spiritual Abuse"

Perfectionistic Standards

Lists of standards, values, and rules make life easier—perhaps not the living of it, but in hard times, when storms come, when difficult choices must be made or during tragedy and change, a visible list of 'dos,' 'don'ts,' 'shoulds' and 'oughts' essentially provides a 'faithfulness measuring stick.' If something doesn't work, a parent can see where they have failed. If something *does* work, one can assert that because they adhered to the rules, they enjoyed success.

Biblical living, as promoted by those who endorse new patriarchy, are man's convictions wrapped beautifully in Scripture—yet, to borrow the words of Timothy, "having the form of godliness but denying its power." If families want to be holy, then they should prescribe to certain roles. If parents want beautifully obedient children, then they must train them according to specific methods. If parents want to obey God, they will keep an open womb and bear an army of children for the kingdom. If parents want unworldly kids, they must homeschool.

This is formulaic. It is standard keeping—teaching as doctrine the commandments of men. Not that these ideals are necessarily wrong in and of themselves, but to place trust in them, to measure one's Christianity and the faithfulness of others by them, is sin. To hold all Christians to one's own values flirts dangerously with fulfilling the role of God in someone else's life, and could very well place stumbling blocks between them and the Lord.

Including in the lives of their own children.

We are called to "walk by faith, not by sight" following the One who desires an intimate relationship with us, who sent the Holy Spirit to lead us into all truth. (Jn. 16:13) Any time someone claims special revelation or knowledge of biblical text and imposes it upon all "true" or "faithful" believers, we do well to question. Works of performance displace faith, whether they are thought to help earn salvation, to merit favor with God to grant power for living, or to merely meet the necessary standards imposed in social settings. Paul tells us, "For by grace you have been saved through faith, and that not of yourselves; it is the gift of God, not of works, lest anyone should boast." (Eph. 2:8-9)

But there is no grace in a perfectionistic system, and little faith.

Imbalance

The final hallmark of spiritual abuse according to Henke is that:

> Abusive religions [usually major on] minor issues such
> as prophecy, carrying biblical law to extremes, or using

strange methods of biblical interpretation. The imbalanced spiritual hobby-horse thus produced represents unique knowledge or practices which seem to validate the group's claim to special status with God. …The Pharisees, quintessential spiritually abusive leaders, were quite unbalanced in their perception of what mattered most to God. Jesus said they "pay tithe of mint and anise and cummin, and have omitted the weightier matters of the law, judgment, mercy, and faith." (Mt. 23:23)[38]

Of course, convictions can be good. Living a peculiar lifestyle because one believes God ordained it is not inherently bad. Imbalance arises when families claim a special grasp on truth or on God not shared by others within the faith, or when lesser doctrines are elevated over greater. For example, many Christians learn through example that withdrawing from the world is more important than fulfilling Jesus' command to "go into all the world and preach the gospel." How can one's light shine, when it is isolated from those in darkness?

As children come of age in this environment, they often develop judgmental or critical biases against anyone "different" or outside, which does not communicate the mercy, compassion, or loving-kindness of Jesus. It is very hard to maintain one's special "truth" without becoming arrogant. And sadly, most elite views are non-essentials of the gospel.

> Therefore, if you died with Christ from the basic principles of the world, why, as though living in the world, do you subject yourselves to regulations—"Do not touch, do not taste, do not handle," which all concern things which perish with the using—according to the commandments and doctrines of men? These things indeed have an appearance of wisdom in self-imposed religion, false humility, and neglect of the body, but are of no value against the indulgence of the flesh. (Col. 2:20-23)

Spiritual Abuse in the Family
Even parents have limits.

---

[38] Ibid.

One of the most subtle and yet spiritually destructive ways a parent can overstep is to infringe on the job of the Holy Spirit, usurping His authority and drawing the hearts of their children to themselves rather than to Him. By doing so, even with the best of intentions, they inadvertently place themselves in a position reserved for God alone—and cause their children to commit idolatry. Until this is corrected, the devastating fruits of dysfunction and sin will continue to delay healing in an adult daughter's life. It is a grave disservice to the heart, soul, body and spirit of a woman when the truth of her own pain is not as important as the reputation of those who inflict it.

Reflection

Abuse, defined simply, is "mis-use." While godly fear of the Lord is the beginning of wisdom, spiritual abuse controls through fear—fear of hell, disappointment, fear of the world, of the flesh, fear of condemnation, labels, judgment, or withheld love. In Quiverfull families, where time and attention are limited or spread thinly, we see how especially tragic this can be, as approval, appreciation, affection, and positive attention are used to manipulate and reinforce desired behavior. Yet emphasis on conduct does little for matters of the heart.

Consider this explanation by Paul:

> But their minds were blinded. For until this day the same veil remains unlifted in the reading of the Old Testament, because the veil is taken away in Christ. But even to this day, when Moses is read, a veil lies on their heart. Nevertheless when one turns to the Lord, the veil is taken away. Now the Lord is the Spirit; and where the Spirit of the Lord is, there is liberty. (2 Cor. 3:14-17)

While neo-patriarchy promotes rules instead of relationship, performance over personhood, and law over grace, Jesus came to do the opposite. He came to fulfill the law and save us through grace. He is concerned not with what we do, but who we are. Jesus came to set the captives—those in bondage to standards and appearance, those who writhe under an oppressive authoritarian environment—free. And He isn't threatened by questions. "Call to Me," says the Lord, "and I will answer you, and show you great and mighty things, which you do not know." (Jer. 33:3) He pleads again—"Until now you have asked nothing in My name. Ask, and you will receive, that your joy may be full." (Jn. 16:24)

Thirteen |

Black

"We were taught that if you have a mental illness, like depression, it's a sign you are not right with God. Everything bad in life is about being "'right with God."' He was in a wreck so he would get right with God. His cousin is dying so he will get right with God. Hurricane Katrina— get right with God!"—Caroline

...for you shall worship no other god, for the LORD, whose name is Jealous, is a jealous God. (Exodus 34:14)

Norm Wakefield, founder of Spirit of Elijah Ministries, is an author and speaker with a tender heart for men and their families. In his article *The Curse of the Standard Bearers: When Idolatry Masquerades as Love,* he tells the story about a young man whose parents crossed a very serious boundary.

> Almost overnight, Marty's life changed. His parents decided to become associated with other homeschooling families whose goal was to raise children with godly character. With the new direction for the family came *more responsibilities and expectations* from his parents. He already felt smothered by their efforts to make him into the type of young person who would give them a good reputation among their peers, but with the change came a tidal wave of standards and goals he felt were impossible to meet.
>
> Marty didn't make it easy for them. In fact, he questioned them constantly as to why they had to live by

all these standards of dress, social etiquette, grooming, facial expressions, entertainment, courtship, attitudes, education, and food. His honest questions brought accusations of rebellion and disrespect, which were not his intentions. Eventually, the conflict became so great that in order to protect their reputation, Marty's parents sent him to live and work with an uncle, hoping God would eventually open his eyes to see the blessing he was rejecting.

Marty's well-meaning parents were *Standard Bearers*. Without realizing it, self-ambition (lust for significance and success) and an idolatrous love of man's approval gained ascendancy within their hearts. The curse of the *Standard Bearers* rested upon them and all the relationships for which they felt responsible. Unwittingly, they looked to *standard bearing* as the solution to parenting Marty and to gaining significance and acceptance for the whole family. Instead of demonstrating a life lived in a relationship with Jesus Christ through the Holy Spirit and leading Marty to do the same, they were caught in the enticing trap of a form of religion. They quickly learned what standards were acceptable and not acceptable among those with whom they wished to connect and then commanded obedience from Marty.[39]

Spiritual abuse, authoritarianism, fear-based control, and neo-patriarchy all have something in common. As we look at our lives, we women who struggle with exhaustive levels of guilt, shame, confusion, low self-esteem, chronic fatigue, and many other heart, soul, mind, body issues, we need to understand that there is *a root under everything*— one that connects the externals, the features of our environment and upbringing, with the hidden places inside of us.

He said to him, "What is written in the law? What is your reading of it?" So he answered and said, "'You shall love the LORD your God with all your heart, with

---

[39] Wakefield, Norm "The Curse of the Standard Bearers: When Idolatry Masquerades as Love." Spirit of Elijah Ministries. November, 2007. www.spiritofelijah.com (20 March 2010) Used by Permission.

all your soul, with all your strength, and with all your mind,' and 'your neighbor as yourself.'" And He said to him, "You have answered rightly; do this and you will live." (Lk. 10:26-28)

Root of Darkness

As humans, we sin and will struggle with sin all of our days. Sin is unrighteousness; it separates us from the Almighty. It's breaking God's law. It's what keeps us from obeying the greatest commandment to love the Lord with our whole heart, mind, soul and strength. Breaking this commandment, we know, is idolatry.

I said in the last chapter that one of the most subtle and yet spiritually destructive ways parents can overstep is to impede the Holy Spirit from both convicting and encouraging their children. The Holy Spirit, dwelling in our hearts, enables and leads us to the worship God reserves for Himself. But when parents place themselves in a position reserved for God alone, they cause their children to commit idolatry.

Think about a garden. Plants need sunlight to grow, to be strong, to produce fruit. Flowers need the sun to blossom and thrive, and yet they are at the mercy of the elements, having no choice over the environment. They don't ask for clouds to come along and hide the sun. They can't make them go away. Yet clouds cut off the source of life. Unless they move, the garden will die.

Like flowers in the sun, we are dependent upon our own Source of life. He is our righteousness. (Jer. 23:5-6) Anything that stands between us and the Lord is sin. Anytime we look to something or someone else as our source, as our justification and righteousness, we commit idolatry. And anything that preoccupies and keeps us from loving the Lord our God with all our heart, all our soul, all our strength, and all our mind is an idol.

Even if it has been erected for us.

We were created to worship God alone which is why we must understand that idolatry is the deepest root of our pain.

White-Washed Idolatry

Wakefield continues,

> At age fifteen and living at home, Marty knew he should obey his parents, but they never led him to deal with his heart relationship with God. Consequently, the parent-child relationship was always about responsibility and expectations. It's no wonder that Marty felt unloved,

controlled, and unvalued. Living by rules and standards cannot build relationships based on God's love and grace. A form of outward obedience may occur, but liberty and love that comes from the Holy Spirit's work internally is overlooked.

Until Marty has a relationship with Jesus, his parents must teach, train, and demand honor and obedience (Eph. 6:1-4). However, once the Holy Spirit indwells him, Marty should be taught to walk by the Spirit in relationship with the heavenly Father. As Jesus told his disciples, "Do not call anyone on earth your father; for One is your Father, He who is in heaven" (Matt. 23:9). As a son starts to walk by the Spirit, an earthly father should encourage his son's decision-making and guidance to come from a personal relationship with the heavenly Father, not himself. To the degree that the father makes the decisions and dictates the lifestyle of his believing son, to that degree he hinders his son's spiritual life. A father's role should decrease just as John the Baptist's role decreased when Jesus appeared (John 3:30).[40]

This is serious stuff. Because there are so many good, godly things that can become idols. That's why our confusion is practically palpable, and why this particular type of dysfunction is so insidious. But godly things are not God, and when they are held up as our source from which we draw life, what controls us, what we serve, and when they become as God to us—a god we can see and measure ourselves by—we become idolaters.

> You search the Scriptures, for in them you think you have eternal life; and these are they which testify of Me. But you are not willing to come to Me that you may have life.
>
> (Jn. 5:39-40)

It's a line so thin as to be almost imperceptible. Often our convictions and beliefs rule us as God. Sometimes it's church. Dad, Mom, even the blessing of children can become idols, cloud-like, obscuring our sun

---

[40] Ibid.

which gives life. Our standards, rules, regulations, even the law itself become our sustenance. Often the Bible is elevated to God's position, and parents, speaking and controlling as God—*but they are still not God.*

As a perfectionist who read the Bible every day and clung to commands to be perfect, holy, and to sin not, I committed idolatry. How? The truth is, Jesus is my perfection. As I listened to voices—my own and others—to keep trying, to press on towards the prize, to not grow weary in doing good, that he who knows to do good and does not do, to him it's sin...I missed the voice that said *Come to Me. Rest.* I thought my obedience was the standard, not the love of Christ. In a curious twist of "I die daily", I killed myself to gain approval, acceptance and "well done." Instead, I found despair, guilt, depression, and shame, in part because I loved the praise of man more than God's.

Of course, we need approval and acceptance. We need to feel love, nurture and affection from others. We need to read the Bible, to have standards, convictions. But we cannot take God and re-create Him into something we can touch, feel, and measure ourselves by. We cannot re-create Him in the image of our parents. Scripture. The law. And by taking God's gifts, and God-given needs, we worship and serve the creature rather than the Creator.

Reflection

Jesus had scathing words for those so entrenched with religion that they forgot their Source of righteousness and caused others to commit idolatry—

> But woe to you, scribes and Pharisees, hypocrites! For you shut up the kingdom of heaven against men; for you neither go in yourselves, nor do you allow those who are entering to go in.
>
> ...Woe to you, scribes and Pharisees, hypocrites! For you pay tithe of mint and anise and cummin, and have neglected the weightier matters of the law: justice and mercy and faith. These you ought to have done, without leaving the others undone. Blind guides, who strain out a gnat and swallow a camel! (Mt. 23:13, 23-24)
>
> Not everyone who says to Me, 'Lord, Lord,' shall enter the kingdom of heaven, but he who does the will of My Father in heaven. Many will say to Me in that day, 'Lord, Lord, have we not prophesied in Your name, cast out demons in Your name, and done many wonders

in Your name?' And then I will declare to them, 'I never knew you; depart from Me, you who practice lawlessness!' (Mt. 7:21-22)

Whoever causes one of these little ones who believe in Me to sin, it would be better for him if a millstone were hung around his neck, and he were drowned in the depth of the sea. (Mt. 18:6)

Sadly, most religious authoritarian families spend ample effort focused on things that ultimately result in shutting up the kingdom of heaven and forbidding others from not only entering, but even seeking it. Many good works, even good beliefs, have overshadowed God Himself. Some have set themselves in places reserved for the Almighty, as final arbiters of right, wrong, and truth, even appealing to Scripture as they do so. This is the ultimate spiritual abuse—white-washed idolatry.

As daughters who yearned to obey throughout our childhoods—or wives who struggled measuring up to the demands of a Quiverfull or patriocentric life—and for all of us who wanted to live holy lives while pleasing God and our husband or parents, what happens the day we look up and miss the sun?

"Do you want to be made well?"

It's a very important question.

He lay there by the healing pool, the crippled man, so close—and yet so far away. I'm sure he blinked up at this stranger in amazement. Dumb-founded, maybe angry a little. Perhaps he sputtered, *"What?"*

"Do you want to be made well?"

And Jesus asks us, too.

Have you been overshadowed by clouds within your life? We now have the ability, and the responsibility (response + ability) to remove the clouds which have kept us in darkness for so long. Jesus wants them to go away and will help us eliminate them from our lives. He whose name is Jealous longs to reach through pain and fog to illuminate and heal the shadow-sorrows crippling our hearts.

And yet, there is no need to feel shame for our hurts, infirmities, or obliterating clouds, for there is no condemnation in Christ.

"Take up your bed and walk," He says.

Move into the sun.

"Go and sin no more."

It is the language of a journey. A new way.

Part Three

The Living Way

Little girl, I say to you, arise.—Jesus

They have made themselves crooked paths;
Whoever takes that way shall not know peace.
Therefore justice is far from us,
Nor does righteousness overtake us;
We look for light, but there is darkness!
For brightness, but we walk in blackness!
We grope for the wall like the blind,
And we grope as if we had no eyes;
We stumble at noonday as at twilight;
We are as dead men in desolate places. (Isaiah 59:8-10)

...Enter the Holiest by the blood of Jesus,
by a new and living way which He consecrated for us,
through the veil, that is, His flesh...
(Hebrews 10:19-20)

Dear Mom and Dad,

To anyone who thinks I might matter (Mom and Dad), I'm just writing to tell you that I can't keep up this shallow, unhealthy relationship. I know you think that I hate you, and that you're right, I'm wrong, and I'll come running home someday. I don't hate you, but this is confusing—we're all good until I say something that you (and no one else) find offensive, and then I spend all day crying because you guys don't care about how I feel nor seem to realize that this has an effect on me. On top of that, you choose to belittle me, my decisions, maturity, and my husband. This hurts more than I can even *begin* to describe. It's insulting and painful because you were the ones who told me I was capable, and when I became capable you decided otherwise. Adulthood isn't up to you. It took me a long time to learn that. Our relationship, as it stands, is hurtful, damaging, and quite honestly makes me physically ill. I can't keep walking on eggshells around the ones who told me not to be scared about what other people thought. Truth is, I *am* scared. I'm scared about what you think, and it keeps me from growing and I can't continue to stay in this pattern. I'm an adult woman, married to a great guy who cares about me and makes me feel safe. I'm growing into a person and I'm different from you, and that's okay. I'm not a clone, right? Until you can accept me and my husband for the adults that we are (and not harp on us for anything you disagree with) I can't have a relationship with you. I'll send presents for the kids. I miss them like nuts. I love you; I just can't do this anymore.

—Hope, a quivering daughter

Fourteen |

Truth

*He shall send from heaven and save me; He reproaches the one who
would swallow me up. Selah
God shall send forth His mercy and His truth. (Psalm 57:3)*

*Say to wisdom, "You are my sister," and call understanding your
nearest kin. (Proverbs 7:4)*

There's an old saying: *If you do what you've always done, you'll get
what you've always gotten.* Remember—the Old Way is the way
we've always gone, the broad way of destruction. Because our minds
have been so twisted by half-truths and whole lies, since we have dwelt
for years in the old ways of thinking, behaving, and performing, it takes
an active re-training to transform our lives. When these things are
cocooned in Scripture, attached to God's name and are the daily
disciplines of well-meaning Christians, sometimes even thinking about
change is frightening!

The New Way is stepping into the unknown. It's doing things
differently, not for the sake of being different, but for the sake of
following the Lord Jesus when He calls. It's trusting God as we walk
the narrow path of righteousness we do not know. Remember Jesus'
question—*"Do you want to be made well?"* It's a serious inquiry, for it
requires faith. And yet He tells us that even if we have faith as small as
a mustard seed, we can move mountains. Do not fear on the way, little
one. He holds you safely.

Seeking Truth

One reason many women do not enjoy lasting healing is that they don't know what to do with lies from emotional, spiritual, and psychological abuse. Jesus, who came to set us free, longs to pierce the darkness with the light of His truth—but first we must be willing to let Him! Before healing can occur, we must admit that our pain is real, and that Christ is the only one who can heal it. We must no longer be the keepers of our family's secrets but with the Lord's help, step out of the kingdom of darkness and into His marvelous light.

For this reason we need to examine some of the lies and thought patterns that keep many Christian women from patriarchal families captive:

"My parents did the best they could."

This common objection to facing childhood wounds is actually a mixed blessing. Scripture exhorts us to be thankful in all things. For most of us, our parents *did* do the best they could, and we can lift hearts in praise to God and sincerely offer thanks to Mom and Dad for this. It also serves to help us stay humble and not think of ourselves more highly than we ought. However, this does not mean we shouldn't examine the roots of our pain and why repeated attempts to heal or grow don't seem successful. Countless times I wailed in frustration, "I feel like I'm back to square one!" However, *"I desire truth in the inward parts,"* says King David. This can be excruciating, and sometimes we dismiss or deny reality—*"That didn't really happen,"* or *"It wasn't that bad,"* or, *"That's not what they meant,"* or even, *"That's not true."* But by its very nature, denial bars truth from entering hidden places. Truth is not always pretty or easy or what we want to hear, yet truth must be our foundation. It means we must look honestly at both our own sin, and the sins of others. When "the others" are Christians, and furthermore our parents or even our husband, examination feels mentally crippling, almost like betrayal.

Unfortunately, telling ourselves "my parents did the best they could" slams the door shut on further introspection. Until we can rest in Jesus and walk through that door, we will continue aching.

> But we have renounced the hidden things of shame, not walking in craftiness nor handling the word of God deceitfully, but by manifestation of the truth commending ourselves to every man's conscience in the sight of God. (2 Cor. 4:2)

"What if I'm wrong?"

My Dad was known to say, "They might be sincere, but they're sincerely wrong." In the final analysis, we know this is true in some cases. But a child is not psychologically equipped to handle the possibility that mommy or daddy might not be right. Because parents are the interpreters of reality, any discrepancy a young child perceives is reinterpreted as her own misunderstanding. In other words, if Susie says the crayon in her hand is "blue" and Mom says, "No, it's red," because Mom is absolute—omniscient in her eyes—Susie accepts Mom's correction and accepts that her own perception is wrong. Obviously, this is God's design for how children are to learn because it mirrors how we learn from Him. And it works when Mom and Dad are right.

But what happens as the child grows and Mom and Dad are wrong? When a Spirit-filled child, sincerely crying out for wisdom from her Lord, *does* hear from Him? When God truly calls her in a direction that challenges long-held family values?

What if Mom was color-blind and Susie was right all along?

Through unique training, our default position is to automatically question and doubt our own perceptions, which makes it hard to shake the belief that Mom and Dad are automatically right, even after we discover their mistakes. We've been raised to trust them to teach us truth, to believe that God speaks through them to us. In our minds, they *should* be right; we want them to be, need them to be. Learning otherwise, if and when it happens, is earth-shattering. This is why making a family *Christ-centered* rather than *father-centered* is so important, and building our house on the Rock, instead of man-constructed theologies. It's why parents need to be humble and quick to acknowledge error and redirect their children to our perfect, heavenly Parent.

When this does not happen consistently, these false beliefs follow children into adulthood. Sometimes we become gripped by an unshakeable sense of trepidation, literally unable to make decisions fearing we will make mistakes. Just as parents help to shape a little one's perspective of God, a young woman raised through subtle messages to believe that, essentially, Mom and Dad are *always right* and she is *always wrong* can encounter extreme difficulty identifying the Lord's voice and understanding His grace and kindness.

When faced with pain or choices or less-than-pretty reality, it can be helpful to ask yourself, "What is the truth of the situation?" And then sit quietly before the Lord and let Him show you. Re-training our minds will take time, but the Father of Truth is eager for you to know it.

> However, when He, the Spirit of truth, has come, He will guide you into all truth; for He will not speak on His own authority, but whatever He hears He will speak; and He will tell you things to come. (Jn. 16:13)

"But a woman is easily deceived!"

Within many Christian homes, children often accept Jesus at early ages. While maturity of course makes a difference in a child's understanding, it is dangerous and arrogant to assume that young people cannot possess godly wisdom. As young women raised in patriarchy begin to wrestle with deeper things in life, they often receive messages that what they're hearing from the Lord can't be true unless it comes through her father. And when those who have established themselves as arbiters of truth insist that a young woman is "deceived" in her understanding of God's will, what then?

Well, she might truly be deceived. If so, hopefully this is communicated with humility (2 Tim. 2:25) and her family safely guides her into proper understanding. But if her misunderstanding is not handled with love and humility, she might internalize it with the belief "I am *always* wrong." This lie can have a devastating effect on a girl's relationship with God. Instead of trusting God, she learns to places her trust in man—in her parents' interpretation of God's will, truth, and Scripture.

And if she is not deceived, such ready proclamations quench the Spirit through causing her to doubt what He has shown her, ultimately veering her off the narrow path and causing her to stumble.

I sympathize with the frustration that exclaims, exasperated, "What should I do then, just let her fall off a cliff if I see her walking towards the edge?" While Christian parents do have a tremendous responsibility to proclaim truth to their children and God gives them wisdom in doing so, He has given parents this task so that each of our hearts will be fully turned to Him. "Work out your own salvation with fear and trembling," says Paul. And often it *is* with fear and trembling as we learn to trust Him, by faith resting in the hope that He will make His will known— for at the end of our days when we face the King of kings, we cannot use our parents as justification or rely on them for protection. James 1:5-6 says, *"If any of you lacks wisdom, let him ask of God, who gives to all liberally and without reproach, and it will be given to him. But let him ask in faith, with no doubting, for he who doubts is like a wave of the sea driven and tossed by the wind.*" God's truth is available to all—male and female—without reproach. He wants your heart—from you directly, not through your father or mother, husband or pastor. And a parent who properly loves Christ first and then his children will recognize the grave disservice he does by placing himself between his daughter and her Lord.

> But God has revealed them to us through His Spirit. For the Spirit searches all things, yes, the deep things of God …Now we have received, not the spirit of the world, but the Spirit who is from God, that we might know the things that have been freely given to us by God. These things we also speak, not in words which man's wisdom teaches but which the Holy Spirit teaches…For "who has known the mind of the LORD that he may instruct Him?" But we have the mind of Christ. (1 Cor. 2:10-16)

This goes for you and for me, who are accepted in the Beloved.

"I can't trust my desperately wicked heart. These desires come from my flesh."

Several years ago I borrowed a book that came highly recommended by many women I knew. I began to read it with eagerness, but as I went along I had serious concerns about its biblical accuracy, lack of grace, and presentation of unwise—even dangerous—ideas. But when I answered the question *"So, what did you think?"* honestly, my concerns were brushed aside—"Women just don't want to submit to their husbands," "Women are rebellious and deceived by nature," and objections to the book and its messages "are the result of the flesh."

I mulled these responses for a while, both in prayer and in Scripture. Growing up I learned that feeling "resistant" towards teachings like the ones in the book was a reaction from my flesh as it warred against the Spirit. Or that when my deceived heart bristled against truth, it was because *the heart is deceitful above all things, and desperately wicked; who can know it?* (Jer. 17:9) And, *for all that is in the world—the lust of the flesh, the lust of the eyes, and the pride of life—is not of the Father but is of the world.* (1 Jn. 2:16)

But what if this teaching was backwards? What if my heart, which belonged to Jesus and became indwelt by the Holy One at a very young age, was right? What if my spirit rightfully grew concerned in response to the old way, the broad way of destruction? What if "my flesh" was actually a word behind me whispering, *"This is the way, walk in it"*? (Is. 30:21) And what if labels—"flesh," "deceived," "wicked"—in actuality quenched the Spirit of truth? These labels, when used unbiblically, simply control our minds and mold behavior—and reject the still, small voice of the One who bids, *"Come, rest."*

A redeemed heart *needs* to be a factor in discovering truth, for that is where Jesus lives and His word resides.

> But the Holy Spirit also witnesses to us; for after He had said before, "This is the covenant that I will make with them after those days, says the LORD: I will put My laws into their hearts, and in their minds I will write them," then He adds, "Their sins and their lawless deeds I will remember no more." (Heb. 10:15-17)

"It's selfish to focus on me and my healing."

Our healing is why Jesus came (Lk. 4:18). Healing is a need (Lk. 9:11), and the Lord God is our sovereign provider (Phil. 4:19). Jesus reminds us that *"Those who are well have no need of a physician, but those who are sick"* (Lk. 5:31). Like the afflicted woman who reached through crowds to grasp His clothes, seeking healing demonstrates our faith—and without faith, it is impossible to please God.

In His wisdom, God sometimes brings about healing in ways we don't fully understand. There are moments that seem especially dark. To cry out to Him for relief is not selfish. It confesses, like the child's Bible song, that we are weak but He is strong.

> Ask, and it will be given to you; seek, and you will find; knock, and it will be opened to you. For everyone who asks receives, and he who seeks finds, and to him who knocks it will be opened.
>
> Or what man is there among you who, if his son asks for bread, will give him a stone? Or if he asks for a fish, will he give him a serpent? If you then, being evil, know how to give good gifts to your children, how much more will your Father who is in heaven give good things to those who ask Him! (Mt. 7:7-11)

"What's so bad about pain?"

Throughout this book we've talked at length about pain and the real need for comfort. Religious lifestyles often emphasize sanctification through hardship and of not growing comfortable or complacent, but welcoming the refining fires of suffering. But sometimes we elevate hardship to dangerous heights. Almost like a holy twist on the phrase, *"No pain, no gain,"* we've learned to measure our current spiritual state by our current level of suffering—or, in positive language, by our degree of will-power and resistance to convenience and comfort.

In an earlier chapter we discussed the issue of idolatry and drawing our source of life from that which is not God—even when our idols have been erected for us. This can be confusing, because much of what we served is necessary and good—our family, Scripture, our convictions. But to help identify where we direct our worship, one thing we can ask ourselves is "For whom am I willing to suffer?" Jesus' suffering was redemptive. The ongoing suffering of quivering daughters is destructive *because it serves the creature, rather than the Creator.* It follows the Old Way, man-made traditions, convictions, interpretations, and the doctrines of men. It is the way that seems right, but the end thereof is death.

However, Jesus did say that difficult is the way which leads to life, and there are few that find it. (Mt. 7:14) With humility, I affirm that Christianity is not a feel-good gospel, and a life lived in obedience still at times encounters darkness and sorrow and pain. But it's suffering with godly purpose, and He who is your Source and in whom you place your trust will comfort you and make all things beautiful in its time.

These three questions—

- Who is my source for all of life?
- Whom do I serve?
- For whom am I willing to suffer?

—will help determine who really holds your heart.

> But even if you should suffer for righteousness' sake, you are blessed. And do not be afraid of their threats, nor be troubled. But sanctify the Lord God in your hearts, and always be ready to give a defense to everyone who asks you a reason for the hope that is in you, with meekness and fear; having a good conscience, that when they defame you as evildoers, those who revile your good conduct in Christ may be ashamed. For

it is better, if it is the will of God, to suffer for doing good than for doing evil…

Therefore let those who suffer according to the will of God commit their souls to Him in doing good, as to a faithful Creator. (1 Pt. 3:14-17, 4:19)

In the garden of Gethsemane, Jesus *"began to be sorrowful and deeply distressed. Then He said to them, 'My soul is exceedingly sorrowful, even to death.'"* (Mt. 26:37-38) Dear sisters, He speaks our language! God-the-Son knows the utter blackness of sorrow and fear that makes us long for the day we die. He then prays, *"O My Father, if it is possible, let this cup pass from Me; nevertheless, not as I will, but as You will."* There is no shame in asking for our cup to pass while remaining committed to the will of God. The trust that surrenders itself to the will of God and accepts suffering is the trust He asks of us. Will we not love our lives to the death?

And this, beloved, is where we find joy—deep wells of healing joy—filled with Living Water, refined by sorrow, and redeemed by the hand of God.

Therefore, from now on, we regard no one according to the flesh. Even though we have known Christ according to the flesh, yet now we know Him thus no longer. Therefore, if anyone is in Christ, he is a new creation; old things have passed away; behold, all things have become new. Now all things are of God, who has reconciled us to Himself through Jesus Christ, and has given us the ministry of reconciliation. (2 Cor. 5:16-18)

The final lie many girls hear or tell themselves is the simplest, most common, and also the most crippling.

"It really wasn't that bad."
This verbal shrug dismisses years of heartache, oceans of tears, countless episodes of emotional, spiritual, and even intellectual and physical abuse. This is denial and it spurns something that matters very much to Jesus.

You.

Your heart. Your soul, mind, and strength.

To be honest, I still struggle with this sometimes. There was a lot of good in my life, growing up. There are many praise-worthy things in my family, things which I love and am glad to be part of. As we saw in the beginning of this chapter, reminding ourselves of this is good because it gives us ways to be thankful in all things. Yet we cannot serve two masters. To remain in denial is to continue ignoring the Father of Truth. We must allow truth to transform darkness and pain for healing to come.

The next time you feel stifled by the lie that "it wasn't that bad," look at a photo of the little-girl you. If you were her mother, what would you tell her? Could you say to her, "Get over it"? Could you say, "It's in the past—move on"? Would you tell her, "It wasn't that bad"?

Instead, look at her through Jesus' eyes—

> But whoever causes one of these little ones who believe in Me to stumble, it would be better for him if a millstone were hung around his neck, and he were thrown into the sea. (Mk. 9:42)
>
> Whoever causes one of these little ones who believe in Me to sin, it would be better for him if a millstone were hung around his neck, and he were drowned in the depth of the sea. Woe to the world because of offenses! For offenses must come, but woe to that man by whom the offense comes! (Mt. 18:6-7)

Reflection

Stumble. Sin. Offense. He takes these things seriously. And as we seek wisdom in the hidden parts, as we uncover the lies we've believed and seek healing from excruciating wounds, recognizing where we remain in denial is a key to overcoming it.

When tempted by denial, it helps to ask: "What is the truth of the situation?" Pray that God will help you see what is real even when confusion and darkness lurks before you. And write it down—seeing it in black and white helps it to sink in.

As you travel the new way, there will be moments when all you see is fog. Since God is not the author of confusion, when you encounter these times it is essential that you stop to consider who is drawing your heart and make a conscious choice. Remember *Source, Serve, and Suffer:* Who am I serving? God? Man? Myself? My convictions? Where do I derive my sense of purpose? Life? Truth? Why am I suffering? Is it for God's purpose or man's?

> Did you receive the Spirit by the works of the law, or by the hearing of faith? Are you so foolish? Having begun in the Spirit, are you now being made perfect by the flesh? Have you suffered so many things in vain—if indeed it was in vain? (Gal. 3:2-4)

Sometimes obedience to God *will be* following certain convictions. However it is imperative to be certain that God is the origin. One way is to remember the words of Jesus:

> Come to Me, all you who labor and are heavy laden, and I will give you rest. Take My yoke upon you and learn from Me, for I am gentle and lowly in heart, and you will find rest for your souls. For My yoke is easy and My burden is light. (Mt. 11:28-30)

If it is from the true God, it will pass this test.

————————————————

We've examined some of the lies that keep women from truly being healed from pain, but something especially tender for many daughters of patriarchy, and one of the biggest spiritual, mental, and emotional hurdles keeping them from that first small step towards recovery is a question I hear nearly every day…

Fifteen |

Honor

In return for my love they are my accusers,
but I give myself to prayer. (Psalm 109:4)

W hat about honor?
One of the more difficult aftereffects of speaking about past hurts and how they've affected us is that doing so often wounds those who are close to us. Even though we try to speak in love (1 Cor. 13:1), some still may feel threatened. "How is this honoring your parents?" they ask. "This does not show respect to your husband!" they might accuse. While truth must be spoken in love, the fact remains that truth is not always pleasant. There are at least two sides to every story—in Quiverfull families, this can mean *many* sides. Someone will likely disbelieve, disagree, blame, or justify. When this happens, we must cling all the more to our Heavenly Father.

Part of being true-hearted means examining ourselves before the Lord, asking, *"Search me, O God, and know my heart; try me, and know my anxieties; and see if there is any wicked way in me, and lead me in the way everlasting."* (Ps. 139:23-24) Seeking truth in the inward parts means *all* the truth, even the messy stuff inside of us. Even what we are responsible for. Paul reminds us,

> For the word of God is living and powerful, and sharper than any two-edged sword, piercing even to the division of soul and spirit, and of joints and marrow, and is a discerner of the thoughts and intents of the heart. And there is no creature hidden from His sight, but all things are naked and open to the eyes of Him to whom we must give account. (Heb. 4:12-14)

As we seek healing, we need to do what we can to make things right. Our exhortation is clear: *"If it is possible, as much as depends on you, live peaceably with all men."* (Rom. 12:18) And again, *"Therefore, beloved, looking forward to these things, be diligent to be found by Him in peace, without spot and blameless."* (2 Pet. 3:14) We need to be above reproach, *"having a good conscience, that when they defame you as evildoers, those who revile your good conduct in Christ may be ashamed."* (1 Pet. 3:16)

If we humble ourselves before God, the Holy Spirit will show us what this means in our particular circumstances. Some of us will need to ask forgiveness from others for hurtful things we've said, or for hurtful behavior. Some of us have apologized our entire lives. Some of us will need to repent and turn away from sinful choices. And some of us will need to endeavor to make restitution, even when we've committed no wrong at all. Jesus preached reconciliation (Mt. 5:23-24), and all who name the name of Christ are our brothers and sisters in the Lord, even if they wear the earthly title of 'husband' or 'wife,' 'mother,' 'father,' or 'daughter.'

This is hard, I know, especially when we may be innocent and have to endure painful rejection, accusations and labels. Please let me assure you that this is not in vain! Regardless of the outcome, even if your approaches are doubted, rejected, or considered "not good enough" in others' eyes, remember that the Lord sees.

> And have no fellowship with the unfruitful works of darkness, but rather expose them. For it is shameful even to speak of those things which are done by them in secret. But all things that are exposed are made manifest by the light, for whatever makes manifest is light.
>
> (Eph. 5:11-13)

Notice that "light is whatever makes manifest." As our souls lie naked and open before the One to whom we must give account, when we humbly obey Him despite our pain and invite Him into the dark, secret places inside, something amazing happens. The Word of God that is living and powerful brings His light of truth. He reveals the hidden things within our hearts, and He doesn't condemn or accuse. He comforts. He strengthens and readies us for the journey that lies ahead, like preparations for labor that results in newborn life. It is a labor to bring restoring grace to our relationships, to find peace through our trials. And when our heart is right before Him, when our intentions and motivations are pure, addressing the effects of others' actions on us becomes a labor of love.

Love with our Eyes Open

Part of loving others means that we must acknowledge truth in our hearts and the truth of how others' choices have affected us. We know the saying "love is blind," but Paul reminds us that *"scarcely for a righteous man will one die; yet perhaps for a good man someone would even dare to die. But God demonstrates His own love toward us, in that while we were still sinners, Christ died for us."* (Rom. 5:7-8) Through His deliberate, willing, intentional love, we have three things: an Advocate who understands pain, for He who knew no sin became sin for us and suffered on our behalf. We have an example to follow as we labor to uncover truth, find grace, and extend forgiveness to others. And, as Isaiah 53 beautifully portrays Christ's work on the cross, we have healing.

But in our quest for healing, while seeking to love like Jesus, to forgive, respect, and honor those who have hurt us, sometimes we face unique obstacles. How do we honor when it's unwanted, misunderstood, or for all practical purposes, rejected? When others insist that honor means to obey, even for those who have left childhood behind? Contrary to what many believe, seeking the truth of pain and acknowledging our struggles does not dishonor our families. And not only does honor *not* mean "obedience," honor is not always a feeling that you give someone. Rather, to honor is to esteem, to place weight, to value. And this is not mutually exclusive to examining or exposing the effects of a dysfunctional childhood or sin.

The Face of Honor

Unfortunately, many authoritarian families attempt to dictate the terms of honor, to redefine it in a self-elevating manner. Some make impossible demands of their adult children, or control their involvement with the family. Some sever communication altogether.

Furthermore, sometimes they blame their wives or daughters causing this.

Blame and accusation are favorite weapons within authoritarian families, and they aren't always overt. Unfortunately, if left unaddressed they succeed only in driving children away, not restoring them in a spirit of gentleness. Especially toxic, these verbal and emotional tactics use the language of the evil one noted in Revelation 12, who is *"the accuser of our brethren, who accused them before our*

God day and night." But this doesn't mean that honoring our accusers is impossible.

In their book, *Forgiving our Parents, Forgiving Ourselves: Healing Adult Children of Dysfunctional Families,* Dr. David Stoop and Dr. James Masteller address the very sensitive topic of parental honor.

> The original Hebrew word used in the passage [Ex. 20:12] literally means "assign weight to." It is as though someone told us something and we replied, "I want to carefully weigh what you've said." If we consider their words and decide that they are important, we are, in a sense "assigning weight" to them. Thus to "honor" our parents means to assign weight—value, importance, significance—to them.
>
> When that original Hebrew word was translated into Greek for the New Testament, the Greek word had to do with "giving glory to" the thing being honored. Both the Greek and the Hebrew carried the sense of honoring people because of the position they held, not necessarily because of intrinsic value.
>
> One way to understand this is to imagine that you are in a banquet hall. Part way through the banquet, your city mayor walks in. Now, let's suppose that you are not particularly fond of this mayor. You didn't vote for him in the last election, and you think he has made some bad decisions. Even so, when he walks into the room, you stand up with everyone else to greet him.
>
> Why? Because he is the mayor, and honoring him is the appropriate thing to do. You assign a certain value, or "weight" to him because of the position he holds. This does not mean you now have to start liking him, or even respecting him, as a person. It does not mean you have to start pretending that you agree with everything he has done as mayor. The honor is accorded to the position he holds, not so much to the individual.
>
> In the same way, we can honor our parents—accord them an appropriate degree of "weight"—because of the position they hold in our lives as parents. Similar to our example with the mayor, the fact that we honor them

does not mean we have to pretend that they have never done anything wrong or hurtful to us. [41]

Forgiveness

Scripture tells us that "love covers a multitude of sins," and it's true. What isn't true, however, is what some would have us believe: that love ignores or blinds us to truth, that love is opaque—non-transparent—or that it even makes sin okay. Like a blanket, we can drape love across the sins of others and through it, offer to them the forgiveness, grace, and mercy that the Lord has shown to us. But this means we need to get uncomfortably close. We need to plunge our fingers into yucky and let Jesus redeem.

Has anyone said these things to you? *"You need to forgive." "Just forgive and move on." "Forgive and forget."* As we seek the Lord for healing and growth in our lives, it's important to understand a few things about forgiveness. Forgiveness cannot be coerced. Forgiveness cannot be rushed. We are exhorted to forgive "from the heart." (Mt. 18:35) Sometimes this takes time. Perhaps if you find forgiveness difficult, concentrate instead on love. It is very hard to hold an unforgiving heart towards someone who you love with Christ's love. *"Owe no one anything except to love one another, for he who loves another has fulfilled the law."* (Rom. 13:8) Likewise, we cannot judge others who are struggling with forgiveness; we can pray for them and encourage them, but their journey with the Lord is intimate and known to Him, not to us. Forgiveness—love—is something that He makes beautiful in the fullness of time.

Do we want to be made well? Digging deeply to identify the roots of pain can be agonizing for everyone—but the Lord is able to sustain, comfort, and make all things new. Our Healer and Helper does not abandon us when we cry, but always lives to make intercession for us—and just as He forgave us, He can help us learn to forgive others.

Reflection

Put simply, honor is a verb—actively giving weight to our parents' work, position, and sacrifice in our lives. Did they raise us to seek truth? To love God and righteousness? To walk in obedience, regardless of the cost? By doing so, we honor them, even if they

---

[41] Stoop, Dr. David and Dr. James Masteller. *Forgiving our Parents, Forgiving Ourselves: Healing Adult Children of Dysfunctional Families.* (Ventura, CA: Gospel Light Books, 1996) pp. 291-298. Used by permission.

disagree with how this looks. We honor them through not settling into apathy but seeking truth, healing, and strengthening our faith. We honor them by fighting the good fight, by obeying God, and by loving Him with all our hearts, minds, souls, and strength. We honor them by maintaining healthy boundaries. This actually is allowing space for God to work, which is an act of love. We honor them by praying for them. Prayer helps us to see our families through Jesus' eyes and have compassion. We honor them through forgiveness. And we honor them through speaking truth.

For in this, we take after our Father, which is what truly sets us apart from the world. (Jn. 8:37-47)

Sixteen

Sanctification

And what agreement has the temple of God with idols?
For you are the temple of the living God.
As God has said:
"I will dwell in them and walk among them.
I will be their God, and they shall be My people."
Therefore "Come out from among them
And be separate," says the Lord.
"Do not touch what is unclean, and I will receive you.
I will be a Father to you,
And you shall be My sons and daughters,"
Says the LORD Almighty. (2 Corinthians 6:16-18)

The King James Version of the Holy Bible uses the term "peculiar" seven times.[42] In Titus, we read what most patriarchal Christians use to motivate their choices while seeking a truly biblical—even holy—lifestyle:

> For the grace of God that bringeth salvation hath appeared to all men, teaching us that, denying ungodliness and worldly lusts, we should live soberly, righteously, and godly, in this present world; looking for that blessed hope, and the glorious appearing of the great God and our Saviour Jesus Christ; Who gave himself for us, that he might redeem us from all iniquity, and purify unto himself a peculiar people, zealous of good works. (Tit. 2:11-14, KJV)

---

[42] Ex. 19:5, Dt. 14:2, Dt. 26:18, Ps. 135:4, Ecc. 2:8, Tit. 2:14, 1 Pet. 2:9

The attitude *"We are to be different. We are a peculiar people"* compels many believers to adopt strict standards of clothing, of physical appearance, and of anti-cultural behaviors to affirm their separateness from the world. Many choose to homeschool, live an agrarian life, or even withdraw from other Christians who aren't "likeminded." But there is something we need to notice in this verse: *our peculiarness is not in our control!* Yes, we should live soberly, righteously, and godly *"in this present world,"* but God is the One who does the work. Our Redeemer is the One who "purifies us unto himself a peculiar people"—I dare add, and not we ourselves, lest we should boast. (Eph. 2:9)

Part of living soberly means to recognize that even when we follow a lifestyle determined by our convictions, such as homeschooling, dresses-only, head-coverings, "doing without," birthing a Quiverfull, not wearing jewelry—that *"These things indeed have an appearance of wisdom in self-imposed religion, false humility, and neglect of the body, but are of no value against the indulgence of the flesh."* (Col. 2:22-23) The truth is, in Christ we are already unworldly. Jesus prayed, *"I do not pray that You should take them out of the world, but that You should keep them from the evil one. They are not of the world, just as I am not of the world. Sanctify them by Your truth. Your word is truth."* (Jn. 17:15-17) And Paul understood this: *"I wrote to you in my epistle not to keep company with sexually immoral people. Yet I certainly did not mean with the sexually immoral people of this world, or with the covetous, or extortioners, or idolaters, since then you would need to go out of the world."* (1 Cor. 5:9-10)

Having Jesus in our hearts, having the truth, is what makes us different.

And this is sanctification.

It means "set apart." We need to understand this as we continue walking the narrow path, because it will grow more difficult along the way.

The daughters of patriarchy know about a special kind of pain. We know the deepest, darkest sorrows that affect the heart, spirit, and soul; the pain of feeling "different" because we don't measure up to what others think we should. We feel as though we don't matter to those important to us, and that we're never good enough.

Scripture tells us that all of us, like sheep, have gone astray. Yet sometimes our parents treat us as though we've not only strayed, but that we've fallen away, even when we seek the will of God and love Jesus. Even when we've come home to His heart. This fear, which usually translates to fear of anything less than mistake-free, cheerful obedience, influences how parents see, speak, and relate their children. Unfortunately, for all practical purposes, this often means *blind* obedience, and that adult children who are, in fact, seeking the voice of the True Shepherd in ways not understood or endorsed by parents are considered lost.

The Disciples of Moses

The sad fact is that sometimes healing creates division within our relationships. Sometimes truth separates. Consider the story of the man born blind. Following his restoration of sight by Jesus, what happened to him?

> They brought him who formerly was blind to the Pharisees. Now it was a Sabbath when Jesus made the clay and opened his eyes. Then the Pharisees also asked him again how he had received his sight. He said to them, "He put clay on my eyes, and I washed, and I see."
>
> Therefore some of the Pharisees said, "This Man is not from God, because He does not keep the Sabbath." Others said, "How can a man who is a sinner do such signs?" And there was a division among them…
>
> So they again called the man who was blind, and said to him, "Give God the glory! We know that this Man is a sinner."
>
> He answered and said, "Whether He is a sinner or not I do not know. One thing I know: that though I was blind, now I see."
>
> Then they said to him again, "What did He do to you? How did He open your eyes?"
>
> He answered them, "I told you already, and you did not listen. Why do you want to hear it again? Do you also want to become His disciples?"
>
> Then they reviled him and said, "You are His disciple, but we are Moses' disciples. We know that God spoke to Moses; as for this fellow, we do not know where He is from."

The man answered and said to them, "Why, this is a marvelous thing, that you do not know where He is from; yet He has opened my eyes! Now we know that God does not hear sinners; but if anyone is a worshiper of God and does His will, He hears him..."

They answered and said to him, "You were completely born in sins, and are you teaching us?" And they cast him out. (Jn. 9:13-34)

Can you relate to this story? Sometimes quivering daughters are cast out, cast aside, rejected—if not physically, then emotionally. Our earthly shepherds might not understand what the Holy Spirit is teaching us, and react out of fear. As we've seen in past chapters, sometimes they try to manipulate and control us using the name of God, much like the Pharisees who railed against Jesus, saying, *"This Man is not from God, because He does not keep the Sabbath...give God the glory! You are His disciple, but we are Moses' disciples."*

While the "disciples of Moses" in our lives might consider us lost as we follow our Shepherd along the way they do not know, take heart knowing that they, too, are being sought by Him. *"What man of you, having a hundred sheep, if he loses one of them, does not leave the ninety-nine in the wilderness, and go after the one which is lost until he finds it? And when he has found it, he lays it on his shoulders, rejoicing...for the Son of Man has come to seek and to save that which was lost."* (Lk. 15:4-5, 19:10) A loving shepherd with a lost sheep doesn't wait around for her to return, nor does he condemn, berate, or judge her when she is found—rather, he gathers her close with rejoicing. *"Those who are well have no need of a physician, but those who are sick,"* He says, and it is to the unwell, the unhealed, the unwanted and wanting, the rejected, brokenhearted, needy, abandoned, ashamed, hungry, broken ones He has come. This goes for everyone—not only we ourselves, but also for our husbands, our parents or pastors, or anyone who might think we've gone astray as we seek the way that leads to life, as we turn from being Moses' disciples and become disciples of Jesus.

And as we are found by Him, we discover how much we do matter.

Reflection

In the quest for living righteously, discovering that you matter to God is a life-altering event. When this truth makes its way from your head to your heart and settles into the bones of your faith, you will never be the same. As you press forward through the fog, confusion, and pain, sifting through what it means to be truly "peculiar", or when others question your motives and doubt your path, keep in mind these words of Jesus:

> And why do you look at the speck in your brother's eye, but do not consider the plank in your own eye? Or how can you say to your brother, 'Let me remove the speck from your eye'; and look, a plank *is* in your own eye? Hypocrite! First remove the plank from your own eye, and then you will see clearly to remove the speck from your brother's eye. (Mt. 7:3-5)

The journey to healing requires us to remove our planks. And just like the idols erected for us, sometimes these planks are placed in our lives by others. We need to address our issues, attend to our needs, and seek health in all areas of life—for not only might we have planks in our eyes, but also in our minds, hearts, and bodies. Sometimes this calls for carefully detailed surgery, which takes time, patience, and precision, in order to be free.

This is part of the beautiful, mysterious way God intimately reveals Himself to you—there is not a formula as to how, when, and where healing will take place, for it is tailored precisely to the shape of your heart. For you are the one He leaves the others to find. You are the one He gathers close, rejoicing. He has given you your eyes to see, for yourself alone. He has given you a mouth to speak. He's given you a mind, breath, feeling, dreams—what about this is not love?

Jesus prayed, *"As You sent Me into the world, I also have sent them into the world. And for their sakes I sanctify Myself, that they also may be sanctified by the truth."* (Jn. 17:18-20) This is the new way, and it's here that we learn the secret to true unworldliness: sanctification.

God sanctified His Son. He sanctified the seventh day—set it apart and called it holy. He sanctified the priests—setting aside a special people. And He sanctifies us, sets us apart and makes us holy. That is how we are different from the world! Remember Jesus' prayer—*"I do not pray that you take them out of the world, but that you protect them from the evil one"?* God is our Source of protection and our sanctification. We become unworldly not by wearing the "right" clothes", remaining under the proper "umbrella", listening to the "right" music, behaving the "right" way, or living the "right" lifestyle—but by surrendering to His transforming work.

In God's exquisite foreknowledge and love, this sanctification cannot be done by us. It is God, who *"chose us in Him before the foundation of the world, that we should be holy and without blame before Him in love, having predestined us to adoption as sons by Jesus Christ to Himself"* (Eph. 1:3-5) that sets us apart. He does not require us to "do" anything to receive this gift. And as we come to Him and rest, as our flesh rests in hope, we too can echo the words of David: *I have set the LORD always before me; because He is at my right hand I shall not be moved. Therefore my heart is glad, and my glory rejoices; my flesh also will rest in hope. For You will not leave my soul in Sheol, Nor will You allow Your Holy One to see corruption. You will show me the path of life; In Your presence is fullness of joy; At Your right hand are pleasures forevermore.* (Ps. 16:8-11)

But we cannot do this alone. We need help.

Seventeen |

Alongside

Two are better than one,
Because they have a good reward for their labor.
For if they fall, one will lift up his companion.
But woe to him who is alone when he falls,
For he has no one to help him up.
Again, if two lie down together, they will keep warm;
But how can one be warm alone?
Though one may be overpowered by another,
two can withstand him.
And a threefold cord is not quickly broken. (Ecclesiastes 4:9-12)

"No matter how hard I tried, I couldn't be exactly what my siblings needed. And I lost my own childhood as well. In fact, I never had a childhood; what I had was spent being a second mother. I know life is not all about fun—I don't mean to imply that at all. And except for feeling tired or guilty all the time, I loved serving my family. But I had very little time to just enjoy growing up, being a child."—Kana

I met Sara when I was thirteen. We've spent more of our lives knowing each other than not, and it's no small thing to have a life-long friend as a child. It meant even more that after much seeking and pleading with the Lord, with tears and prayer for wisdom regarding my steps, I moved in with her when I left my childhood home.

Having Sara as my roommate and soul-sister cemented the bond we knew already. Her own life has curved through dark, painful places, yet having our paths intersect in youth and run parallel even unto now causes me to rejoice in the One who connected us in His book—the One He wrote before we were even born (Ps.139:16).

The Lord blessed me again when I spied blue eyes across a crowded room, and my lover came into my life. Through the love and help of my husband, the one who is literally alongside me every day, years of healing have taken place. My Troy believes in me. He loves and supports me; he challenges my mind and encourages me in my relationship with the Lord. He's given me the freedom I've needed to run the race of faith. He makes me laugh and blesses me with freedom. He helps me stay balanced—through his unique sense of humor, He reminds me to laugh when I've remained serious too long. He is like God's hands and feet, ministering love, protection, and sacrifice to me. He lays down his life for me daily. Through him I've caught glimpses of what *should* be, and through his outpouring of grace, I feel safe. And because I'm safe in his love, I can rest and allow soul-wounds to heal.

The Lord brings others along, as well. He brought Cindy, who has been invaluable in the release of this book. He's brought Alisa, my dear, dear friend, who prays for and encourages me in every struggle, every joy, and every endeavor. He's supplied Lily, who is like an aunt to me. Because He is my Source, He provides those I need to come alongside.

For we cannot go the way alone.

Helpmeets

It is our responsibility to step out of denial and seek the truth regarding our hurts, our struggles, and our past. But in our quest for healing from a dysfunctional childhood and the effects of sin, we need support. Jesus fulfilled His promise to send us a *parakletos,* the Holy Spirit who would be our Helper. The Greek word for "helper" means *"one called alongside [to help]"*. In Scripture, our Helper comforts, advocates, encourages, strengthens, consoles, enables, protects, defends, and intercedes on our behalf. He knew how desperately we would need help through the battles of life, how much we would need reassurance that He cares for us daily.

Jesus also knew the value of physical companions. In Gethsemane He brought His closest followers to watch and pray during His darkest moments of need. For us, this might be godly mentors and friends who will counsel, guide and encourage us on the journey. Sometimes it means we will need professional helpers—those trained in matters of deep emotional, spiritual, and physical pain and abuse. There is no shame in needing others to help us. Sara and I often asked each other to "be my eyes when I cannot see"—because sometimes the unknown way is dark and confusing, and eyes strain while meeting only blackness.

The Lord has always given me the right helpers—including *the* Helper—at just right time, because it is part of His faithful promise. Who has He sent you? Perhaps a friend who faithfully lifts you before the Father, or someone you can call at 3 AM? A "Titus 2" woman who can help you flesh out what it really means to be a daughter of God?

The key is to find someone you trust, someone safe and wise who will gently hold your heart while you make your way through the valley of the shadow. For example, Sara listened patiently while I raged, wrestled, and fought both myself and old voices. She challenged me, prayed for me, and shared God's wisdom. She let me repeat the same things over and over until I needed to no more. She weeps when I weep and rejoices with true, overflowing joy when I rejoice. Her friendship is a gift from the Lord and I pray that He blesses you with your own Sara.

Facing a lifetime of pain is no small feat—but a godly companion can help you see your way through the darkness, and can help you stand strong as you confront the lies that have torn at your faith and hope.

Facing Abuse in the Christian Family

As women from deeply religious, conservative families, most of us can say without a doubt that our parents truly desired to live righteously and raise us in a godly manner. Drawing from biblical texts, through prayer and selective external influence, our parents did the best they knew how to ensure we would grow up to seek the Lord, to love Him, and to walk in obedience to His voice. To have a pure heart and to take a stand against worldliness, and be strong Christians. While exceptions may exist, I have not heard from one young woman who believes her parents intentionally, willfully tried to damage her.

And yet, abuse and heartache abounds. Where does this leave us? We can ignore it and pretend it goes away. We can live our days in denial. Or we can let the Healer do what He came to do—to heal the brokenhearted and to bind up our wounds. (Ps. 147:3) But in a sad, strange irony, those who attempt to face issues of childhood pain, abuse, and family dysfunction often encounter objections.

- "You are just blaming your parents."
- "Why can't you take responsibility for your own sin?"
- "Love covers a multitude of sins."

- "They did the best they could. You shouldn't judge."
- "Just forgive."
- "If you honored your parents, you wouldn't bring this up."
- "Leave the past in the past."

While seeking wholeness, what common objections have you heard? Are you told that you're just whining, or that you are "too sensitive", or that "well, others had strict parents too, so what are you complaining about?" Do people tell you that you're being influenced by feminism or psychology? Or that you're selfish?

These responses are unhelpful and crippling at best, with potential for inexpressible emotional, spiritual, and physical damage at the worst. Dismissing real concerns offends the One who came to save. For most of us, healing occurs when we surrender to the Spirit of Truth and invite His light into our pain and abuse—even when we can't recall everything that happened in our past and even if we think it doesn't matter. Sometimes God allows us to forget certain things, or will bring them to remembrance in His timing. Either way, this can get messy. Parents get defensive. Daughters feel torn. Yet Scripture teaches that the fruits of doctrine, teachers, and those in authority reveal whether something is good or bad, healthy or unhealthy. And in most cases, the fruits of patriocentric, authoritarian doctrines are bad. As we've seen, depression, chronic fatigue, self-injury, attempted suicide,[43] and murder[44] are just a few serious ramifications from doctrines of man perpetuated in patriarchal households.

Consider that it is actually honoring to parents for children to examine the abusive environments that affect them even into adulthood. Because this way they can heal, and learn how not to perpetuate the same lies, the same hurts within their own families.

Parents, especially Christian parents who claim to want to "be a light" or a "witness" or to "transform the culture", should be humbled and overjoyed that their offspring seek recovery from false teaching, lies, and spiritual, emotional, psychological and physical abuse, even if they do not understand the dynamics. But instead, sadly, many continue to impede the work of God and quench the Spirit.

---

[43] Bennett, Vyckie *"I Was Too Wiped Out and Overwhelmed to Enjoy the Fruits of My Labor"* No Longer Quivering. www.nolongerquivering.com (22 February 2010)

[44] Clark, Owen *"Deadly Child Abuse Case Linked to Biblical Chastisement"* khsltv.com February 10, 2010 www.khsltv.com (22 February 2010)

Millstones

When seeking to understand the roots of your struggles, you will be faced with the naked, raw, brutal reality of abuse. And you will become angry. Christian girls taught that they should never be angry need to know truth: anger is not always bad. Anger is not always ungodly. Properly directed, it can be a healthy tool for recovery. Scripture tells us to "be angry and do not sin." Don't let anger become your source from which you draw life, or allow it to control you, but have the Lord purify, sculpt, and allow your wrath to be a window to truth—because anger towards your pain is the first stepping away from denial. Godly rage agrees that what happened to you was wrong. It places you on the side of Jesus—

> Whoever causes one of these little ones who believe in Me to sin, it would be better for him if a millstone were hung around his neck, and he were drowned in the depth of the sea. Woe to the world because of offenses! For offenses must come, but woe to that man by whom the offense comes! (Mt. 18:6-7) Assuredly, I say to you, inasmuch as you did it to one of the least of these My brethren, you did it to Me. (Mt. 25:40)

To those who are often treated as the least of these within neo-patriarchy, let me say: Jesus calls *you*. And He has nothing good to say to those who would place idols as stumbling blocks at your feet. For how you, daughter, are treated is how your parents, your husband, or pastor or teacher treats Jesus Christ.

Sorrow

One necessary part of healing isn't always expected. "It's overwhelming when you learn that what you've been taught isn't true," says Carla. "And that the people you love taught it to you."

Hannah writes, "I love my brothers and sisters so much. But in many ways I sacrificed, too—and I love to sacrifice for them. But I get sad sometimes that I couldn't feel free; I always had to be so responsible because of all the little eyes watching me. I felt like most of my life I walked around stiff and careful, holding my breath. And now everything's just so bottled up and if I don't let it out I think I'll burst..."

Sifting through hurts can summon a host of emotions—sometimes one at a time, and sometimes all in a rush, leaving you shaken, disoriented, and completely inundated. We've looked at anger. Sometimes you might feel envious of those who didn't have such strict control. Perhaps you will feel resentment at times—and in the midst of these, more guilt because you know envy and resentment are wrong. *Remember that resentment cannot be forgiven and healed if you do not admit it exists.*

And at some point you will feel overwhelming oceans of grief.

It's important both to anticipate and welcome it when it washes over you—because sorrow unlocks deeply rooted, carefully hidden and tender places. And yet, when there is grief, know also that there is hope.

For grief is the voice of Luna.

Sometimes Mommies

It's hard to pull apart internal, heavy, insulating drapes and bring soul-stains to light.

I know.

One of my favorite writers spilled healing ink into my heart when she wrote: [45]

> *We never cease to be with child.*
> *Those of us who have birthed, and those of us who never have.*
> *—Ann Voskamp*

She didn't know that I've always wanted a little boy. I'd name him Gabriel, and he would wear blue eyes and dark hair, like us, and maybe even dimples like one of his uncles.

I sit with Luna, sometimes, when I think of Gabriel. I've immersed myself into her world, to listen, to hear what she wants to say, to feel what she wants me to feel. When she first began to cry I had to listen—really listen—and teach her what was true. I had to nourish the fury that welled inside, for within that fierce protectiveness she began to see the light of Jesus.

If you had a little girl of your own, how would you respond to her?

If you had a little girl and she told you stories that mirror your own, the same stories you hide away inside, how would you answer? Would you tell her that those things didn't really happen? That it wasn't that bad; others had it worse? Would you insist she's exaggerating, craving

---

[45] Voskamp, Ann *"Mother's Day Hope: Wombs May Always Swell With Soul."* A Holy Experience. May 9, 2009 www.aholyexperience.com (10 May 2009) Used by permission.

attention? That her pain doesn't matter anymore, because it was so long ago?

That's not what Jesus would say.

> Then they brought little children to Him, that He might touch them; but the disciples rebuked those who brought them. But when Jesus saw it, He was greatly displeased and said to them, "Let the little children come to Me, and do not forbid them; for of such is the kingdom of God. Assuredly, I say to you, whoever does not receive the kingdom of God as a little child will by no means enter it." (Mk. 10:13-15)

When she began to stir this time, I could not say those things to her—to my own little Luna. Rather, I faced a choice. Truth—or denial? Listen—or turn away?

How would I mother her? How did I re-mother her?

I listened, and I said to her:

I am so sorry you had to hug him. You should never have to hug anyone you don't want to, ever. He told you he was a sex addict? And nobody listened? He told you that God said you'd move in with him when you turned 18—and you were terrified, and prayed that God wouldn't?

But then you remembered that your wants are "of the flesh" and we should die to our flesh. That it's best to get what we don't want so that we learn godly character—how to deny ourselves. So you secretly feared you really were *going to live with him, even though he was gross and fifty and you were eight and he drooled and his mouth was yucky and he smelled. And you had to help clean his house, because he lived by himself. He kept chasing you around with his arms out. And kept tickling you.*

But he was a "ministry."

Luna, what happened was wrong. God is sad—angry—that you felt abandoned inside, that you, your heart, and your feelings weren't important enough; that you didn't matter. That you wondered if anyone cared.

But it was an opportunity for you "to learn." A chance to "be Jesus." To do hard things and sacrifice.

Even though your family didn't celebrate Christmas because it was "pagan" and "materialistic," you still acknowledged the day for him, because it meant something to him. And when you tried to avoid him, others grew offended and accused you of rudeness, of embarrassing them, even though they knew the other stuff, the yucky stuff.

You wanted to scream, "But I am your daughter!"

You should scream it, because it's true. You should never have to wonder, even a little, if they care how you feel. Yet because you needed "to learn," your needs and feelings became material for sacrifice, and you were left uncherished.

You wanted to scream, "Take my side!"

They never took your side? No. They wanted to "broaden your horizons" and show you different perspectives because "it's not all about you, Luna!" They said you "needed to think." That they were "stretching your mind." They considered you selfish, shallow; they said you thought you were "too good" for them. Luna, that was wrong. You do not need to feel guilty for wanting to be validated, nurtured. Parents should find something to support in their daughters— especially when it comes to grown men who make you feel uncomfortable; even grown men you do not like. Not everything has to be a lesson at your expense. Dear Luna, even as a little girl, it was important that your mind and your side be heard and validated. You talk to God a lot; He shows you things, too! They could have learned from you if they listened without interrupting or making you feel stupid. But they didn't want to hear your thoughts, did they? Well, they did, only so they could tell you what was wrong with them, or how they could be better. They asked those "leading" questions all the time, the ones with an "agenda" so you felt trapped no matter what you said, and no matter what you said, thought, or felt, it was always wrong. And they kept you up at night for hours and hours, and you cried and cried, because there were lectures and training sessions that you "needed" because you were "becoming worldly" or "drifting away from the family" or "full of worldly values." Because you were bad. Because you weren't the kind of daughter they wanted. Because you were always wrong.

That makes me so sad, Luna. You aren't "just another kid" but a sister in Christ. But you were treated as a responsibility, a job. As a threat to godliness—a threat, almost, to God himself; a selfish sinner in need of correction and training and rebuke—constant rebuke. There wasn't much you did, besides work, which brought praise. Sometimes you cleaned your mama's room as a surprise for her, and it made her happy, which made you happy. You got the good kind of attention then; otherwise, you were just a bundle of foolishness that needed the admonition of the Lord. And there was never any letting up—because good parents are consistent, conscientious.

So there was no relief. This is why you crave relief now. This is why you love autumn, because it brings relief from the scorching summer that always made sweat drip down your legs while you stood in the burning kitchen washing dishes, flies buzzing around your skin which was streaked with mud because the sweat mixed with the dirt—because you conserved water and bathed only when it was really necessary, sometimes once every week or two—and created ugly rivulets down your legs which were already ugly to you, because you thought you were fat. They said you were. And the flies that didn't climb all over you and bite at the saltiness got stuck in fly papers which hung from the kitchen ceiling—grotesque mobiles loaded with knobby black corpses, pasted to the stickiness like bees to a honeycomb, with live flies crawling over the dead and resting, smug that they escaped a tacky fate, and laughing with disdain that you were embarrassed whenever people came over and had to duck to avoid hitting those vile swaying things.

And so you love relief, when the heart and mind and soul and body can rest and be and breathe. This is why you love softness and beautiful things that are "unnecessary and worldly" because they bring relief to roughness and ugliness, reminding you that not everything is soulless and brown and hard. This is why you love art and music, and wish you were ethereal so you could waft through life, loving and being loved, wanting and being wanted.

Like Jesus wants you.

Like He prays, "You have hidden these things from the wise and prudent and have revealed them to babes. Even so, Father, for so it seemed good in Your sight. All things have been delivered to Me by My Father, and no one knows the Son except the Father. Nor does anyone know the Father except the Son, and the one to whom the Son wills to reveal Him. Come to Me, all you who labor and are heavy laden, and I will give you rest." (Mt. 11:25-28)

Luna, you are His precious child. A babe, loved tenderly by Him. He calls you. He wants to give you rest, to bring you back to life.

Mothering

Remember how we discussed the importance of finding someone safe? The silenced child must find her cry. She-who-is-broken, whose spirit is fractured, whose heart lies in pieces *must* spill her secrets—if only to you. *You might be her "alongside".* Will you listen to the little girl you were? Let her speak. Be gentle. Believe what she whispers; believe her secrets and the hidden things which make her sad. *Let them be important to you.* Be to her the mother she needs. Will you honor her stories, her pain? Will you be patient as she weeps with grief so deep she makes no sound? Will you care for her, tenderly, as you would your own aching little girl? Will you carry her to Jesus?

When you meet her for the first time, give her a name. Acknowledge her personhood. Did she not feel unimportant throughout her life? Teach her truth: *Jesus cares more for her than He does rules or behavior.* It's okay if she makes mistakes. It's okay if she doesn't measure up to Mom and Dad's expectations. It's okay if she says the wrong thing; if she fails or falls. You know why? Because she is held by Emmanuel, and while she may stumble along the way, while she might trip in the lines of His palm, she will never fall out of His hand.[46] He is her sanctuary. He makes her whole.

I read Ann's words again to Luna, because they give her a whispering of life:

We may not be with child.
But we can be with the abandoned, the elderly, the needy.
We need not ever let our wombs languish empty.
We may always open and welcome another person
to find nourishment and comfort
within the empty places we have made just for them.
Regardless of age or fertility, we can make spaces within
for the growing of souls. For the unfurling of people's dreams,
their stories, their hurts, their lives.
Do we not line our lives with the stretch marks of love?
—Ann Voskamp

I cherish all the little girls I've met, the ones who lurk, the ones who spill their pain, then run away. The ones unfurling at every age, like newborn flowers straining for the sun. I think of the little girls who frantically grasp for nourishment and comfort; who cry and argue and defend and ache.

They grieve and delight me, like any child would.

I have empty places.

I close my eyes and whisper, *Gabriel.*

---

[46] Although some claim salvation can be lost, consider that Jesus teaches that no one can be snatched from the Father's hand. (Jn. 10:27-29) This means not even by you, yourself.

Reflection

We cannot allow the sin of others to control us any longer. Just as we are to work out our own salvation with fear and trembling, as we can approach the throne of grace directly through the work of Jesus needing no other mediator, we are also responsible for our hearts, our attitudes, and what we do with our pain. This includes the aching of the little girl you used to be. What stories do you hold close, lurking half-forgotten, yet swimming in grief? What would you say to the pearl-child of frozen moments and of memories?

Perhaps you might say—

Want to know how a daughter should be treated? A little girl should feel safe. She should feel that her mind, body, and heart are all tucked in at night, with the door cracked just a little so it is not quite so dark, with the low murmur of voices trickling in from the living room telling her that mommy and daddy are still there.

A little girl should feel wanted. She should make her parents smile, just because she walks upon the earth, and make their hearts glad—not because of what she does, but because of who she is. A little girl should have her needs met; she should thrive, and not be required to learn survival and fear as a constant way of life. A little girl should be encouraged, not broken. She should hunger for nothing...for bread, shoes, or love. A little girl should be given room to breathe, not smothered by the old way. Not bound upon the old way. Not stifled, strangled, cast out into the open field.

How did the little girl, the one that *you* were, live her life?

Let our tender loving Savior call to her:

> And when I passed by you and saw you struggling in your own blood, I said to you in your blood, "Live!" Yes, I said to you in your blood, "Live!" (Ez. 16:6)

We can pursue truth with determination and passion. We can seek wholeness; seek to understand why we struggle, why we ache, why we have wounds that need healing. We can throw ourselves at the feet of Jesus and writhe and weep and rage, for He will not turn us away, or tell us we are not perfect enough, or that we aren't good enough.

In fact, we need to stop trying to be good at all.

Stop.

Eighteen

I do not set aside the grace of God; for if righteousness comes through the law, then Christ died in vain. (Galatians 2:21)

Several years ago a sister sent me a letter. "I've been thinking about perfectionism," she wrote, "and how we are commanded to be perfect. Doesn't this mean it is possible? Why would God command us to be perfect, unless it means we can be?" As one whom the drive for perfection almost killed—literally—I told her I wanted to think about it before replying. It's long overdue, dear one, but here's my answer.

If it were not for the command, we'd never try to obey it.

If we never tried to obey it, we wouldn't learn it's impossible.

If we didn't learn it's impossible, we wouldn't see how we fall short and need Jesus. *"For the law made nothing perfect; on the other hand, there is the bringing in of a better hope, through which we draw near to God."* (Heb. 7:19) *"Therefore the law was our tutor to bring us to Christ, that we might be justified by faith."* (Gal. 3:24) "There is none righteous," says Scripture, "no, not one." And so the command of God is good, holy—for it brings us to the One who *is* our righteousness, who is our perfection.

And this is how we learn grace.

Come, Rest

Many of us have spent our entire lives trying. Trying to be joyful, trying to be holy, obedient and loving, trying to measure up to both God's standards and man's. To be a good girl, a good Christian, a good wife, a good mother. When we fail, we've learned to repent and try again, yet sometimes it feels like our walk of faith is one tired circuit instead of following Jesus onward and upward.

Scripture exhorts us to *"make straight paths for your feet, so that what is lame may not be dislocated, but rather be healed."* (Heb. 12:13) What does this mean for those who have grown weary and haggard on the same old paths, plodding in circles? Who fight the same old depression, shame, thought patterns, and the same thorns for years, with only temporary victory? Paul writes,

> Concerning this thing I pleaded with the Lord three times that it might depart from me. And He said to me, "My grace is sufficient for you, for My strength is made perfect in weakness." Therefore most gladly I will rather boast in my infirmities, that the power of Christ may rest upon me. Therefore I take pleasure in infirmities, in reproaches, in needs, in persecutions, in distresses, for Christ's sake. For when I am weak, then I am strong.
>
> (2 Cor. 12:8-10)

Here is a gentle challenge: what if you stopped trying to measure up? What if you no longer felt pressure to conform to all of the standards others—and yourself—hold for you? What if you ended this futile cycle of trying? What if you abandoned the old way?

It's a little scary, because doing this plants you firmly in the path you do not know. It's the way that requires seeing with eyes of faith. *For indeed the gospel was preached to us as well as to them; but the word which they heard did not profit them, not being mixed with faith in those who heard it...For he who has entered His rest has himself also ceased from his works as God did from His.* (Heb. 4:2, 10)

I understand that to stop striving seems like giving up; abandoning all of our efforts feels contrary to Paul's caution to not grow weary in doing good—but what if you already *are* weary?

"Rest!" Jesus pleads, *"Come—My yoke is easy and my burdens are light!"*

> Now to him who works, the wages are not counted as grace but as debt. But to him who does not work but believes on Him who justifies the ungodly, his faith is accounted for righteousness...but Israel, pursuing the law of righteousness, has not attained to the law of

righteousness. Why? Because they did not seek it by faith, but as it were, by the works of the law. For they stumbled at that stumbling stone. (Rom. 4:4-5, 9:31-32)

Will you have faith? Will you rest; will you "not work" and trust the One who justifies the ungodly? In the last chapter I said that the next step to healing is to *stop trying to be good.* Jesus reminds us that we cannot serve two masters, and as we continue *trying* to be good we serve the works of the law.[47]

You see, it's not about what we do. It's about who we are, and God wants us to know this. He wants our hearts.

The Fruit of the Vine
We've seen the Old Way, the beliefs, practices, abuses, and the white-washed idolatry that places stumbling blocks in our paths and pain in our hearts. We have scars on soul and skin; we have spirit wounds. Destructive fruits. Jesus tells us what happens to those who bear bad fruit:

> Do men gather grapes from thornbushes or figs from thistles? Even so, every good tree bears good fruit, but a bad tree bears bad fruit. A good tree cannot bear bad fruit, nor can a bad tree bear good fruit. Every tree that does not bear good fruit is cut down and thrown into the fire. Therefore by their fruits you will know them. Not everyone who says to Me, "Lord, Lord," shall enter the kingdom of heaven, but he who does the will of My Father in heaven. Many will say to Me in that day, "Lord, Lord, have we not prophesied in Your name, cast out demons in Your name, and done many wonders in Your name?" And then I will declare to them, "I never knew you; depart from Me, you who practice lawlessness!" (Mt. 7:16-23)

The protests are real—"But Lord! Look what we did for You! Look at how we lived. Look at how we raised our children, how separate we are from the world. Look at how biblical we are. We did all this for You!" *"Lawlessness,"* He says. Those religious deeds—fruit from a bad tree. In contrast, however, He shows us what we do need:

---

[47] Mt. 7:21-23, Rom. 2:28-29, 13:8-10

157

> Abide in Me, and I in you. As the branch cannot bear fruit of itself, unless it abides in the vine, neither can you, unless you abide in Me. I am the vine, you are the branches. He who abides in Me, and I in him, bears much fruit; for without Me you can do nothing.
>
> (Jn. 15:4-5)

These words of Jesus are like a key to the narrow gate that leads to life—a key to the Door. (Jn. 10:9) But what does this look like to us, as women who understand keenly our own shortcomings and failures? Our mistakes and lack of measuring up?

As branches dependent upon our Source of life, what is it to abide?

We have a wonderful example in a tale of two sisters whom Jesus visited. *"Now it happened as they went that He entered a certain village; and a certain woman named Martha welcomed Him into her house."* What an honor, to be hostess to the Son of God! *"And she had a sister called Mary, who also sat at Jesus' feet and heard His word."* We can imagine that she nestled close, eyes fixed upon Him eagerly while feasting on His words of life. *"But Martha was distracted with much serving, and she approached Him and said, 'Lord, do You not care that my sister has left me to serve alone? Therefore tell her to help me.'"* Martha—distracted, Scripture says. And not with the ways of the world, or sin, or anything inherently bad. Martha's distraction was something that all of us want, something we all make a priority in our lives—*she wanted to serve her Lord.*

Yet He gently reminded her of what is good, what is important and necessary. We can hear Him lovingly offer grace, see Him perhaps lay a tender hand on her arm—*"Martha, Martha, you are worried and troubled about many things. But one thing is needed, and Mary has chosen that good part, which will not be taken away from her."* (Lk. 10:38-42)

Mary rested. And in so doing, she enjoyed intimacy and nearness with Christ. And do you see what He did? *He defended her.* He protected her. He stood up for her against something that wasn't bad, it just wasn't the best for her at that time. But He didn't stop there—he continued to offer compassion and grace to her accuser, her sister.

Abide, all you who labor and are heavy laden! On this, your healing, new way journey, stop trying to be good. *Abide*—fruit just *is*. It grows naturally from healthy stems and branches that rest and draw nourishment from the vine. Rest. Heal. Grow. Become a healthy branch. And the fruit, the precious fruits of love, joy, peace, longsuffering, kindness, goodness, faithfulness, gentleness, and self-control—the fruits that are birthed when we draw our life from the Vine—will come.

Faith like Abraham

When we've traveled one way for a long time, a way we're used to and familiar with, one that looks safe and is accompanied by our friends and family, to change isn't easy. It's important to be prepared for this, to be aware of the pits that gape and lurk along the way. Whenever you actively turn from things that tear down and pursue things that build up—body, soul and spirit—it feels like you're going to another extreme. Consider, however, that you are on a line, with patriarchalism on one end and, as an example, secular feminism on the other. Because your starting point is an extreme, to move toward balance initially appears like rushing to another extreme.

On the new way, the straight and difficult way that leads to life (Mt. 3:3, 7:14), it's important to challenge the practices and beliefs we've held throughout our lives. This won't mean that all of them are wrong—but they need to be tested. They need to be held with open arms so that God can thresh them—and what is good, what is life-giving and sustaining, will remain (Jn. 15:16). Part of this is allowing the Holy Spirit to transform you through the renewing of your mind (Rom. 12:2). This means that you may need to stop often to consider an idea, thought, a belief, a way of doing something that you've always had, and question it. Flip it around, view it from a new angle. Is this really rebellion, as some might claim? Or is the truth that, for the first time, you are finally hearing the voice of God?

As you journey, it's imperative to know in whom you believe. Just like Abraham, who set out on the way he did not know, you must trust that He who calls you is faithful and will lead you unto life. Because when you become free and can no longer rely upon your upbringing, your parents, your daily prayers, fastings, and spiritual disciplines…at first it feels as though you're hurtling through space, surrounded by nothingness, with nothing to hold, nothing to grab, nothing to say you're doing the right thing.

You must be willing to make mistakes. To not measure up. To not know. To not be a "good Christian". To go against everything you've ever known out of faith that a better way has come, a narrow way that leads to life. You must be willing to give up everything, to strip yourself naked and lay yourself on the cornerstone, a living sacrifice. It is here, reborn and shivering in the arms of the Good Shepherd, we find grace.

And His grace is for sinners.

Reflection

I didn't know what to expect when I stopped trying. I felt rebellious, although if you asked what I rebelled against, at the time I didn't know. But when I began to feel "the shoulds" nipping at my heels—*you should read the Bible today; you shouldn't be depressed; you should go to church today; you should clean the house today; you should pray more*—I deliberately didn't do them. Gradually they began loosening their hold and one day I realized that my thought patterns had changed. The little voice inside said, *"You know, it would be easier if you went ahead and did the laundry today instead of putting it off until tomorrow."* Or, *"It might help to pray about that. Why don't you grab your coffee and sit outside and just talk to Jesus?"* As I continued to be set free through the grace of God, the day came when I grabbed my Bible because I *wanted* to. Oh! Can you imagine my joy? Or when I flung myself face down in a pile of soft sheets and poured out my heart to God, day after day, because I *wanted* to, not because that's what "good Christian women" do—can you fathom the love for God that poured out of my heart?

And it hasn't stopped since.

Unlike the pseudo-love we knew—old way love, which is legalistic, conditional, austere, withheld, obsessed with perfectionism and control—Jesus' love is messy love. His hands are bloody and He is not afraid of darkness. He dispels it with His glorious light. He does not heap oppression on our souls or give us more to do. He leaves the flock to seek us and rejoices when He finds us. He is our Healer. And His love is unconditional, surprising, jealous, feeling, and willing to get dirty.

New way love.

It is here, into your pain, that our Savior invites you. Here, into the darkness, where His light can shine. Here, into the brokenness, where His hands can heal. Here, into the unknown, so that He can become known.

Known by you.

I told you this is a love story.

Nineteen |

Mercy

I am still an earthling, stumbling
Drinking deeply of grace
And running through sweet droplets of mercy.—Luna

For I desire mercy and not sacrifice, and the knowledge of God more
than burnt offerings. (Hosea 6:6)

As little girls who often felt like the "least of these", we often find it hard to accept grace. It's hard to wrap our minds around this new way love. Luna asks her Heavenly Father, "Why me? Why did you come after me?" But we serve a God who's jealous. Who created us to be in unity with Him—will not the God who created heaven and earth move them to bring us home? He says,

> I will bring the blind by a way they did not know; I will
> lead them in paths they have not known. I will make
> darkness light before them, and crooked places straight.
> These things I will do for them, and not forsake them.
>
> (Is. 42:16)

In fact, our journey and the love of God are beautifully illustrated in Hosea. The Father who already knew our names when He separated light from darkness said to the prophet,

> Say to your brethren, 'My people,'
> And to your sisters, 'Mercy is shown.' (Hos. 2:1)

Mercy. It is foreign to many of us who know little but law and judgment, withering beneath relentless criticism, fear, authoritarianism, shame, and exhaustive control. For mercy is relief—overflowing, comforting relief for the heart. Mercy enables us to run and not grow weary, to walk and not faint. Mercy allows the soul to breathe. As we walk the old paths, *"Mercy!"* is our spirit's cry.

What does the Lord require of us? Micah reminds us that we are to do justly, to love mercy, and to walk humbly with our God. We learn to love it through the brutal torment of life without it. And the only way we can know mercy is to *do* or *be* something, or someone, in need of it.

> So speak and so do as those who will be judged by the law of liberty. For judgment is without mercy to the one who has shown no mercy. Mercy triumphs over judgment. (Jas. 2:12-14)

Do you want to see mercy in action? Even before we've broken away from idols erected for us, before we come against the lies we've heard and believed, before we seek truth and healing, while we still are like those who have long been dead (Ps. 143:3)—we are named, known, and loved by the true God. And as the little girl comes forth to the gentle voice of Jesus—"Arise"—we are brought to life. Let's arise and meet the true God.

The heart of God

> Bring charges against your mother, bring charges; for she is not My wife, nor am I her Husband! Let her put away her harlotries from her sight, and her adulteries from between her breasts; lest I strip her naked and expose her, as in the day she was born, and make her like a wilderness, and set her like a dry land, and slay her with thirst. I will not have mercy on her children, for they are the children of harlotry. For their mother has played the harlot; she who conceived them has behaved shamefully. For she said, "I will go after my lovers, who give me my bread and my water, my wool and my linen, my oil and my drink." (Hos. 2:2-5)

Remember the Source—who gives us our good things, the things we need for life, for sustenance? Through the Lord's outcry to the prophet we see His agony, His broken heart when we look elsewhere to have our needs met. He wants to be your Source. And you must actively choose Him over the Old Way—over what you were handed and taught. Over those who have stood in His way, even over the good people, good intentions, over righteous and necessary things.

Because of His great, jealous love, He will "slay us with thirst"— how many of us have craved living water? Craved relief? Wandered in a wilderness? How often does it seem we are aimless, without purpose, that our lives are futile? What old, tiresome paths! Yet when we tire, when we are weary and worn, what do we need? Rest. Not more to do. And Jesus meets *all* our needs. "There remains therefore a rest for the people of God. For he who has entered His rest has himself also ceased from his works as God did from His." (Heb. 4:9)

So what does this God do—the God who called us by name even when we didn't know Him?

> Therefore, behold, I will hedge up your way with thorns, and wall her in, so that she cannot find her paths. She will chase her lovers, but not overtake them; yes, she will seek them, but not find them. Then she will say, "I will go and return to my first husband, for then it was better for me than now." For she did not know that I gave her grain, new wine, and oil, and multiplied her silver and gold—which they prepared for Baal. Therefore I will return and take away My grain in its time and My new wine in its season, and will take back My wool and My linen, given to cover her nakedness. Now I will uncover her lewdness in the sight of her lovers, and no one shall deliver her from My hand. I will also cause all her mirth to cease, her feast days, her New Moons, her Sabbaths—all her appointed feasts. And I will destroy her vines and her fig trees, of which she has said, "These are my wages that my lovers have given me." So I will make them a forest, and the beasts of the field shall eat them. I will punish her for the days of the Baals to which she burned incense. She decked herself with her earrings and jewelry, and went after her lovers; but Me she forgot, says the LORD. (Hos. 2:6-13)

Remember the suffering with purpose? Whom the Lord loves He chastens—and yet His chastening is taking away the false good so He can replace it with true, living, lasting goodness. "I am the LORD, that is My name; and My glory I will not give to another, nor My praise to carved images." (Is. 42:8) *Look at Me!* He implores. *You are mine. I am your source, your provider—the others are false loves. They do not satisfy.* Our God—He wears His heart on His sleeve; He loves with abandon. He rages, weeps, gives and takes away, driven with love and jealousy.

Are we not spent by false loves? The ones we've served? Even endless chasing is not good enough. We will never measure up to them or their standards. We pour out our hearts and exhaust ourselves, seeking approval, attention, love—and are left wanting.

Our true Love says, *"Rest."*

Our true Love says, *"Seek and you shall find."*

Our true Love says, *"Mercy."*

> Therefore, behold, I will allure her, will bring her into the wilderness, and speak comfort to her. I will give her her vineyards from there, and the Valley of Achor as a door of hope; she shall sing there, as in the days of her youth, as in the day when she came up from the land of Egypt. And it shall be, in that day, says the LORD, that you will call Me 'My Husband,' and no longer call Me 'My Master,' for I will take from her mouth the names of the Baals, and they shall be remembered by their name no more. (Hos. 2:14-17)

Scripture is full of the Lord's plea to remember Him, mourning when those whom He creates and loves will not remember. "Do not forget Me," He says. "But forget your false loves—the ones who had no mercy. The worthless masters who did not love you, who oppressed you." To our Heavenly Father, remembrance is synonymous with love.

> Can a woman forget her nursing child, and not have compassion on the son of her womb? Surely they may forget, yet I will not forget you. See, I have inscribed you on the palms of My hands; your walls are continually before Me. (Is. 49:15-16)

Sometimes our wildernesses are good. When the Lord is there, when He allures us away into dry, barren places, when we are empty and lacking—this is when we are most ready to receive His comfort, His living water. And who but the Lord can bring forth a vineyard from wasteland?

If you have been burdened, broken, lost, barren, swallowed up by darkness and the shadow of death…it is to you He gives the Valley of Achor—the door of hope. What are doors for but to pass through? In Hebrew, "Achor" means "trouble."[48] Do you see? How many times have we tried to be good, tried to overcome, tried to rise above? He says, *"I will give you the treasures of darkness and hidden riches of secret places, that you may know that I, the LORD, Who call you by your name, am the God of Israel."* (Is. 45:3)

For you to be made whole, you must rest. Trust in the One who justifies the ungodly. Embrace the midnight of life—for our God is there. Take heart. As you pass through sorrow let Him comfort you. It is here He is victorious.

This is His dream for you.

> I will betroth you to Me forever; yes, I will betroth you to Me in righteousness and justice, in lovingkindness and mercy; I will betroth you to Me in faithfulness, and you shall know the LORD. It shall come to pass in that day that I will answer, says the LORD; I will answer the heavens, and they shall answer the earth. The earth shall answer with grain, with new wine, and with oil; they shall answer Jezreel.[49] Then I will sow her for Myself in the earth, and I will have mercy on her who had not obtained mercy; Then I will say to those who were not My people, 'You are My people!' And they shall say, 'You are my God!' (Hos. 2:19-23)

He wants to be known by His beloved. That is the heart of the true God. He wants to be seen; He longs for—waits eagerly for—the gasping breath of newness as we are reborn. He waits for the dawning of knowledge and awe and life, for us to turn to Him and say, "You! You are my God. You are the one who answers my wanting, who meets my needs, my desires. You are my God." Unlike the gods we served which left us drained, blinded, stumbling, exhausted and dead on the Old Way, the true God gives life—and that, more abundantly.

---

[48] Strong's H5911: *Trouble, disturbance.* Other words for trouble include suffering, torment, struggle, sorrow, heartache, mess, anxiety, danger, discontent, pain, affliction, failure, stress, grief

[49] Jezreel: "God sows."

> He shall be like a tree planted by the rivers of water, that brings forth its fruit in its season, whose leaf also shall not wither; and whatever he does shall prosper. (Ps. 1:3)

Can you rest? Can you stop and just be? His promises are good, and our God is faithful. As we are healed, as we are renewed and established, He manifests Himself in our lives. We don't have to focus on what we do, how we behave, or how well we perform.

He asks,

> Is this not the fast I have chosen, to loose the bonds of wickedness, to undo the heavy burdens, to let the oppressed go free, and that you break every yoke? Is it not to share your bread with the hungry, and that you bring to your house the poor who are cast out; when you see the naked, that you cover him, and not hide yourself from your own flesh? Then your light shall break forth like the morning, your healing shall spring forth speedily, and your righteousness shall go before you; the glory of the LORD shall be your rear guard. Then you shall call, and the LORD will answer; you shall cry, and He will say, "Here I am." If you take away the yoke from your midst, the pointing of the finger, and speaking wickedness, if you extend your soul to the hungry and satisfy the afflicted soul, then your light shall dawn in the darkness, and your darkness shall be as the noonday. The LORD will guide you continually, and satisfy your soul in drought, and strengthen your bones; you shall be like a watered garden, and like a spring of water, whose waters do not fail. Those from among you shall build the old waste places; you shall raise up the foundations of many generations; and you shall be called the Repairer of the Breach, The Restorer of Streets to Dwell In. (Is. 58:6-12)

The Lord God alone is our Healer, our Protector. He gives us wisdom, meets our needs, and plants vineyards in our wastelands. He satisfies our souls. He brings us home—He *is* our Home. Abide in Him, and as we enter His betrothal, the new covenant of a faithful husband, He drenches us in mercy. He sows us in the earth; He plants us. And we bear fruit, and live.

Reflection

> Therefore, since we have this ministry, as we have received mercy, we do not lose heart. But we have renounced the hidden things of shame, not walking in craftiness nor handling the word of God deceitfully, but by manifestation of the truth commending ourselves to every man's conscience in the sight of God. But even if our gospel is veiled, it is veiled to those who are perishing, whose minds the god of this age has blinded, who do not believe, lest the light of the gospel of the glory of Christ, who is the image of God, should shine on them. For we do not preach ourselves, but Christ Jesus the Lord, and ourselves your bondservants for Jesus' sake. For it is the God who commanded light to shine out of darkness, who has shone in our hearts to give the light of the knowledge of the glory of God in the face of Jesus Christ. (2 Cor. 4:1-6)
>
> Therefore, from now on, we regard no one according to the flesh. Even though we have known Christ according to the flesh, yet now we know Him thus no longer. Therefore, if anyone is in Christ, he is a new creation; old things have passed away; behold, all things have become new. Now all things are of God, who has reconciled us to Himself through Jesus Christ, and has given us the ministry of reconciliation. (2 Cor. 5:16-18)

Dear ones, this is the language of renewal. It is present tense. As you go forth on the way that leads to life, carry with you and remember that through the Lord's mercies we are not consumed; His compassions fail not and are new every morning. "Therefore I have hope," says Jeremiah.

You have need of one thing more.

> Therefore, brethren, having boldness to enter the Holiest by the blood of Jesus, *by a new and living way* which He consecrated for us, through the veil, that is, His flesh, and having a High Priest over the house of God, let us draw near with a true heart in full assurance of faith,

having our hearts sprinkled from an evil conscience and our bodies washed with pure water. Let us hold fast the confession of our hope without wavering, for He who promised is faithful. Therefore do not cast away your confidence, which has great reward. For you have need of endurance, so that after you have done the will of God, you may receive the promise. (Heb. 10:19-39, emphasis added)

Endurance. When the new way is dark, and dry, and cold, and secret—beloved, *endure*. It won't be long. "But to you who fear My name, the Sun of Righteousness shall arise with healing in His wings." (Mal. 4:2)

For you were once darkness, but now you are light in the Lord. Walk as children of light (for the fruit of the Spirit is in all goodness, righteousness, and truth), finding out what is acceptable to the Lord. And have no fellowship with the unfruitful works of darkness, but rather expose them. For it is shameful even to speak of those things which are done by them in secret. But all things that are exposed are made manifest by the light, for whatever makes manifest is light. (Eph. 5:8-14)

Our God will come and bring salvation. He will take the little girl by the hand, look at her with love, and say,
"Awake, you who sleep,
Arise from the dead,
And Christ will give you light."

Epilogue |

Luna of the Sorrows

I will go before you
And make the crooked places straight;
I will break in pieces the gates of bronze
And cut the bars of iron.
I will give you the treasures of darkness
And hidden riches of secret places,
That you may know that I, the LORD,
Who call you by your name,
Am the God of Israel.
For Jacob My servant's sake,
And Israel My elect,
I have even called you by your name;
I have named you, though you have not known Me.
I am the LORD, and there is no other;
There is no God besides Me.
I will gird you, though you have not known Me.
(Isaiah 45:2-5)

Sparrows flutter, falling
And the King of Heaven sees.—Luna

The little girl trembled. Her teeth chattered as she lay curled in midnight, curled in mud. Tiny stars eddied through squeezed, tear-stained lashes. "What are you asking of me? I can't do this, you know I can't!" She opened her eyes to meet the gaze of smothering darkness, and choked on its bitterness. "I tried to be good," she whimpered, clutching at her flesh as though tearing away ugliness. "You said if I did what you asked, you would love me!" But once again, she'd failed. And once again, she crumpled—alone, unwanted, ashamed, abandoned.

"Abba," she whispered. Hot tears carved paths down her cheeks. *"Abba—"* Her clammy fingers wrapped around her arms in a feeble attempt to ward off sinister, sticky cold. "Where are you?" Sobs escaped her lips as her hands groped in darkness, finding nothing. Yet she knew, somehow, that she must keep going for it was a matter of life or death.

She pushed herself up, up, shuddering, out of the dank soil, and inched her foot ahead. Her way unfolded with step by agonizing step, breath by labored breath. Weariness filled her flesh. "I want my mother," she mourned, yearning for the comfort and warmth which lay distantly in memory. "I can't do this anymore! I must to stop now!"

But no end, it seemed. Relentless, merciless brutality compelled her forth. Heavy air's gloom oppressed heaving lungs. The little girl grew tired, so tired—weary of flesh, of the blindness and nothingness in her eyes. Laden shoulders burned with sorrow. *Why didn't you want me!* She ached all over with bruises which never faded. Her spirit grieved. *I don't know where I am!* Rocks slid beneath her feet and she faltered. The little girl's feet slipped. And without warning, she tumbled, plunging through oblivion, fragile body slamming against rocky interfaces. Her eyes closed against calamity, for surely, death became destiny. *Hurry,* she willed her soul, welcoming her fate. *I cannot go on.*

She crashed against the earth with violence. Broken whimpers crossed her lips. "At last," she whispered, and sighed with relief. And peaceful blackness settled in.

The ground felt cool and wet. The little girl couldn't see and pushed herself up, head throbbing with the ache of tears. She sensed warmth trickle down her leg; felt bitter sting as raw torn skin met frigid night air. *"Noooo!"* she screamed, distraught to find she lived, still. "Help me! You have to help me! Help me, now!"

In taunting chorale, echoes reverberated through eternity—mirrored anguish reflecting off of unknown places. "Am I too bad, even for death? Not worthy to die, and escape this shame?" Silence followed the echoing. "You can't do this to me! You can't!"

She shrieked and sobbed with horror and despair over the denial of immortal rest. And then she felt rage—rage that she'd been thwarted and forced to exist, still. Fueled by this, she struggled to her feet and stumbled forward, wounded limb leaving bloody trail. Extending her arms, she reached hysterically, longingly—but for what? She did not know.

Then with surprise, she noticed that she could see the rough silhouette of her hands. Shadows! She caught her breath and lifted tear-streaked face. The shadows moved gently all about, lilting and rippling with varying degrees of darkness. Eyes searched, lungs heaved with emotion as revelation pierced soul-surrounding fog. *Where there is shadow, there is light!*

In the distance a glimmer haunted, delicate and ethereal, obscured by timbers. "Wait!" she called, but her throat was hoarse and dry. *"Wait..."*

With all of her strength, the little girl dragged crippled leg behind and staggered towards the light. As she neared the wondrous luminary which lured her soul, shadows subsided enough to see the depth of the valley where she had plummeted. She convulsed and recoiled with shock. Grievous pits gaped at every turn; boulders lurched overhead, waiting to fall at will. A maze of despair, her path—twisting, circling a thousand times and more. Quicksand pulled on every side while ominous creatures slithered along the way. "Abba," she gasped with fear. "Keep going...don't look at it," she said to herself, eyes grasping for any errant ray.

The air lightened and she reached the edge of the forest. And yet more forest, more valley, more paths sprang to life before her eyes. The little girl stopped, exhausted. "Where am I? I don't know!" she cried. "I don't know where I am going. I don't know where I am, or what I am supposed to do." Leg and heart throbbed in rhythmic pulse of overwhelming pain, and she collapsed to the forest floor. Motionless, broken, once again her eyes closed and spirit weakened. Perhaps now she would find rest.

A soft breeze began to brush her cheeks, as though hidden kisses blew warmth to skin. Her eyes drifted awake, and blinked in languid wonder. Trees above began to sway, undulate—graceful branches moving gently and revealing hints of violet sky. Peace, drifting soft like cashmere, settled around her body.

And there he was.

He stood before her humbly, this creature of mystery and light. His eyes glowed with tenderness. A hand extended, dream-like, and rested tenderly on broken places. As he leaned in to heal and nourish, she caught a glimpse of herself, mirrored in his eyes.

"But I was a little girl!" she gasped, her eyes searching his as reflections of womanhood mirrored forth.

"Luna." He spoke her name as warmth and brilliance—the sun? She couldn't tell—spilled across the sky. She couldn't move or speak. She couldn't articulate all that encompassed this moment.

"Who are you?" she whispered, uncertain and shy.

He took her by the hand, drew her to her feet. They stood in the midst of the forest while mysterious glimmers of life swirled about on starlit wings. Luna could see the darkness which gaped through the trees—but strangely, she didn't feel afraid.

"I have brought you through the valley," the humble being said to her. "I know it was hard, little one. I watched you grieve, and my heart wept." His voice, like healing balm, caressed her restless soul, spilling into wounds. Something pressed into her hand. "This is a gift for you," he continued, "more precious to me than all of the rubies or diamonds or emeralds in the world. Take it with you, so you remember."

Luna uncurled her fingers to find a luminous crystal which danced on the rays of sun. Movement swirled inside chiseled facets. It seemed to be alive, this prism, suspended in her palm. "What is it?" she asked, voice soft with unworthiness. *Why me?* She wondered. *I am such a wicked little girl—how can this be for me?*

The gentle creature of mystery took both of her hands in his and clasped the jewel within. "Dear, sweet Luna," he said, eyes searching her face with a beloved's hope and passion. "This vial contains every tear you have ever shed. They were so precious to me; I couldn't let them go. I caught every one, before they hit the ground." He grew intense. "I was there, and I cried with you."

She began to tremble—not with fright, but with the dawning of hope. He went on. "My arms longed to snatch you out of the valley, but you had to make your way through, in order to see. I want you to see! If it were not for the valley, you would not know."

Her eyes swam with tears. "Know what?" Her mind strained to comprehend. "It was so dark there, and heavy; I couldn't breathe, and I wanted to go away and be no more."

He embraced her with a paradox of fierceness and tenderness which connected all of the dark, empty, aching places and replaced them with light and goodness and truth. "If it were not for the Valley of the Shadows you would not have known how much I love you." His arms tightened protectively. "How we wanted you—oh, how you were wanted! We looked forward to the day of your birth, and celebrated in the heavens when you were brought into the world. You have such a beautiful life, a beautiful destiny. And you are good, worthy of love and wisdom and all things lovely, *for I have made you so.*"

174

Luna closed her eyes as the words washed over her soul. *This is too good to be true,* she wanted to say, yet hesitated because she knew somehow that it *was* true. After long silence and reflection she whispered, "Why me?"

"We knew that you would be faithful to the gifts we placed within you," he enumerated with quiet joy. "You have been set apart, and filled with wisdom and strength. Your mind perceives beauty in the desolate and forsaken; you feel compassion for the lost and weary." He leaned forward and kissed her eyes softly. "Partake of the path of life. I have made all things new."

Her eyes still closed, Luna felt the world spin. Comfort and nourishment coursed through her frame; unexplainable joy lighted her spirit. Eyelids warm from kiss, she opened them slowly. And instantly her Way burst forth! Living light radiated from every creature; dewdrops glistened with lucent fire upon every tree and grass and baby violet which peeked shyly from the earth. Breath came sweetly as the fragrance of life, the fragrance of this radiant creature, entered her being.

She could still see the distant pits which lurked and the ominous slithering creatures, but they didn't frighten her, for the darkness was gone. The beautiful, humble being beside her laughed softly as she inhaled with relief. "This is for you," he said, extending his hand towards a narrow trail that glowed through the wildwood. "Walk along this path; there are many things for you here, and this is the way you must go."

Luna felt breathless. Inklings of life stirred within—unfamiliar sensations, but heady, intoxicating. "Where does it go? What do I follow?"

The being of mystery and light stepped aside and smiled with reassurance. "I will go before you," he said. "You will never be alone, even if you stumble on the journey. You will hear my voice saying to you: this is the way, walk in it." He squeezed her hand and sighed deeply with jubilance. As she watched, he turned to the path and walked strong and steady until he disappeared from sight.

She stood alone, yet warmth remained, and she did not feel abandoned as before—for it was as though he'd never left. The way drew clearer and she exhaled, pressing foot into a hesitant step. As she moved towards it, Luna started in amazement. Her limp was gone! She stopped and traced her fingers down her leg; all that lingered were the edges of a scar which bore testimony to the darkness of the valley.

"Abba!" she whispered, overcome. She lifted her face in reverence and wonder. The wind undulated, a symphony of light resonating along her way. Truth infused her soul. "You are here, in this very place!"

Wind moved softly, delicate and balmy against her flesh. Words spilled into her heart. "I have always been with you, since before you were born. I have created you, I have called you by name, and you are mine."

Her spirit exulted, and she leapt on the path with joy.

I heard a loud voice from heaven saying, "Behold, the tabernacle of God is with men, and He will dwell with them, and they shall be His people. God Himself will be with them and be their God. And God will wipe away every tear from their eyes; there shall be no more death, nor sorrow, nor crying. There shall be no more pain, for the former things have passed away." Then He who sat on the throne said, "Behold, I make all things new." And He said to me, "Write, for these words are true and faithful."

(Rev. 21:3-5)

Afterword

The Body's Silent Weeping

By Cynthia M. Kunsman, RN, BSN, MMin, ND

The connection between stress and certain physical health problems is well acknowledged by medicine. Recent advancements in science now indicate that a host of health problems relate directly to the affect that stress hormones have on nearly every system of the body. Cortisol, for example, alters the metabolism of cholesterol and fats, hormone production, cellular repair, connective tissue integrity, inflammation, and immunity, creating both long and short-term health problems. When a person experiences intense stress on a regular basis, they can develop symptoms related to high, chronic level of cortisol. Many of these problems related to chronic stress also contribute to the major health concerns in our nation today.

Doctors have noted that people who experience a high degree of stress, emotional difficulty or conditions such as Post Traumatic Stress Disorder often share medical conditions, such as adult onset asthma, gastrointestinal conditions, headache, chronic fatigue, fibromyalgia and other pain syndromes. What the traumatized person does not express directly as emotional or psychological pain manifests indirectly as disease.

In Greek, the word for "body" is "soma," so this phenomenon of transforming stress into health complaints has been named "somatization."

Health problems related to chronic stress in children

While neurohormonal imbalance in the brain causes certain aspects of depression to increase the experience of pain and fatigue, depression also causes a cluster of other physically debilitating conditions. There is a strong correlation between depression and overlapping health problems in children who live in highly stressful conditions. For example, parents with personality disorders that cause erratic parenting styles have children with a high incidence of allergies, asthma, gastrointestinal disorders, and headaches. These types of findings were general and based upon anecdotal information that was not specifically subject to statistical analysis. New research indicates also specifically that children who experienced neglect, mistreatment and abuse also manifest a higher incidence of both migraine and osteoarthritis. [50] [51]

Other studies that require more intensive and specific investigation report strong preliminary correlations of childhood mistreatment with cancer, high blood pressure, high cholesterol, and inflammation associated with elevated C-reactive protein which mediates all sorts of cardiovascular disease such as heart attack and stroke.[52]

Based on what we now understand about the effect that our emotions have on our body medicine now recognizes that our minds and our emotions are intimately connected to our physical health. As one specialist in trauma notes, "the body keeps score,"[53] and our physical bodies will grieve and mourn if we do not deal effectively with our psychological and emotional baggage. Our bodies will cry through illness and pain if we do not learn to do so ourselves.

Unfortunately, it seems that once our minds learn to translate our emotional pain into physical illness, the damage can never completely be undone. The body then learns to cope by way of disease and this

---

[50] Fuller-Thomson E, Stefanyk M, Brennenstuhl S. A robust association between childhood physical abuse and osteoarthritis in adulthood: findings from a representative community sample. Arthritis Rheum. 2009 Nov 15;61(11):1554-62.

[51] Tietjen GE, Brandes JL, Peterlin BL, Eloff A, Dafer RM, Stein MR, Drexler E, Martin VT, Hutchinson S, Aurora SK, Recober A, Herial NA, Utley C, White L, Khuder SA. Childhood Maltreatment and Migraine (Part I). Prevalence and Adult Revictimization: A Multicenter Clinic Headache Study. Headache 2010;50:20-31.

[52] Danese A, Moffitt TE, Harrington H, Milne BJ, Polanczyk G, Pariante CM, Poulton R, Caspi A. Adverse childhood experience and adult risk factors for age-relted disease: depression, inflammation and clustering of metabolic risk markers. Arch PediatrAdolesc Med. 2009 Dec; 163(12):1135-43.

[53] Van der Kolk B. The body keeps score: memory and the evolving psychobiology of post-traumatic stress. Harv Rev Psychiatry. 1994 Jan-Feb;1(5):253-65.

survival and coping mechanism opens up a Pandora's Box of health issues with lasting consequences. One cannot "unlearn" this tendency, though a person can learn strategies to deal with a painful past and the physical results. Unfortunately, many parents have caused physical diseases into their children despite the best intentions of spiritual benefit.

Hope for Healing
The following list includes many problems experienced by quivering daughters who have been brave and honest in sharing information about the difficulties they face as adults. Do any sound familiar to you? If you are a Quiverfull or patriocentric daughter, or a woman with a dysfunctional childhood or abusive past, and you experience a great deal of frustration from habits or health problems that you struggle to overcome, you may find that other Quiverfull sisters also face the same kinds of ongoing and recurrent problems listed here:

- Depression, anxiety, fear, or irritability
- Loss of interest in things, difficulties making important decisions due to fear
- Problems with motivation, self-care, or a sense of futility
- Repetitive or compulsive behaviors associated with anxiety
- Any behaviors that cause harm to the body, thinking about wanting to die, or suicide attempts
- Allergies and asthma
- Immune system problems (fevers, frequent infections, lymph node enlargement, chronic sore throat)
- Tightness, heaviness, or pain in the throat or chest
- Heart rate irregularities
- Chemical or food sensitivities
- Skin inflammation (both intermittent and chronic)
- Hormonal problems including thyroid disorders and adrenal fatigue
- Reproductive problems including Polycystic Ovarian Syndrome
- Issues with weight or appetite (high or low)
- Digestion problems, ulcers, stomach pain, or nausea
- Lower bowel pain, diarrhea, or irritable bowel
- Headaches, migraines or sensitivity to light and sound
- Dizziness, lightheadedness, or problems with balance

- Fatigue, lack of muscle strength, or muscle pain
- Neck or back stiffness or pain
- Joint stiffness or pain
- Sleep disturbances

If our bodies have wept for us because of the neglect that helped us survive, there is hope. In our own experiences with pain, we have learned that very specific pains generally mean we are ignoring anger, an emotion we were not permitted to express openly while growing up. ("Good Christian girls shouldn't get angry.") Anger in and of itself is not evil but is most often protective, so long as we don't sin in anger. We've learned to be grateful and to honor our pain because it "keeps us honest" by reappearing when we fail to deal with emotions properly. We had to learn how to honor all of our emotions, too, even the ones that bring us discomfort. We have learned to be grateful for these gifts that God placed in us for His ultimate glory, learning to embrace them as opportunities for the Lord to show Himself strong when we are weak.

We should take care of all aspects of ourselves, spirit, soul, and body, because Jesus calls us to be good stewards of all that He has given us. He has entrusted our bodies to us, and those bodies have needs. In respect to overall health, we should attend to our physical care and our needs for nourishment and rest. Many health problems overlap with depression and emotional pain, but that does not mean that we should forego medical care. If you have a physical condition, get a proper medical diagnosis from your physician and follow their instructions for good health and healing. Caring for our bodies also includes proper exercise and good nutrition, as well as any medications that our physician prescribes. Healing the body helps to heal the mind, and exercise does have a very beneficial effect on emotions.[54]

Recovery from trauma comes in stages, and in order to heal, you must first find a safe place that encourages the healing process. It is very difficult to heal from battle wounds if you are still in the midst of an ongoing scrimmage. As much as possible, put distance between yourself and your point of struggle. Find an oasis with safe people in a safe place. Working though the good and bad elements of your life and your beliefs can be difficult, and doing that with safe and supportive

---

[54] Amen DG. Making a Good Brain Great: The Amen Clinic Program for Achieving and Sustaining Optimal Mental Performance. New York: Three Rivers Press, an imprint of Random House (2005), pp. 167-76.

people will help you. Trauma and discouragement break us into pieces, splintering our identities, so it is essential that we sift through the rubble to choose that which we want to keep. We also have to decide what elements we want to discard, making peace with ourselves and forgiving others after we've purged ourselves of the pain, anger, and confusion we endured. We need to honor these painful experiences by acknowledging them for what they brought into our lives so that we can move through them. Through this process of putting things together in a way that helps us make sense of our experience, we will reintegrate who we are and what we believe into wholeness. When we find this wholeness, we can more easily connect with others in healthy ways, finding our new way in the world.[55]

If we have been brought up in a home where we failed to learn good communication skills and were taught unhealthy ways of dealing with our emotions and thoughts, we will have to spend time learning new ways of health so that we can be good stewards of our souls. Accepting Jesus as our Savior does not divinely transfer these skills into our heads, as if Jesus were the magic pill for all of our ills. (It reminds me of the old joke about the man who asks if he can play piano after his broken arm heals, knowing full well that he could not play before the injury!)

We must devote time to "unlearning" the bad patterns that were given to us as God's highest and best ways by examining them, and we must replace them with the "new planting" that God wants to do in our hearts and minds. Friends and professional counselors will provide a sounding board for you, serving as a "mirror" for you to see yourself more clearly. Find good counsel with someone who can comfort you with the comfort they have received in this area. Ask others for referrals for help from counselors and good sources of information that were helpful to them. There are many of us who can help you as we help one another in places like private email lists and online forums. Learn to walk on a new path in a new way, and let other people love and help you. As you learn from others, you will find that they are also learning from you.

If you read books about emotional recovery, they generally recommend "cognitive behavioral therapy" which may sound strange, exotic, and intimidating. Let me explain it in more Biblical terms. For the Christian, this therapy can be explained as bringing our thoughts

---

[55] Herman JL. Trauma and Recovery: The Aftermath of Violence – From Domestic Abuse to Political Terror. New York: Basic Books, (1997).

captive and looking at how our thoughts and emotions interrelate and thus influence our behavior. Keeping a daily journal is an excellent way of doing much of this work on your own. I love Chris Thurman's book, "The Lies We Believe" which explains how we can journal every day about troubling emotions, linking them to irrational thoughts or "lies" that lead us astray through bad patterns of thinking. Once we develop the habit of emotional awareness and how our thoughts and emotions influence one another, they can become tools to help guide us through better ways of thinking by holding them up to the standard of the Bible. In this way we bring our thoughts captive to the Word and heal the wounds in our hearts and our minds. Two other good books on this subject that were written by Christians (Dr. Daniel Amen's "Change Your Brain, Change Your Life" and Dr. Earl Henslin's "This is Your Brain on Joy") discuss this same type of cognitive therapy through countering what they call ANTs (Automatic Negative Thoughts) with optimistic and realistic thoughts. You must learn to kill the ANTs!

There are many other options available for exploration of healing of anxiety, behavior and lasting emotional pain. New therapies such as Eye Movement Desensitization and Reprocessing tap into the healing that eye movement can bring to the brain, specifically its overactive emotional and anxiety centers.[56] Rhythmic movement of both sides of the body such as mindfulness during walking or liturgical dance which involves attending to how the body feels as it moves brings healing to these same areas of the brain. Physical movement does help healing of the emotional center in the brain, in addition to the general health benefits that it brings. [57] How poetic is it to consider that when the body has learned to manifest stress that movement of the body can also be used to harness its own physical and emotional healing? Explore safe and healthy options of mindful physical activity that will heal both body and mind, some of which heal the mind more effectively than anti-depressants and other medications.

There are many options available to bring healing after loss. I would like to encourage you to remind yourself that emotional healing

---

[56] Van der Kolk B, Spinnazola J, Blaustein ME, Hopper JW, Hopper EK, Korn DL, Simpson WB. A Randomized Clinical Trial of Eye Movement Desensitization and Reprocessing (EMDR), Fluoxetine, and Pill Placebo in the Treatment of Post-Traumatic Stress Disorder: Treatment Effects and Long Term Maintenance. J Clin Psychiatry 2007 Jan;68(1):37-46.
[57] Baer RA. Mindfulness-Based Treatment Approaches: Clinician's Guide to Evidence Base and Applications. Burlington: Academic Press, Inc. (2005).

is different from physical healing. Emotions heal in layers, and you will often find yourself "backtracking" to what seems like lessons you learned before, as though you are failing to make progress. Think of emotional healing like peeling an onion. As the onion grew, the framework of every layer drew water and nourishment from the same source, putting some of those nutrients into each layer as it grew. As you progress into deeper levels of healing, each layer will greet you with reminders of the old paths of pain that shaped your past. When you peel each new layer, your eyes will burn and tear with the grief over the disappointments and loss concerning that past. This is normal and healthy, and it is not something to be feared. That is just how emotional healing takes place. There will always be a few tears of grief as you mature, getting down into the deeper places when deep calls unto deep. This is a good sign of positive growth, something that should encourage you with hope.

—*Mrs. Kunsman writes about spiritual abuse and thought reform at undermuchgrace.blogspot.com.*

Stories

I wish I could have included every experience that was sent to me. They are all priceless glimpses of heartache and pain, of silenced voices yearning to make sound and to be acknowledged. I've chosen these three because they echo the same tragic emotional and physical reality I hear time and again.—H.M.

"Skin"

I can tell you anything you want to know about shame. You know how you feel when you never do anything right? Well that was me my whole life. Trying to please, trying to do the right thing, to go above and beyond. Doing all as unto Jesus. It was a constant drive—I wanted to do the best job I could to make God happy and my parents proud. What hurt, though, was when I worked real hard to do something as perfect as I could for them, craving just a smile or a word of praise— and not only would they dislike it, but they'd actually HATE it. I mean, I know I was an example to little eyes, but the lectures I always got about trying harder, doing all as unto Jesus—they hurt so bad because I was already doing my best! Didn't they see that if I could do better, I would! Ugh. It made me feel embarrassed and stupid and ashamed, all at once.

I think I dreaded those lectures more than anything else growing up. Whenever Mom or Dad started in, I got this crazy feeling of panic and sadness, like I was in a hole with no bottom. It felt like my body was dying. My stupid, imperfect body.

Puberty held one blessing for me—someone must have set a rule that I could be in the bathroom alone. It almost felt safe in there; sometimes it was quiet too, except for my own crazy thoughts—anxious voices, critical ones—I was harder on myself than anyone ever thought of being. "How could I be better?" "If I try harder or better—but I did!"

But puberty came with a price. I'll never forget the day something I did distracted Mom from her own busyness, and she looked directly at me. I mean, for once, I had her full attention. For almost a whole minute she stared at me—not at my eyes, but at my face, at my little blemishes. I stood there, thirteen years old, almost trembling under that burning scrutiny. When she opened her mouth, I think I flinched.

"You know you have dirt and fat coming out of your pores?" She stared and stared. "Your face is disgusting. I wonder where you got that. My skin never looked like yours." I started to shrink away, but she grabbed my arm and made me stand still so she could peer even closer. "Do you even wash yourself? That is awful." I'm surprised she didn't get the magnifying glass from our bug and scientist kit to look at me. I felt exposed, helpless, like a bug under glass. She let go of my arm and I stumbled away, reeling. *My skin makes my mother sick.* I wanted to throw up, myself, from embarrassment and shame.

Still in shock, I didn't cry right away. It took a while to sink in—but when I went to bed that night, I cried until my pillow was soaked. In the dark I traced my nose, my cheeks and forehead with my fingers, and could feel some little bumps under my hands where Mom was looking. I hated that feeling; it felt like the dried scabs on my arms where sticker bushes in the woods scratched me. I'd pick those scabs off so people wouldn't see them, because I wanted my skin to feel smooth. But this was worse; I had dirt and fat in my skin—horrible yuckiness coming from inside my body, and I wanted to get it out! I'd always heard about parasites and now it seemed like I was trapped in my own, real-life horror movie about a girl with parasites inside her skin. In a panic, I clutched at my face and sobbed harder. "I have to get them out! I am horrible and terrible because I can't do anything right; it's so bad that it's even coming out of my skin! I have to get it out! Maybe if I get it out of my skin, I can get it out of my deceitful heart? Then I can do better!"

I wanted to be beautiful like my mother, but she was never bad, so bad like me. The terrible thing that happened to me, the one I can never tell anyone about, did not happen to her when she was young and pure. My thoughts screamed at me. *I am hopeless. I want to die. I feel like I am dying...or maybe I'm already dead. I know I will never really be pure, and no one will want me when it comes time to marry. I will have to tell him—whoever it is that would want to marry me—about IT. And he will leave, too. Because no one will want me.*

And so I find myself in the safety of the bathroom. The house is quiet; everyone sleeps soundly, peacefully, purely.

There is me in the mirror. I look at my face. Ugly, ugly, ugly. I reach up and feel my skin. Bumpy. My fingers move to the swollen pores and without thinking, I start picking. Squeezing. Methodical, robotic movements that transform my skin and soul. *Ugly, ugly...clean and smooth. Ugly, ugly...clean and smooth.* My eyes catch sight of an old scrape on my arm, crusted and scabbed, and I pick at that, too. *Clean and smooth.* I have to get this out of me—I must! All the hot water in the world can't boil me enough to cleanse me of this disgusting evil. I have to pick and squeeze it.

Suddenly, I become very calm and very tired. I return to bed and sleep so deeply, I have trouble waking in the morning. I still have red marks on my face—but I am satisfied, almost proud of what I have accomplished. I've done my best, and I'll keep trying till I've gotten it. Step by step, I'll become pure. Sweet. Beautiful, like my Mom.

I don't realize it, but I've just performed my first ritual purging.

Mom teaches me to use a bobby pin to clean the deep pores. I experiment too, and find that the looped end of the back of a wire hair barrette works well. I can get the ugly plugs out of the pores myself, but using the wire leaves only a little redness, compared to the pinching and picking. The day the front part of the barrette breaks and Mom throws it away, I think I'll die and that it's the end of the world. The ugliness under my skin pulses, screams, and my thoughts torment me. I'm dying, I'm dying. I'm sick. I'm sweating. I'm throwing up. I'm so tired!

Of course that was years ago; I'm grown up now. When I feel so overwhelmed that I could die, when it seems impossible to live through the disappointments which have no beginning or end—I still pick my skin. I must get the ugly, ugly filth out of me. It's a ritual, like you might have coffee. I've learned ways to hide the redness, but I'm not always successful. People try not to stare but I know it's obvious. I found a thing that beauticians use, and a friend of mine says it looks like what doctors use to do D&Cs or abortions, scraping the uterus inside just like how I press into and drag across my skin. You know, in a way, I'm aborting myself when I do this. I've got it down in a warm, predictable pattern. First I feel like such a failure, then I wish I was never born, and then I scrape my skin with metal so I get out the ugliness and the evil—the evil dirt my body makes because I am alive and horrible and helpless to be better.

Hurry! Hurry! My mind cheers me on. *Clean and smooth. Clean and smooth. Clean and pure. Get it all, Jesus. Get it all. Make me clean. I can't do anything else right, but at least I can get this ugliness out of me.*

Panic, I panic; I feel like I am being washed down a drain, spinning in a whirl of water that never really makes me clean. *I am not real. I don't exist. But I would not hurt so much if I didn't exist! Hurry! Hurry! Hurry! I hate myself. I hate my ugliness.*

And then tired calm sweeps over me; my thoughts grow slow and sleepy. I must sleep; when I wake, maybe life will be better. Maybe I can pretend to be clean for a little while, until the next time I feel the ugliness and shame. Oh, why was I born? Why do I have to hurt so bad? Love is not supposed to hurt, is it? If living and loving is hurting, I don't want to hurt anymore. I'm so tired.

"The Secret"

I can't pinpoint it, that nagging feeling, the true beginning of the obsession—the hunt.

The day starts like any other. Same routine, same job, same life, but something triggers it—something I never quite name, never quite find. The call beckons me as all else fades away. Tunnel vision increases. Whether the children are crying, the boss is calling, or the husband bellows or croons, the only thing that matters is answering the call. Satiating the hunger.

It is like a worm in my mind. At first it whispers, and is quite easy to get through, but then it grows and overtakes me. However sometimes, whilst the worm still whispers, I go ahead and stretch the steel to stop it, before it gets too hungry…before I get too desperate. But not this time. No, this time I have waited too long. I had no other choice. Things did not line up properly today, and I have been pushed to the very edge.

My voice quivers as I answer mundane questions. I fight back tears and anger. I hold on to the thread that soon, very soon, the cold blade will take away, replacing all with a singular pinpoint of pain.

Something I can see; something I can name.

The moment before relief comes, there is one last loose end. I am already anticipating, already sweating. I can barely see. Sometimes I must endure annoying, bright places, but not today. I almost run down the hall to my small shelter of refuge. Today I have the solace of semi-darkness, my sacred hiding place. I hide IT not only from my loved ones, but, too, from myself, hoping someday to lose it forever. But today I ache for the cold steel. My mouth waters and blood rushes in my ears.

I do not cut merely for the blood. Sometimes, if I am away from my chosen implement, I use any sharp object that will not draw much—or any—blood at all. But when I do bleed large swollen drops it seems more purposeful, and holds me over longer.

The tunnel vision overwhelms me and nothing will stand in my way. I look down to choose the spot to work. To make my marks— something I can hide under clothes, but easy enough to reach. Sometimes I clean first with alcohol wipes, but not this time. I have waited too long and I can bear it no longer.

My arm looks "right."

The first cut is light, superficial. The cold rush of adrenaline beckons me further. I continue to score lines, and pale flesh turns crimson. A smile lights my face. My eyes grow drowsy with pleasure-pain, and my heart slows. The blood in my ear no longer pounds, and that awful, hungry, whispering, pleading worm retreats.

I rest the blade on my lap. For now, I am finished. I know, with the same mystery that lured me, that I have "completed" this session. I hesitate to stand, relishing the emptiness of anxiety as I wipe the blood and watch it bead a little longer. I rise, and take myself to the mirror. Sometimes I am surprised at what I've done—the "harshness" of it. Other times, I see beauty there.

This time I am quite detached and grab a few Band-Aids to slap on the wounds. I step drowsily out of the bathroom, and the first question pummels and rings reality in my ears.

"What happened to your arm, Mommy?"—his little eyes wide with care. I answer the only way I know how.

"Mommy hurt her arm, baby…"

"The Cost"

Even though we homeschooled and there were tons of us, my parents tried to be lenient where they could. They didn't want to be like those we always heard about, the legalistic, weird ones. We were "normal." I think they prided themselves on this. We listened to contemporary Christian music, we didn't wear denim jumpers. Sometimes we bought t-shirts from the Christian store with our own, hard-earned money so we felt like we owned something cool. But haircuts in the kitchen, hand-me-downs, and never really knowing how to act in public made our "cool" shirts look dorky and desperate—despite our best efforts, we still had that "homeschool look." But we shouldn't care, right? 'Cause that's pride.

But despite this, they did want to control something. They wanted our minds. Our thoughts, conscience. They'd never admit it, of course. But they needed them because they wanted a whole set of little spiritual champions, to raise up the next generation to be "set apart." A light in the darkness. To be free thinkers in a world that believes everything it's fed—hook, line, and sinker.

To be holy.

Some things we went along with, even agreed with. Other times we didn't really have a choice—like "courtship," for example. And some of my sisters did end up following the party line, you know, the conservative, Christian, homeschooling "vision." But others of us weren't sure what to make of it. We wanted to be holy just as much. It wasn't that we didn't love God, because we did. It just didn't quite make sense, what we were being taught versus what the Holy Spirit was telling us.

As we got older, those of us who didn't buy the latest homeschool-guru endorsement noticed a subtle change, a shift. Somehow, we became one of *them.* The world. At least they viewed us that way. There was no big disagreement or act of defiance. It was what we *didn't* do. Like when everyone jumps into the water and yells for you to jump too, but instinct holds you back, because something tells you that what lies under the surface isn't safe. And when they notice that you haven't joined them, they yell, cajole, call you a sissy, 'fraidy-cat...or rebellious.

Looking back today—or better yet, looking forward to Heaven when all will be revealed—there's a strange, beautiful irony. My parents did achieve what they always wanted—the set-apart child who pursued

192

God and His ways even when it wasn't popular. The child who stuck to their convictions even when the cost was high.

Even if the cost was their family.

Appendix B |

How Does Jesus Love You?

By Eric M. Pazdziora

The story goes that somebody once asked a great theologian—nobody's quite sure which theologian, but so the story goes—what was the most profound doctrinal statement he had ever heard. The theologian thought for a moment and replied:

> "Jesus loves me; this I know
> For the Bible tells me so."

We smile at the irony of a distinguished scholar singing a ditty for children. But I think he knew his stuff. Unless you become like a little child, after all, you won't get into the kingdom of God. Out of the mouths of infants and babes, God has perfected praise. In those three little words we all sang as children is everything we really need to know: "Jesus loves me."

Is the statement too simple? It might seem that way, especially if (like me) you learned those words just as soon as you were old enough to sing them. Like most simple truths, it's easy to overlook it, to neglect it, to assume we know it and move along. But some things shouldn't be overlooked—at least, not according to the Bible that tells us so. "This is My commandment," said Jesus, "that you love one another as I have loved you" (John 15:12). "The life which I now live in the flesh," wrote Paul, "I live by faith in the Son of God, who loved me and gave Himself for me" (Galatians 2:20). It's even in the Bible's most-quoted

195

passage on marriage: "Husbands, love your wives, just as Christ also loved the church and gave Himself for her" (Ephesians 2:25).

Jesus' love for us is not just a simple truth for children, though it is that. It's not just a comforting thought for when we're feeling lonely, though it is that. It's not even just a doctrinal proposition, though you can make it that if you like. If these verses are anything to go by, it's nothing less than the foundation of everything to do with the Christian faith and the Christian life.

This leads to an obvious question, a question so obvious that I'm not surprised so few people think to ask it. How, exactly, does Christ love the church? What does the Bible mean when it says Jesus loves me?

It may be an obvious question to ask, but it's not a trivial one to answer. The answer you give to it will do more to shape your life than anything else will. Or perhaps it's that the shape of your life reveals the answer you've given to this question.

Maybe that's part of the reason Jesus was so furiously opposed to spiritual abuse. When a Christian husband is domineering, harsh, or controlling toward his wife, it sends the message that that's how Jesus treats the people He loves. When a pastor is legalistic, arrogant, browbeating, or manipulative toward his congregation, it sends the message that that's how Jesus treats the people He leads. When a church leader withholds his approval until you've met his arbitrary standard, it sends the message that that's how Jesus dispenses His love.

Is Jesus manipulative? Can Jesus' love be earned? Does Jesus micromanage? Does Jesus demand perfection? Does Jesus use "love" as a tool to compel our servitude? Does Jesus withhold His love from those who aren't good enough? Does Jesus force submission? Is Jesus harsh and authoritarian? Does Jesus reject those who don't love Him enough?

I admit that if we looked for the answer to those questions in the way we've been treated by some people who called themselves Jesus' followers, we might come up with an unflattering picture. (Trying to calculate from Christians in my own experience, I'd estimate two negative for every positive, evening out more lately.)

But that's where the second line of the song comes in. It doesn't say "Jesus loves me; this I know / for my pastor treats me so." Or my parents, or my friends, or my employers, or anybody else. To see what Jesus' love is like, we have to start with Jesus Himself, and the most reliable representation we have of Jesus is in the Bible. Once we know what Jesus' love is really like, then (and only then) we can determine whether something else shows Jesus' love correctly.

The minor difficulty here is that trying to find the parts of the Bible that talk about God's love is a bit like trying to find the parts of Moby Dick that talk about whales. What parts don't? And I can't just go slapping all 1,189 chapters into one article or we'll be here all month. It might be worth mentioning, though, that Jesus Himself advocated reading the whole Bible in just that way—looking for the truth about Him in every part. "And beginning at Moses and all the Prophets, He expounded to them in all the Scriptures the things concerning Himself" (Luke 24:27). You could do a lot worse than, whenever you read a passage of Scripture, asking yourself, "How can I see the love of Jesus here?"

There are some verses, though, where it's especially easy to see.

Jesus' love is real and knowable.

He who has My commandments and keeps them, it is he who loves Me. And he who loves Me will be loved by My Father, and I will love him and manifest Myself to him. (John 14:21)

And I pray that you, being rooted and established in love, may have power, together with all the saints, to grasp how wide and long and high and deep is the love of Christ, and to know this love that surpasses knowledge—that you may be filled to the measure of all the fullness of God. (Ephesians 3:17-19)

To people with a skeptical nature, this whole notion of the love of Jesus can seem to border on absurdity. I get that. It's easy enough to appreciate where the skeptics and atheists are coming from on this one. There's a person you can't see, yet you're certain He loves you? Isn't that just having an imaginary friend?

I respect an honest skeptic. So does Jesus. He doesn't propose what would surely turn off any doubting inquirer, a glib assertion that "you've just gotta have faith." Instead, He asks us to observe a particular commandment: "This is My commandment, that you love one another, just as I have loved you." (John 15:12. This also explains the verse that trips up some readers: "If you love me, you will keep my commandments." The commandment in question is not to practice legalism but to love others.)

If you try this, Jesus says, "I will manifest myself to [you]." In other words, if you want to see whether Jesus' love is real, find out how His love is described and try loving other people that way. Then you'll know—although, as Paul says in Ephesians, you will "know this love that surpasses knowledge." There's a lot more to it than knowing: it's like the difference between knowing someone's name and having them as a friend. Or, if you like, the difference between having an imaginary friend and having a real friend.

Jesus' love is like the Father's.

As the Father loved Me, I also have loved you; abide in My love. (John 15:9) Some people give the impression that God the Father was itching to smite us with His wrath until Jesus stepped in and showed us some love instead. Those people are wrong. Jesus said He does nothing but what He sees the Father do (John 5:19). So anything that's true of the love of Jesus for us is true of the love of His Father for us.

However, this declaration moves it to another dimension: Jesus said His love for His disciples—and therefore, the Father's love for His disciples—was just like the Father's love for Him. The Father's love for His Son is eternal and unchangeable, a greater constant than the universe itself. It's a part of His essential nature: "God is love" (1 John 4:8). Jesus loves you exactly the same way.

Jesus' love takes the form of a sacrifice.

This is My commandment, that you love one another as I have loved you. Greater love has no one than this, than to lay down one's life for his friends. (John 15:12-13) And walk in love, as Christ also has loved us and given Himself for us, an offering and a sacrifice to God for a sweet-smelling aroma. (Ephesians 5:2) By this we know love, because He laid down His life for us. And we also ought to lay down our lives for the brethren. (1 John 3:16)

Loving someone means wanting what's best for them. Truly loving someone means giving up something voluntarily so they can get what's best for them. It can't be forced or manipulated by anyone else—real love makes sacrifice come naturally. The more someone truly loves, the more they freely sacrifice.

R. A. Torrey put it directly: "The love of Jesus Christ manifested itself in His giving Himself, laying down His life for us. His was a self-sacrificing love. The death of Christ was not the only sacrifice He made, but the crowning one. His whole life was a sacrifice, from the manger to the cross. His becoming man at all was a sacrifice of immeasurable greatness and meaning. (See Philippians 2:6-7.)" (What the Bible Teaches, Ch. 4).

This shows that Jesus' love won't demand, compel, or manipulate. Jesus never says, "Well, now that I've given so much, it's time for you to do something for me." He follows His own commandment to "give, expecting nothing in return" (Luke 6:35).

He just gives. He gives everything.

He gives Himself.

Jesus loves people when they don't deserve it.

Very rarely will anyone die for a righteous man, though for a good man someone might possibly dare to die. But God demonstrates his own love for us in this: While we were still sinners, Christ died for us. (Romans 5:7-8)

The greatest kind of love we can imagine (as Jesus said) is someone giving up their life for someone they love. We could probably picture ourselves trading our lives for somebody we love who loves us back— our child, our spouse, our best friend. But how about taking a bullet to save an enemy? Drowning to rescue somebody who hates you? Consider your mind staggered.

Sin, by definition, is an action that goes against God's nature. Lies are sinful because God is the truth; adultery is sinful because God is faithful; resentment is sinful because God is forgiving, and so on. God hates sin because it puts us at odds with Him: our choice to sin makes us God's enemies (compare Colossians 1:21, James 4:4). But God didn't wait for us to turn our lives around, to become "good enough" to earn His love and approval.

Jesus died for us while we were His enemies.

If you have ever thought that you had to be good enough for Jesus to love you, or that Jesus would stop loving you if you did something bad, or that the better you were the more Jesus would love you, now would be an appropriate time for you to crumple that thought up and toss it in a wastebasket to hell.

Jesus' love makes people pure and beautiful.

Husbands, love your wives, just as Christ also loved the church and gave Himself for her, that He might sanctify and cleanse her with the washing of water by the word, that He might present her to Himself a glorious church, not having spot or wrinkle or any such thing, but that she should be holy and without blemish. (Ephesians 5:25-27)

Why did Jesus sacrifice Himself for us? We all know the Sunday School answer: "To take away our sins." However, that doesn't fully answer the question of "why"—it tells the result but not the motive.

What was His motive? He wants to make us pure and beautiful, like a bride in white. He wants to make us glorious, flawless, and spotless. He wants to show that He considers us beautiful and unique and special. He wants to take away anything that might make someone think otherwise. He wants us to be whole, and complete, and cleansed, and made new and lovely. He wants to celebrate us, delight in us, rejoice over us.

And that's exactly what His sacrificial love for us accomplished.

By the way, that verse is written to tell Christian husbands how to treat their wives. So if you ever wanted to see one verse that singlehandedly demolishes the false teaching of Patriarchy—well, there you go. To Jesus, to love and lead means to serve and sacrifice.

Jesus' love nourishes and cherishes.

For no one ever hated his own flesh, but nourishes and cherishes it, just as the Lord does the church. (Ephesians 5:29)

This verse continues the previous thought, part of the same admonition to husbands. A godly husband applies the Golden Rule to his wife—he loves her as he loves himself. He nourishes her—he makes sure she has everything she needs to be healthy and grow. He cherishes her—he lets her know how special he thinks she is. He shows her every day that he's thankful for the blessing of having her in his life. He encourages her and builds her up. He makes room for her to be vibrant and to flourish.

He got that idea from the way Jesus treats the church.

Jesus' love lifts the lowly.

He raises the poor from the dust
and lifts the needy from the ash heap;
he seats them with princes,
with the princes of their people. (Psalm 113:7-8)

200

For you know the grace of our Lord Jesus Christ, that though He was rich, yet for your sake He became poor, so that you through His poverty might become rich. (2 Corinthians 8:9) God's love for us is not from the top down but from the bottom up. Jesus didn't wait for us to get our acts together; He got His hands dirty. The story of the Incarnation is the story of a king who laid aside His crown for the love of a beggar. Then, a beggar Himself, He gave the beggar He loved His crown and all His kingdom.

Jesus loves the neglected, the poor, the lowly, the outcasts, the overlooked, the untouchable. Jesus loves the disenfranchised, the misfits, the minorities, the friendless, the victims. He loves them so much that He came to earth and became one of them Himself.

Jesus was not ashamed of your lowliness; He made it His own. Jesus does not wait for you or anyone else to lift yourself up; He lifts you up. Jesus' love doesn't put us down in our places. It lifts us up to His place.

Jesus' love is friendship.

No longer do I call you servants, for a servant does not know what his master is doing; but I have called you friends, for all things that I heard from My Father I have made known to you. (John 15:15)
Jesus doesn't just love you in a vacuous general sense, like a recorded message that says, "Your call is very important to us." Jesus doesn't just love you because He's somehow obligated to. Jesus doesn't just love you because He loves everybody as a collective group. Jesus loves you as an individual. More than that—Jesus likes you.

Jesus isn't interested in having mindless servants who blindly obey. Jesus wants friends who will hang out with Him. Jesus wants friends He can talk with (His favorite topic, again, is His Father). Jesus thinks you're the kind of person He'd like to get together with over coffee. Or, if you're in England, tea.

Jesus' love is constructive.

"As many as I love, I rebuke and chasten. Therefore be zealous and repent." (Revelation 3:19). This verse may rub us the wrong way if we've been abused by authoritarian leaders. In reality, it shows us how Jesus finds a middle path between two extreme misunderstandings of discipline. A parent who destructively abuses and controls their child does not love that child as Jesus does, but neither does a parent who carelessly lets their child do whatever they please. Jesus instead gives us constructive training and guidance to help us develop into free and healthy individuals. As Paul put it, "The kindness of God leads you to repentance" (Romans 2:4, emphasis mine).

The fact that Jesus loves us does not guarantee that our life will be all flowers and sunshine and rainbows—often, quite the opposite. Jesus allows suffering and hardship in our lives to teach us and (sometimes) to correct us. It's not that suffering always means we've done something wrong—though our actions do have consequences—but that it often gives us an opportunity to see our faults with a bit more clarity. (For instance, having to wait in a long line at the bank reveals to me that I'm woefully impatient.) That in turn gives us an opportunity to change and to become more enthusiastic about our walk with God.

Jesus' discipline and training is not about controlling us but about helping us to grow. When Jesus points out our faults, weaknesses, or sins, it's never to make us feel guilty or inferior but to get us to turn away from them and turn instead to His grace and the transforming love and power of His Spirit.

Jesus' love is compassionate.

A bruised reed he will not break, and a smoldering wick he will not snuff out. In faithfulness he will bring forth justice… (Isaiah 42:3) If you're bruised, or wounded, or hurting, it may seem like people want to cast you aside, throw you away, or (worst) make you think it was all your fault. What good is a bruised reed except to break and throw away? What good is a smoldering candle except to blow out? What good is a broken person except as a cautionary tale to avoid?

Not to Jesus. Jesus isn't in the business of discarding things other people have broken. Jesus is in the business of finishing the good work He started. Jesus treats the bruised and broken things of the world with the tenderness they need to recover and return to life.

Jesus is all about resurrections.

Jesus' love identifies with our suffering.

For even Christ did not please Himself; but as it is written, "The reproaches of those who reproached You fell on Me." (Romans 15:3)

In all their affliction he was afflicted, and the angel of his presence saved them; in his love and in his pity he redeemed them; he lifted them up and carried them all the days of old. (Isaiah 63:9)

When Shadrach, Meshach, and Abednego were thrown into a fiery furnace for their convictions, the king who put them there was astonished to see a fourth man in the flames with them—one who looked like "the son of a god" (Daniel 3:25). Jesus does something infinitely better than keeping us from ever going through suffering and hardship. He experiences our suffering and hardship right along with us. He's not just with us in our suffering, or even just "carrying us" like in the old "Footprints" poem, but actually experiencing our suffering as much as we are.

In His life on earth, Jesus experienced what it was to be hurt, abandoned, beaten up, misunderstood, mocked, laughed at, scorned, slapped, betrayed, tempted, and even seemingly forsaken by God. "For we do not have a high priest who is unable to sympathize with our weaknesses, but one who in every respect has been tempted as we are, yet without sin" (Hebrews 4:15). Jesus' suffering absolved not only our sins but also our griefs and our sorrows (Isaiah 53:4). When someone insults you, hurts you, or abuses you, Jesus feels it too. He's been there before, and He's there with you now.

Jesus' love is unilateral.

"We love him, because he first loved us." (1 John 4:19) Once in a while, it helps your interpretation if you look very closely at what the Bible doesn't say. For instance, this verse doesn't say, "We have to strive to love Him if we want Him to love us back." It doesn't say, "He loves us when we love Him and do our best to be well-behaved and attractive." It definitely doesn't say, "He won't love us until we're good enough." You get the idea.

Lots of people like to use the phrase "unconditional love," which is accurate as far as it goes—Jesus' love comes with no strings attached. But the Bible goes even further than that phrase does. A friend of mine, a theologically minded woman, once suggested the phrase "unilateral love": as far as Jesus is concerned, His love for us is entirely His idea and exclusively His initiative. I like the phrase.

Jesus' love for us is the cause, and our love for Him is the effect. If you want to love Jesus more, don't waste your time trying to strive or to do good things or to work up your passion and emotions. Just think

203

about Jesus' love for you, and how much He had to do with it, and how little (nothing) you had to do with it.

A little girl in London once asked her Sunday School teacher—his name was Mark Guy Pearse—how she could learn to love Jesus, since she didn't. Pearse thought for a moment and replied, "Little girl, as you go away from here today, keep saying to yourself, 'Jesus loves me,' 'Jesus loves me,' and I believe you will come back next Sunday saying, 'I love Jesus.'"

It worked.

Jesus' love is invincible.

Who shall separate us from the love of Christ? Shall tribulation, or distress, or persecution, or famine, or nakedness, or peril, or sword? Yet in all these things we are more than conquerors through Him who loved us. For I am persuaded that neither death nor life, nor angels nor principalities nor powers, nor things present nor things to come, nor height nor depth, nor any other created thing, shall be able to separate us from the love of God which is in Christ Jesus our Lord. (Romans 8:35-39)

(To be followed by the "Sevenfold Amen.")

Conclusion: Abiding

Well then. In the words of a scholar who taught me many of the principles of applied hermeneutics and exegesis—"So what?" Was this all a pointless intellectual exercise, or does it make a difference to the life we'll face on a Monday morning?

If you were expecting a list of things to do here, I'm going to have to disappoint you. The first thing Jesus tells us to do about His love is to stop doing things about it. His word of choice is "Abide": "As the Father loved Me, I also have loved you; abide in My love" (John 15:9). "Abide" means "Make yourself at home." Stay, relax, hang out, take a load off, pull up a seat, put down roots; you can stay forever. Jesus wants us to live in His love.

What does it mean to live in Jesus' love? It means you can know you will always have someone who loves you. As the psalmist sang, "Though my father and my mother forsake me, the Lord will take me up" (Psalm 27:10).

It means that you never have to worry about being good enough for Him to love you. Jesus loved you first. Your behavior had nothing to do with it either way. You don't have anything to live up to. You're already good enough.

It means you don't have to worry whether you will be loved or not. You just have to know that you are loved, and that therefore you are worth loving. You can lose the worries of legalism, perfectionism, and authoritarianism. You can feel the freedom to love yourself. You can feel the security of being unconditionally loved.

If you still insist on doing something, there is one thing you can do: You can love other people the same way Jesus does. Jesus said, "This is My commandment, that you love one another as I have loved you" (John 15:12). Of course, that's impossible, except for one thing: abiding in Jesus' love changes us and makes us more like Him. The more we see what Jesus' love is, the more we become able to love that way ourselves. It's not the kind of commandment you have to struggle to live up to; it's the kind of commandment you grow into and live out.

One other thing. Don't accept substitutes. Don't believe the lies. Once you see what Jesus' love is like, stay there. Don't put any other person or place or idea in that place, especially not one that's a lie. Nothing can separate you from Jesus' love for you. Nothing can stop you from being loved forever.

Anything that says otherwise isn't Jesus.

—Eric M. Pazdziora is a freelance composer, pianist, worship leader, author, and editor who works for a variety of publications and venues. He is a graduate of Moody Bible Institute with a B.Mus. in sacred music composition. Eric lives in Chicago with his beautiful wife Carrie and their spoiled cat Eloise. His writing and music can be found online at www.ericpazdziora.com.

Appendix C |

Biblically Refuting Cultic Criteria

By Hillary McFarland

In a study of authoritarianism and the levels of control within some families, it can be argued that some traits are necessary for those seeking godliness—such as separation from the world and the pursuit of holiness. As Christians, we believe that Jesus Christ is the Son of God, the Way, the Truth, and the Life. We confess our trespasses to one another, and pray for one another. (Jm. 5:16) These views can certainly be pulled right out of established cult criteria and appear to be forms of elitism, of "us versus them," of confession and purity. Taking known characteristics of cults and hallmarks of spiritual abuse, let's look at Scripture and how it relates to faith and family.

Milieu Control—

The best way to understand milieu control is *"total life micromanagement,"* although that doesn't even suggest the toxic levels present within high demand, closed groups. Biblically, we are to be self-controlled. (2 Pet. 1:5-7) This is actually one of the fruits of the Spirit. (Gal. 5:23) When a child receives the Holy Spirit through salvation, a parent should trust God with their child and appropriately give Him space to work and produce fruit. This doesn't mean that a parent won't still have influence or even the "final word" in many cases. God has provided the home as a safe place for a child to learn vital lessons about life and spirituality, but when parents endeavor to control every aspect of life—physically, mentally, emotionally, financially, spiritually—they actually quench the Spirit by fulfilling the role of God in someone else's life. In this case, home becomes unsafe and stumbling blocks occur. While there are times, of course, when controlling another person is necessary, such as legal restraint of criminals or those who intend to inflict harm on themselves or others, *this only becomes necessary **after they have ceased to control themselves.***

Authoritarian Structure—

Jesus preached humility. Through His life we have an example decidedly anti-authoritarian, whether we are wives, husbands, mothers, fathers, pastors, teachers, or government officials. He who is the eternal I AM *"...made Himself of no reputation, taking the form of a bondservant, and coming in the likeness of men. And being found in appearance as a man, He humbled Himself and became obedient to the point of death, even the death of the cross."* (Phil. 2:7-8) He did not come to be served, but to serve, to pour out His life. Godly leaders will pattern themselves (Jn. 13:1-17) after the One who knelt before His followers. *"...having loved His own who were in the world,"* writes John, *"He loved them to the end."*

Image Conscious—

Jesus concerned Himself with truth, not with the appearance of evil. He sat among sinners (Mt. 9:9-11) and even defended His actions. (Mk. 2:16-17) He wasn't afraid of associating with prostitutes, nor of allowing them to touch Him. (Lk. 7:36-50) And our perfect, holy Lord offers Himself as our example.

Suppresses Criticism—

God is not afraid of questions. "If any of you lacks wisdom, let him ask of God, who gives to all liberally and ***without reproach,*** and it will be given to him." (Jm. 1:5) (emphasis mine) He will not annihilate your soul for coming boldly to the throne. 'Call to Me, and I will answer you, and show you great and mighty things, which you do not know.'

(Jer. 33:3) He remembers our frame (Ps. 103:14) and can take our questions, our rages, our criticism, and our doubts.

Perfectionistic—

Our God is merciful. (Neh. 9:31) He is patient and suffers long. We make mistakes, but He still loves us. Shall we sin, that grace abounds? Certainly not, but as Paul reminds us, *"For the good that I will to do, I do not do; but the evil I will not to do, that I practice. Now if I do what I will not to do, it is no longer I who do it, but sin that dwells in me."* (Rom. 7) And in Christ there is no condemnation. He is both our Priest *and* our sacrifice, who "always lives to make intercession" (Heb. 7:20-28) for us. He calls us to be holy, but He is the one who *makes* us holy. (Rom. 4:4-6)

Imbalanced—

"Jesus Christ is the same yesterday, today, and forever. Do not be carried about with various and strange doctrines. For it is good that the heart be established by grace..." (Heb. 13:8-9) In Christ we have stability. God does not change. *"Do not be deceived, my beloved brethren. Every good gift and every perfect gift is from above, and comes down from the Father of lights, **with whom there is no variation or shadow of turning.**"* (Jm. 1:16-17) This means we can trust Him. He has proven Himself faithful.

Manipulation—

Mystical: Through manipulation, one seeks his own glory. God is not manipulative. While He is a jealous God and seeks His glory, He seeks it because He is true and knows that glory belongs to Him. The false humility we often encounter in ourselves and others is not truth. God recognizes the truth of who we are *and* the truth of who He is. And He is our Creator who loves us and freely gives us all things. "If you then, being evil, know how to give good gifts to your children, how much more will your Father who is in heaven give good things to those who ask Him!" (Mt. 7:11) Sometimes this means that He operates supernaturally in our lives. *Emotional:* While we were yet sinners, Christ died for us. He doesn't love us only when we behave, when we perform to standard. Not only do we love Him because He first loved us, but it is His goodness that leads us to repentance. (Rom. 2:4) He doesn't play with our hearts; He doesn't dangle a carrot before us. He didn't wait to see (Rom. 5:6) if we'd accept Him as Lord before He went to the cross. He did it; and *"it is finished,"* He said.

Cognitive Dissonance—

God is Truth. Mixed messages lead to confusion, and God is not the author of confusion (1 Cor. 14:33) but of peace. We can trust the One who cannot lie (Tit. 1:1-3) and who will not deceive us. Sometimes we experience the natural consequences of our actions, and even then, God can use them for good. (Rom. 8:28) When there is something we do not understand, we can come boldly unto His throne, and He will teach us. (Ps. 32:8)

Separatism, or Demand for Purity—

Separation from the world, purity, and God's command to "Be holy, for I am holy" are key tenets within many families and churches—both healthy ones, and cultic ones. It is important to recognize that separation, or to be "set apart", means sanctification—something done by God. "But know that the LORD has set apart for Himself him who is godly; The LORD will hear when I call to Him." (Ps. 4:3, also: John 17:17, Eph. 5:26-27, 2 Thess. 2:13, Heb. 13:12) He is the one who justifies us, who makes us holy, and saves us, and not we ourselves. (Eph. 2:8-10)

Confession—

Cultic environments reek of secrecy and lack of trust, but note the difference with Jesus: "No longer do I call you servants, for a servant does not know what his master is doing; but I have called you friends, for all things that I heard from My Father I have made known to you." (John 15:15) Love rejoices in the truth. (1 Cor. 13:6) In a trusting environment—**a *godly* environment, for God is safe and trustworthy**—we can confess our trespasses (Jm. 5:16) and find non-shaming encouragement, support, and comfort. (2 Cor. 1:3-5)

Loading the Language—

As we worship the Lord, we might have intimate language, like that between lovers or friends, but in context of a closed group, special, inner language serves to feed elitism. As we are called to evangelize, what good is it if we cannot speak in a way others understand? Even within our own culture—and for some, this is *limited* to family—we are called to be missionaries. We have a unique example through the experience of Paul in Acts 17: *Then Paul stood in the midst of the Areopagus and said, "Men of Athens, I perceive that in all things you are very religious; for as I was passing through and considering the objects of your worship, I even found an altar with this inscription: TO THE UNKNOWN GOD. Therefore, the One whom you worship without knowing, Him I proclaim to you..."* Through Paul's entire dialogue, we see that: he met them on their level—intellectually and culturally equipped to relate to them; he reasoned with them with their own language: that of philosopher; he involved himself in community and their daily life; he made himself visible, willing, and available; he was observant and relevant; he engaged the culture where he found himself, even able to quote a poet of their own—without sinning, without being snared by the world.

Sacred Science—

The Truth of God is absolute, but it is available for all who call upon the name of the Lord. It isn't limited to gender or role. Many cultic families and groups teach that wives and daughters can only hear from God through their husbands or fathers, but consider the woman who approached Jesus herself: *But the woman, fearing and trembling, knowing what had happened to her, came and fell down before Him and told Him the whole truth. And He said to her, "Daughter, your faith has made you well. Go in peace, and be healed of your affliction."* (Mark 5:33-35) We are all responsible for seeking both the knowledge of God and the voice of God. Look at another verse that uses the words 'fear and trembling': *Therefore, my beloved, as you have always obeyed, not as in my presence only, but now much more in my absence, work out your own salvation with fear and trembling; for it is God who works in you both to will and to do for His good pleasure.* (Phil. 2:12-13) This is not exclusive—this means to anyone, man, woman, child, slave, free, Jew, Greek, Gentile...

Doctrine Over Person—

While cultic groups, familial or otherwise, elevate doctrine above individuals, Jesus came to challenge this by His very existence on earth. Jesus shows us person over doctrine, valuing souls, hearts and bodies above religious practice. *"And behold, there was a woman who had a spirit of infirmity eighteen years, and was bent over and could in no way raise herself up. But when Jesus saw her, He called her to Him and said to her, "Woman, you are loosed from your infirmity." And He laid His hands on her, and immediately she was made straight, and glorified God. But the ruler of the synagogue answered with indignation, because Jesus had healed on the Sabbath; and he said to the crowd, "There are six days on which men ought to work; therefore come and be healed on them, and not on the Sabbath day." The Lord then answered him and said, "Hypocrite! Does not each one of you on the Sabbath loose his ox or donkey from the stall, and lead it away to water it?"* (Luke 13:11-15) The Way came to die for *people,* not for a way of life. The Truth came to serve *people,* with humility, not to be served. The Life came to pour out His own so that *people,* not doctrine, would have it for eternity.

Dispensing of Existence—

Jesus did not reject anyone. Even the Pharisees, whom He loudly and often corrected, were loved. (Jn. 3:16) While hanging on the cross, He pleaded with God to forgive those who crucified Him, *"for they know not what they do."* (Lk. 23:33-34) To reject those who do not prescribe to group ideology, especially in the name of God, counters Christ's example of sacrificial love. Communicating that others are "dead to me", as some proclaim, or that others are less than, or don't matter, denies the gospel—especially when they are members of one's family.

Conclusion

"Cultic" is a distasteful, loaded, even offensive term for many. In our context, in its basic form, it describes a culture that utilizes non-Christlike means of getting something—*even something good and godly*—while trying to change someone else. That is strictly the Lord's responsibility. Those who perpetuate this generally mean well, want only the best for their families, and don't realize what happens until it seems too late. But it is never too late. God is great and can restore the

years. (Joel 2:25) Even if a lack of faith has led parents to take desperate steps, God can strengthen and restore it.

Recovering from a cultic environment takes time and continually searching for truth and wisdom. But anyone can do this. We do not have to be naturally strong, naturally "good" Christians, naturally perfect. Sometimes we need professional assistance. We need those who can help us, support us, pray for us, encourage us, listen to us repeat the same thing over and over until it is spent. It can be hard, for over the course of life it will involve pain, anger, grief, and forgiveness. But Jesus said that *"difficult is the way that leads to life."* (Mt. 7:14) Yet He also says *"...I am with you always, even to the end of the age."* (Mt. 28:20) In cases when one has a pre-cult identity, trying to remember the past is only a step towards healing—but it is a step of faith and will help you find the right path. Those who do not have this can find their identity in Christ, who Himself is the Way, Truth, and Life. Healing is a journey, and if it is taken with Christ, the soul will find rest.

—*For more, please visit www.watchman.org. This article first appeared on www.quiveringdaughters.blogspot.com.*

The Myth of Normal

By Hillary McFarland

When I was young, I envied those who told breath-catching testimonials of how they came to Christ. I listened, enraptured, to stories featured on our local religious radio station and dreamed of how thrilled God must be with these dramatically-acquired souls. Many met Him in death-defying places; others spoke of time in prison or gang life, and how God transformed them into amazing teachers or evangelists of the gospel. I hung on every word, and then slowly returned to the dishes or laundry or the care of my younger siblings— my own daily reality. My parents said that I always wanted adventure—an observation implying *bad,* branding me with the label "discontent".

In hindsight, I think that I wanted *to matter.* We read Martyr's Mirror, and my thoughts drifted to foreign lands, where somehow I took the place of innocent young women patiently waiting their fates— *my fate*—while remaining faithful and devoted to God. And while sore fingers scratched page after page of stories in faded gray pencil, my characters reflected the inner angst that yearned to do something great for God—something glorious, that made Him say, "Well done." I wanted approval. I wanted that certain air of pride that comes, not from selfish ambition, but rather from the sense that *"She's mine. And that is a good thing."* I wanted to matter, to have a purpose, and to make a difference—yet it seemed that every day was exactly the same.

In every movement and every culture—religious or otherwise— there are extremes. Within the homeschooling, conservative, and Quiverfull world, there are some families who go to great lengths to observe dogmatic, legalistic, and austere patriarchal standards. These are the ones who often gain national attention as the waves of public interest ebb and flow, inciting controversy and awareness of "peculiar" lifestyles and beliefs.

However, there are others within this Christian sub-culture—typical, traditional families, with perhaps a few non-mainstream practices. Not often found on the covers of magazines or the subject of articles or books, many are still well-known and well-liked within their church and community. Perhaps they aren't dresses-only; some do not live on a farm, others might have "only" three or four children. Some home-school, yet participate in local sports or other extra-curricular activities.

No one has hurt me, so why do I feel hurt?

Daughters within these conservative yet non-extreme households face a unique challenge that I believe is not shared by their more dogmatic sisters. Many of the same emotional and spiritual struggles which arise from this lifestyle impinge them as well, but with a twist that can potentially crush life from the spirit.

These young women feel that since their external situation or lifestyle is not that "bad", it would be fraudulent to acknowledge the mystifying internal effects that such an upbringing can have. They embrace denial rather than admitting pain. Using phrases such as, "Well, that doesn't apply to me," or "That's not how it happened in my family" tends to dismiss deep, lurking, real hurts which need the healing touch of Christ.

A lovely young wife and mother writes:

> My story was far from extreme, yet I have the same wounds from the same lies as the extreme cases. But they're harder to identify. My parents said things like "You have a rebellious heart", "You're going to lead all your siblings astray", "If this were God's will for you, He would tell us", "You should want to spend time with your family more than your friends", "You're too independent", etc. We were forced to wear dresses because "beauty is dangerous and you could defraud your brother". And on it went. Yet, on the outside, we didn't look too different, except for our dress. My dad was a teacher in the church and my mom very active in our church community. They counseled many families

and many marriages. We went everywhere and had every opportunity you could imagine. But on the inside, our hearts were broken and there was much fear, shame, and guilt. They used guilt and the Bible to keep me from going to college, from getting married…Then when I prayed and sought the Lord and still chose to do those things, they acted like I had rejected God and our family.

The myth of "normal"

The roots are the same—shame, fear and guilt—but they are made much more insidious by the choking fog of confusion. How can you acknowledge something you can't identify? How do you verbalize something you can't explain or understand? It is like watching blood slowly trickle down your arm and yet not find a scratch or mark. This is very disorienting—there is no apparent source. One is left troubled and aching, without knowing why—and especially not knowing how to address the issue and seek healing.

Those who have born years of emotional and spiritual abuse, neglect, shame, and depression find it easier to brush all aside when external factors do not make sense. It is easier to succumb to pressures that insist you are making it all up, that you are crazy and imagining things, or that the problem lies within you. The reality of alone-ness is compounded knowing that those closest to your family would not believe you, if you told them what you feel and what has been said or done; when you consistently hear, "What good kids you have!" gushed to your parents; when your family is held up as a model of virtue or shining example; when your parents think you are either over-dramatic or simply can't understand your own conflicting emotions. This internalizes, and places another layer of shame and confusion upon a slowly withdrawing heart. *It must all be me--hormones, or something,* you might tell the pain which dwells within, effectively shutting her up for one more day.

When we strip all away, a foundation rife with falsehoods can be often found at the core of our being. Believing these lies exacerbates all of the problems; until the light of Jesus illuminates error and transforms the heart, symptoms will only grow worse. It is amusing when little children insist they are not tired. Yet they go willingly to bed after gentle reminders that they didn't take a nap, that their eyes will not stay open, and that they are face down in their mashed potatoes. It is similarly ironic when those who insist they are well, but flushed cheeks, warm skin, glassy eyes and lethargy indicate fever. Have you ever staunchly refused to believe something until finally faced with a list of symptoms, the truth is undeniable?

Even if your family appears normal within this conservative movement, if you are exhibiting the symptoms of deep, serious issues, I beseech you to sit with these things in stillness and prayer before God, asking Him to reveal to you what it is that you need to know. It is my humble belief that God desires truth to be known by you—the truth of the source of your pain. Abuse is abuse—whether it is physical, emotional, sexual or spiritual—and all of it grieves the heart of God. Minimizing it and shrugging it away does not honor God nor does it bring the healing that He longs for you to have. Wait on Him and His timing, trusting that whatever it is you find He will give you strength to bear. In the meantime, He will never leave you nor forsake you.

Signs and times

In most cases, symptoms and features indicate that something is wrong. In our fallen world, peopled by sinful creatures who bear the image of God and yet tarnish His name, the sad reality is that we have all been hurt at some point in our lives. When these wounds are caused by those meant to protect, nourish, and love us the most, we bear the most excruciating pain. Our loyal tendency is to excuse and dismiss hurtful actions—"They were just doing the best they could," or "It's okay," or "That was so long ago; I don't even really remember that," or "I was just a baby."

As I have written before, forgiveness does not mean it's okay. Forgiveness is a separate issue; forgiving someone who has wronged you—while a godly spiritual discipline—does not miraculously ameliorate the scars inflicted upon you. That is the work of our Heavenly Father—who sometimes allows symptoms to smolder under the surface, occasionally erupting until they become present enough to sustain your attention.

It is here that He meets us, in our woundedness and vulnerability, in the shame of our nakedness, in the raw and the wild. It is here that He is glorified, for His strength is made perfect in our weakness. In the secret shadows of pain He infuses the light of His truth—redeeming, revealing, and restoring.

If you feel as though you are the proverbial "middle child" within Christian culture—not as extreme as some, yet more conservative than others—and stumble trying to find your voice among the confusing messages you receive, take heart, dear sister. You have been created and chosen, *as you.* Your wounds and your words have equal validity. You matter dearly to God, and He has a purpose for you. Perhaps your testimony will not elicit ooohs and ahhhs from the congregation; likely you will not become a martyr from foreign lands. As you dwell faithfully however, daily showing your devotion to God, it is quite possible that somewhere, your story might cause an exhausted young woman in the midst of dishes and laundry to catch her breath in hope— and keep going for just one more day.

—This originally appeared on www.quiveringdaughters.blogspot.com

Encouragement for Stay-at-Home Quivering Daughters

By Hillary McFarland

Facing the truth about spiritual abuse and emotional abuse is hard, especially for daughters—even years after the fact. Years after we are safe, loved, and growing in the Lord. But what about when it isn't years after? When it's right now? Today?

Once I assisted an instructor with an important project. He repeatedly criticized my work in front of other students, belittled me, and treated me with condescension to the point that others asked, often, "Why are you still helping him? Why do you put yourself under that?" Although the situation made me sick inside, I could only reply, "Because I am trying to be a good student. It's about who I am, not about who he is."

When we try to do all things as unto the Lord, we aren't bound by the behavior of others. We can still treat them with integrity, respect, and honor because we are respectful. We are women with integrity. We are women of honor. We are women who love the Lord, and want to walk worthy of the calling with which He calls us. This includes our positions as friends, employees, students, wives, mothers, teachers, writers, missionaries, doctors, hairstylists, chefs, and daughters.

If you are an adult daughter still living at home, you probably hear from "outsiders" that you need to move out, get a job, or go to school. But from those "likeminded", you hear that such ideas are worldly, unnecessary, unbiblical, and that you need to remain under your father's headship until he transfers this authority to another man—specifically, your husband. But what about in the meantime?

"In the meantime" really can feel "mean" sometimes. For many adult daughters, it's the 'in-between'—your home education is complete, and normal family life continues to bustle around you, while you wonder what God has planned for your life. For some, it seems to stretch without end, without hope. The purpose of this article is not to devalue family life or to suggest that one way is better than the other, for truly, I can't say what you should do. Move out? Stay home? Start a home business? Get a job? Take a class? Will a young man enter the picture? The options are overwhelming, especially in light of mixed messages and your own emotional, spiritual, mental, and physical struggles. I realize that many of you do these things already, but as you seek the Lord's will, may I humbly offer some encouragement?

- Repay no one evil for evil. Have regard for good things in the sight of all men. If it is possible, as much as depends on you, live peaceably with all men. Beloved, do not avenge yourselves, but rather give place to wrath; for it is written, "Vengeance is Mine, I will repay," says the Lord. (Rom. 12:17-19)

While you wait upon the Lord, do everything within your power to be at peace with your family. Not to defend sinful actions, but to understand—it's hard for many parents to see their little girls grow up. They often react out of fear, pride, and other issues that they themselves might not realize. For some families, this might be a love of power and control. Or they may truly believe that you are going to hell and yearn to stop you. Ask God to give you compassion for your parents, brothers, and sisters, even when they react in an unChristian manner to your walking in obedience to the Lord's calling.

- But sanctify the Lord God in your hearts, and always be ready to give a defense to everyone who asks you a reason for the hope that is in you, with meekness and fear; having a good conscience, that when they defame you as evildoers, those who revile your good conduct in Christ may be ashamed. For it is better, if it is the will of God, to suffer for doing good than for doing evil. (1 Pet. 3:15-17)

Accusations, when unfounded, are violent words that break peace and sever relationships. Do everything you can to ensure that before the

Lord, you live righteously and in love. Notice that even angels do not accuse the ultimate Accuser: *Yet Michael the archangel, in contending with the devil, when he disputed about the body of Moses, dared not bring against him a reviling accusation, but said, "The Lord rebuke you!"* (Jude 1:9) Live your life in such a way that when others blame, scapegoat, revile, and accuse, their words are meaningless. The Lord knows the truth. Trust Him and rest in this.

- but, speaking the truth in love, may grow up in all things into Him who is the head—Christ— from whom the whole body, joined and knit together by what every joint supplies, according to the effective working by which every part does its share, causes growth of the body for the edifying of itself in love. (Eph. 4:15-16)

As a Christian family, your parents are your brothers and sisters in the Lord. Sometimes we need to speak truth and exhortation unto them. However, we must do this with the goal of edification in love. This means that we must speak to them in ways that show kindness, gentleness, longsuffering, and humility—even when we are right. *So then, my beloved brethren, let every man be swift to hear, slow to speak, slow to wrath; for the wrath of man does not produce the righteousness of God.* (James 1:19, 20) Unfortunately, you may not always be heard. Your thoughts, ideas, and beliefs might be ridiculed, criticized, and you might be cast aside. But hang onto the Lord, and *Let your speech always be with grace, seasoned with salt, that you may know how you ought to answer each one.* (Col. 4:6) *Let no corrupt word proceed out of your mouth, but what is good for necessary edification, that it may impart grace to the hearers.* (Eph. 4:29) Perhaps you will help bring grace unto the graceless, and in so doing, so fulfill the law of Christ.

- Likewise you younger people, submit yourselves to your elders. Yes, all of you be submissive to one another, and be clothed with humility, for "God resists the proud, but gives grace to the humble." Therefore humble yourselves under the mighty hand of God, that He may exalt you in due time, casting all your care upon Him, for He cares for you. (1 Peter 5:5-7)

It is important to be clothed with humility, for like an old saying goes: "Make your words sweet, because someday you may have to eat them."

But even more importantly, when we are humble we make ourselves like Christ. We need to understand that humility doesn't equal allowing your personhood to be maligned, but rather states the truth of who we are in Christ—both to yourself and to others.

- "Honor your father and mother," which is the first commandment with promise: "that it may be well with you and you may live long on the earth." And you, fathers, do not provoke your children to wrath, but bring them up in the training and admonition of the Lord. (Eph. 6:2-4)

Much literature is devoted to children obeying parents, and for adult children to honor parents. Unfortunately, not so much is written to parents who exasperate, provoke, discourage, or defraud their children. However: the fact that one does not do their part does not excuse the other. Colossians 4:6 suggests how and why: *And whatever you do, do it heartily, as to the Lord and not to men, knowing that from the Lord you will receive the reward of the inheritance; for you serve the Lord Christ.* So for adult daughters, what does this look like? How can an adult daughter honor a parent who discourages her? Who exasperates her? Who perpetuates a lifestyle that quenches the work of the Holy Spirit in her life? Who provokes, defrauds, and stands between her and her Lord?

Honoring the dishonorable

- But the wisdom that is from above is first pure, then peaceable, gentle, willing to yield, full of mercy and good fruits, without partiality and without hypocrisy. Now the fruit of righteousness is sown in peace by those who make peace. (James 3:17,18)

Adult daughters who walk in obedience to God and who seek the Lord's will inevitably become faced with choices. Sometimes they can be confusing, especially in an authoritarian environment. The core of authoritarianism is self-seeking, and James says, *But if you have bitter envy and self-seeking in your hearts, do not boast and lie against the truth. This wisdom does not descend from above, but is earthly, sensual, demonic. For where envy and self-seeking exist, confusion and every evil thing are there.* (James 3:13-16) Coming into adulthood can be convoluted enough without adding authoritarianism, spiritual abuse, emotional abuse, and other stumbling blocks to the dynamic. Whether or not you are called to leave the home is between you and Father God, but choosing to respect the non-sinful wishes of another person is an important fruit of wisdom, even when you are disrespected and mistreated in return.

Regardless of your living situation, remember that a parent is honored when you obey the Lord, even if it isn't in a manner they wish. A parent is honored when you love the Lord and stand up for righteousness. A parent is honored when you seek truth. When you put the Lord first in your life, your parents are honored, which means that when you take your eyes off your parents and place them on Jesus, this brings them honor.

I want to humbly offer a difficult but important reminder for adult daughters still living at home, who struggle with oppressiveness or depression, with trying to hear the still small voice of the Lord and to follow His commandments. Just as we respect the home of anyone we visit, even in things we think are unimportant, certain things must be honored while living under your parents' roof. A parent's sinfulness doesn't release us from God's commands to love others, to put others first, or to be kind—and these are things we can do wherever we are. But it's another matter when your home is unsafe. If certain things make you contemplate death or destructive behaviors, please find someone safe, some place safe, and take steps to seek the healing life offered by Jesus. You can love others from a distance, if necessary. Even Paul knew when boundaries and separation were needed. (Acts 15:38-40)

But if, for the moment, you are called to remain at home, rest knowing that He who sees a sparrow fall does not forget you ~ and is even now making *"intercession for us with groanings which cannot be uttered. Now He who searches the hearts knows what the mind of the Spirit is, because He makes intercession for the saints according to the will of God. And we know that all things work together for good to those who love God, to those who are the called according to His purpose."* (Romans 8)

Take heart; it may seem like the "meantime" draws on for eternity, but trust God that He sees you and cares for you. Keep listening to His voice—whether He calls you to leave, or calls you to stay. He will make known His will for you. As you spend your time seeking first the kingdom of God and His righteousness, seeking His will, purpose, and plan, He says "All these things will be added unto you." In the meantime, take care to remain above reproach; *"be diligent to be found* by Him in peace, without spot and blameless." (2 Peter 3:14) *Who is wise and understanding among you? Let him show by good conduct that his works are done in the meekness of wisdom.* (James 3:13) He loves you, and will show you the way you should go.

—This originally appeared on www.quiveringdaughters.blogspot.com

Appendix F |

Notes from Christian Families on the Edge: Authoritarianism and Isolationism by Rachel D. Ramer

1.   R. J. Rushdoony, "Founder's Foreword: Family and Government" (paper presented at the California Home Educator's Association meeting, Anaheim, CA, 1997), 1.
2.   "Is It Right to Be Family-Centered?" *Patriarch,* 25 July 2001, http://www.patriarch.com/article.php? sid=19.
3.   Ibid.
4.   "When Is It OK to Leave a Church?" *Patriarch,* 30 July 2001, http://www.patriarch.com/article.php? sid=59.
5.   Ibid.
6.   Jonathan Lindvall, "Sheltered Homeschoolers and Evangelism," *Home School Digest* 9, 3 (1998): 29.
7.   Don Veinot, Joy Veinot, and Ron Henzel, *A Matter of Basic Principles* (Springfield, MO: 21st Century Press, 2002), 208.
8.   Michael Pearl and Debi Pearl, "Training Roseanna's Flesh," *No Greater Joy* 4, 1: 1.
9.   Ibid., 1, 2.
10.   Kelly Crespin, review of *To Train Up a Child*, by Michael Pearl and Debi Pearl, *Eclectic Homeschool Online,* 2001, http://www.eho.org/reviews/individualprint.asp?revid=160.
11.   Reb Bradley, *Child Training Tips* (Fair Oaks, CA: Family Ministries, 1995), 44.
12.   William Dedrick and Colleen Dedrick, *The Little Book of Christian Character and Manners*, 1st ed. (Elkton, MD: Holly Hall, 1992), 54.
13.   William Dedrick and Colleen Dedrick, *The Little Book of Christian Character and Manners*, 2d ed. (Port Angeles, WA: Christian Tutorial Books, 1993), 5.
14.   Michael Pearl and Debi Pearl, *To Train Up a Child* (Pleasantville, TN: Pearl, 1994), 23. See also Bradley, 70.
15.   Dedrick, 1st ed., 54.
16.   Jonathan Lindvall, "A True Romantic Betrothal Example," Bold Christian Living, 1997, http://www.boldchristianliving.com/articles/romance3.php.
17.   Les Carter, *Imperative People: Those Who Must Be in Control* (Nashville: Thomas Nelson, 1991), 26–28.
18.   Jeff VanVonderen, *Families Where Grace Is in Place* (Minneapolis: Bethany House, 1992), 117.
19.   J. Richard Fugate, *What the Bible Says about Child Training* (Tempe, AZ: Family Building Seminars, 1996), 50.
20.   Ronald Kirk, "Facing Sin in Education," *Chalcedon Report,* August 2002, 7.

21.   Tedd Tripp, "Foundational Concepts, the Centrality of the Heart in Parenting," *Shepherding a Child's Heart: Video Series*, Shepherd Press, n.d., videocassette 1.

22.   VanVonderen, 138–40.

23.   Pearl, *To Train*, 85.

24.   VanVonderen, 140.

25.   Gary Busselman, "Personality Disorders Caused from Physical and Emotional Abuse," www.freeminds.org/buss/disorder.htm.

26.   Rick Seelhoff, e-mail to author, 13 September 2002.

27.   John W. Thompson, "God's Design for Scriptural Romance, Part VII," *Patriarch*, 31 July 2001, http://www.patriarch.com/article.php?sid=90.

28.   Pearl, *To Train*, 45.

29.   Dedrick, 1st ed., 59.

30.   Ibid., 20.

31.   Steve M. Schlissel, "Laws and Order (Part II)," 1 November 2000, http://www.messiahnyc.org/ ArticlesDetail.asp?id=254.

32.   Michael S. Horton, *Where in the World Is the Church?* (Phillipsburg, NJ: Presbyterian and Reformed Publishing, 2002), 43.

33.   Ibid., 44.

34.   Ibid., 45.

35.   Ibid., 46.

36.   Ibid., 48.

37.   Ibid., 51.

38.   Gordon D. Fee and Douglas Stuart, *How to Read the Bible for All Its Worth* (Grand Rapids: Zondervan, 1981), 151.

39.   Horton, 40.

40.   Fee and Stuart, 71.

41.   Ibid., 68.

42.   Steve M. Schlissel, "Tattoo You?" *Messiah's*, http://www.messiahnyc.org/article.php?sid=133.

43.   Ibid.

44.   Fee and Stuart, 157.

45.   Thompson.

46.   Fee and Stuart, 92.

47.   Wayne Griess, phone interview with author, 12 June 2002.

48.   John Holzmann, in the Sonlight Curriculum Ltd. 2002 Catalog, 115.

49.   John Fischer, *Fearless Faith* (Eugene, OR: Harvest House, 2002), 15.

50.   Ibid., 8.

Acknowledgments

There are no words to adequately express my gratitude to all who have given support, encouragement, and prayer throughout the writing journey of Quivering Daughters. May my humble words give you a tender glimpse of what's in my heart to say, and I pray that the Lord blesses you tremendously on my behalf.

My heartfelt appreciate goes to my editor, Megan Lindsay, for her willingness to meet this project on her knees. Thanks to her expert eye and ability to grasp the scope of *Quivering Daughters*, this book is blessed to be sculpted through her hands. She expressed concerns with grace, offered helpful suggestions, and poured herself forth to see this project through completion for the glory of God.

I am blessed that Rachel D. Ramer graciously allowed me to feature her article, *Christian Families on the Edge—Authoritarianism and Isolationism*. As a newlywed in my early twenties, this document was literally the first publication I ever read which addressed these serious issues, gave words to the concerns in my head and heart, and provided a ray of hope.

To Elizabeth Esther—thank you for agreeing to write my foreword and for your commitment to exposing the abuses of fundamentalism. BIG HUGS. To E. S. Hansen, thank you for lending your eyes in the final stages! You are a sweetheart. And to Abigail Paul, who created the cover for this volume—you are amazing. Thank you for your patience with me and for interpreting my wordy suggestions into beautiful art; I am thrilled with the result.

This book would not be the same without Cindy Kunsman, who, like a midwife, helped bring forth this child and then carry her to my sisters. Like that of Caleb and Joshua who held up the arms of Moses in the hardest, darkest moments of battle, her support has been a godsend to me. On behalf of both myself and Quivering Daughters—thank you, with much, much love.

My deep, inexpressible appreciation to Mom and Dad, who gave me the gift of life and provided a solid foundation of Scripture and home education. Dad, thank you for staying up late to quiet the fear in my six-year-old soul; Mom, thank you for the prayers and sacrifices you've made on my behalf. I love you both very much.

To my brothers and sisters: I am so glad that each one of you belongs to my family. I'm sorry for being impatient with you when we were growing up, and for not encouraging you more. I miss you. You have no idea how much, and I hope that one day the Lord will let you see how much I love you.

I am eternally grateful for my friend Angie, whose support, encouragement, and nurture are the richest of blessings to me—much love to you; for Ramsie, who found my soul at seventeen and will always be precious to me— xo; and Tonia P., who is the reason I first began to understand grace. To Monika, you make me smile. Keep seeking, keep listening, and keep reaching. I love you. To Lily, who God placed into my life at a very pivotal time— let's get coffee soon, okay? I love you and thank you for everything.

I fall on my face to God in praise for my dear Alisa, my prayer-warrioress-sister. I could not have done this without you and your support and love. Thank you for being such a precious part of my life. I love you dearly.

Ah, Sara-my-Sara, my soul friend. My eyes when I couldn't see. When God wrote our book of days, He penned us into each other's pages. How to even begin thanking Him for this, thanking you? Thank you for launching me into the new way and for being with me in both dark and light. Love, love, love you.

To my husband, Troy—I know you don't like sappy stuff but it's late and I can't think of anything funny. So can I just say WOW? Because of you, I've discovered the love of God. Because of you, I've found freedom and the richness of life. Thank you for your patience and support—technical support, too—throughout all of this—the journey, the tears, the struggles, the writing, the late nights. Thank you for believing in me and encouraging me in everything I do. I love you so much.

To all of you who have prayed for me and this book, and sent words of encouragement, you are a treasure to me. You have no idea how much and I wish I could tell you in person. I'm humbled by your kindness and look forward to the day we meet; the day God wipes away all of our tears and where there will be no more pain. May the Lord bless you.

To my quivering daughter-sisters—you inspire me with your courage and bravery. Every day I wish I could throw my arms around you; thank you for reaching, for asking, for searching. Thank you for your faith, for seeking the narrow way that leads to life. Thank you for loving truth, even when it hurts. Thank you for living, even when it hurts. For daring to step into the unknown so that He may become known.

Emmanuel.

Hillary McFarland

In memory of Lydia Schatz
2003-2010

267

Thank you for taking the time to read *Quivering Daughters—Hope and Healing for the Daughters of Patriarchy*. For comments or feedback, the author may be reached by email at hillary@quiveringdaughters.com, or by writing:

c/o Darklight Press
PO BOX 796511, Dallas, TX 75379

www.quiveringdaughters.com
www.hillarymcfarland.com

www.generationrejects.com

(Coming soon. For more information, please write to generationrejects@gmail.com)

268

Breinigsville, PA USA
24 November 2010
250034BV00004B/133/P

9 780984 468607